MW00327222

Win Business with Relationships

Win Business with Relationships

Communication Strategies Inspired
by Entrepreneurs & Taoism

Dr. May Hongmei Gao

Kaleb,

09/05/23
Kennesaw. GA

Hope you enjoy reading
this Book!

May H Gao

BEP
BUSINESS EXPERT PRESS
Leader in applied, concise business books

Win Business with Relationships:
Communication Strategies Inspired by Entrepreneurs & Taoism

Copyright © Business Expert Press, LLC, 2023.

Cover design by May Hongmei Gao

Interior design by Exeter Premedia Services Private Ltd., Chennai, India

All rights reserved. No part of this publication may be reproduced, stored in a retrieval system, or transmitted in any form or by any means—electronic, mechanical, photocopy, recording, or any other except for brief quotations, not to exceed 400 words, without the prior permission of the publisher.

First published in 2023 by
Business Expert Press, LLC
222 East 46th Street, New York, NY 10017
www.businessexpertpress.com

ISBN-13: 978-1-63742-450-6 (paperback)
ISBN-13: 978-1-63742-451-3 (e-book)

Business Expert Press Corporate Communication Collection

First edition: 2023

10 9 8 7 6 5 4 3 2 1

Description

In this *fun* and data-rich book, you will discover how you can *win business* through cultivating meaningful *relationships*, nourished by *listening, respect, trust,* and *cultural sensitivity*. This business development *guidebook* illustrates relationship building and leadership strategies with quotations from entrepreneurs, communication theories, business case studies, Taoism metaphors, and real-life stories. You can apply ideas from this book for career success and work–life harmony.

Are business relationships still important in the digital age? Do you want to develop new business leads and grow profit from existing relationships? What are the different communication preferences of Baby Boomers, Gen X, Y, and Z? Are social media and online reviews important for business? How can a leader motivate his/her employees through passion, vision, and mission? How should we deal with change? Is work–life harmony possible?

This concise book strives to satisfy your search for up-to-date and effective business development strategies. Connecting Western theories with Taoism philosophy, this applied business relationship *guidebook* illustrates complex relationship building strategies with metaphors from gardening and stories from business leaders. Synthesizing field-notes from 12-year participant observation in fundraising and over 500 pages of transcripts from interviews with 20 multicultural business leaders and entrepreneurs, this book debuts communication strategies for win–win–win results. While flipping through the book, whether in uninterrupted or fragmented time slots, readers may be entertained and inspired by the case studies, infographics, quotations, concepts, and discussions on business relationship cultivation. Smart, sophisticated, and busy readers can apply ideas from this book in their relationships at work and life instantly.

Keywords

business communication; business development; business relationships; client retention; consumer behavior; corporate communication; customer service; entrepreneurship; international business; leadership; multicultural marketing; organizational communication; rainmaking; listening; respect; servant leadership; social media and online reviews; trust and branding; work-life balance; work–life harmony; dialogue; Asian studies; Asian communication; Taoism; relationship selling; relationship marketing; networking strategies

Contents

Testimonials

"Win Business with Relationships *is a sheer joy to read! The quotes and case studies illustrating the six-step process of building long-term relationships with customers and the communities are backed up by research and ancient wisdom. May Gao is a master storyteller!"*—**Dr. Jagdish N. Sheth, Charles H. Kellstadt Professor of Business, Emory University**

"*Dr. Gao's book,* Win Business with Relationships, *takes a deep dive into what drives success in the highly competitive business environment of sales. The case studies from various industry icons gives readers a roadmap that can be uniquely tailored to their environment. When implemented properly, the insights she pulls from her interviews provide readers with profound perspectives for success. Epic.*"—**Dan Forsman, Chairman, Berkshire Hathaway HomeServices Georgia Properties**

"*Dr. Gao's work takes us across cultures, generations, and theories, all explained with real-life examples. It does not get any better than this book if one tries to understand business development. A must read for anyone in the relationship business.*"—**Athar Khan, Director, International Specialty Sales, Delta Air Lines**

"*May Hongmei Gao has crafted a book with the perfect mix of practice-driven, research-oriented, and principles-grounded approaches for complex workplace interactions. This book will speak not only to business decision-makers but also to students in various disciplines. Readers will be entertained, educated, and inspired by the case studies and the elucidation of concepts. It will be on many bookshelves for years to come, finding solutions for the full range of complex communication strategies.*"—**Dr. John R. McIntyre, Professor of Management, Executive Director, Georgia Tech CIBER**

"Dr. Gao shows us the way for business success with approaches in effective communication across generations and trust-based relationships around the globe. This content-rich book is filled with experiences and ideas for closing business deals. Dr. Gao has a unique style of leveraging wisdom from Taoism to develop leadership skills and business strategies."—**George Mui, Managing Partner, Global Consultants United**

"With her outstanding academic intelligence and high EQ, Professor Gao presents a book with rich content for entrepreneurs at all levels. We benefit from our social circles. Prof. Gao truly understands how relationships help business grow to next levels."—**Jinsong Yang, Managing Member, McKinley Homes**

Foreword

With the advent of advanced communication technologies and the emergence of global markets, interpersonal relationships—not bricks and mortar—have become the load-bearing structures of every business. The COVID-19 pandemic has only served to accelerate this transition from organizations as defined locations to organizations as far-flung networks of connections.

One implication of this shift is that well-established principles of how to succeed in business are being questioned, and the desire for reliable guidance has created a hunger for new ideas and practical solutions. In this unique and inspiring book, Professor Gao uses a combination of provocative cases, questions, ancient wisdom, and contemporary advice to offer a roadmap for how we might think about work in the future.

The central idea of the book is that trusting relationships are the heart and soul of a successful business. This notion shapes her approach to communication in important ways. All too often, businesspeople focus almost exclusively on broadcasting messages and far too little on analyzing the preferences of audiences and the extent to which they understand what is intended. A better approach, according to Gao, begins with the proper stance toward communication, one that is characterized by presence, humility, openness, and respect. Such a stance sets the stage for the development of trusting relationships, which are the true secret to success in the long run.

Another important point that Gao makes reinforces the idea that business leaders should think about more than shareholders and should extend their communication and relationship building to a broad array of stakeholders (she calls this a *win-win-win model*). Doing so makes sense both in terms of social responsibility (how is my business impacting the communities it serves?) and as a means for extending a broad network of positive influence. One of the best parts of the book is the extended discussion of intermediaries, individuals in one's network that can support and advocate on behalf of you and your vision.

Drawing on Eastern philosophies, Gao augments each chapter with important parallels between contemporary challenges and ancient wisdom principles. Describing some core principles of Taoism, she underscores the importance of patience, timing, and waiting for the right moment to act. This reminded me of Peter Senge's observation that we cannot force employees to accept our vision; people enroll in an organization's vision when they are ready to do so.

Readers will be interested to examine her analysis of two particularly contemporary challenges, accelerated customer feedback and work–life harmony. Most executives today are highly attentive and responsive to customer postings on social media, addressing service issues that in the past would have been invisible and likely ignored. Gao emphasizes the importance of making peace with the speed of change by adopting an adaptive and organic mindset—always growing, always learning. Regarding work–life harmony, she rejects the old metaphor of *balance* and advocates instead for a world where work–life boundaries are both more fluid and also mutually beneficial. While challenging to accomplish in practice, this is certainly a conversation that must be had, given the changing values that emerge in an intergenerational organization.

In summary, Professor Gao has written an insightful and useful book that successfully straddles the worlds of theory and practice, contemporary business challenges, and ancient wisdom. We are fortunate to have such a book at a time when the fundamental narratives of communication, business, and work are in the process of being re-written.

—Dr. Eric Eisenberg
Professor of Communication; Senior Vice President of
University-Community Partnerships, University of South Florida

Acknowledgments

I have to start by thanking my awesome husband, Todd Sachtjen, a relationship manager at his bank for commercial loans. From bouncing ideas about this book, to reading manuscript drafts, he was as important to this book getting done as I was.

Special regards need to be paid to the leadership team at Kennesaw State University (KSU) for allowing me to organize the Symposium on ASIA-USA Partnership Opportunities (SAUPO) since 2011. From SAUPO, I connected with accomplished business leaders and entrepreneurs. A heartfelt *thank you* to the 20 global business leaders and entrepreneurs I interviewed for this book. I hope to share your experience, insights, and wisdom with people around the world. This project was made possible by the *Tenured Faculty Enhancement Leave* grant offered by KSU and *Developmental Editing Fund* offered by KSU's Interdisciplinary Studies Department (ISD). Thank you for these blessed relationships and rewarding opportunities!

I am grateful for the input and feedback of my graduate and undergraduate students in Communication, Business, Public Administration, Asian Studies, and American Studies. I appreciate their eagerness for knowledge. I am indebted to my graduate assistant Chet Wallace for his thorough and intelligent proofreading work.

Finally, I appreciate the publication opportunity provided by Scott Isenberg, managing executive editor at Business Expert Press. Mr. Isenberg has been very encouraging and entrepreneurial. I would like to recognize his guidance.

CHAPTER 1

Relationships Matter for Business

Quotations to Ponder

It's about Win-Win-Win! In my case, it should be a win for my company, a win for my clients, and a win for our shared consumers.
—Brad Taylor, former Brand Strategist
The Coca-Cola Company

Real estate is a people business, and our clients are the heart and soul of everything we do.
—DeAnn Golden, President and CEO
Berkshire Hathaway HomeServices Georgia Properties

It makes a huge difference, if you invest your time and efforts to read the EQ[1] of people, interpret their body language, and get a good understanding of what this person cares about.
—JR Wilson, Vice President for Tower Strategy & Roaming
AT&T

Good salespeople practice active listening and genuine keeping up. They know it's all about the people, and it's all about giving people reasons to like them.
—Alex Gregory, former President and CEO
YKK Corporation of America

---

[1] *Emotional quotient (EQ) or emotional intelligence* reflects one's ability to understand, display, and manage emotions when communicating with others. A person with high EQ usually strives to empathize with others, defuse conflicts, and work collaboratively. EQ often reflects different skills than intelligence quotient (IQ), which is a score derived from a set of standardized tests designed to assess human intelligence.

Business is about relationships. Companies do business with compa-
nies, but at the end of the day, it's an individual who's made a con-
nection with another individual that allows that business to proceed,
whatever that business line might be.

—Rick Cole, former Senior Vice President
Turner Broadcasting System[2]

Water is the softest thing, yet it can penetrate mountains and earth.
This clearly shows the principle of softness overcoming hardness.

—Laozi (also known as Lao Tzu老子), Author
Tao Te Ching（道德经）

---

[2] *Turner Broadcasting System, Inc.* was an American media conglomerate, founded in1965 by the legendary Ted Turner and based in Atlanta, Georgia, which later launched CNN in 1980. The company merged with Time Warner (later Warner-Media) in 1996. More recently, the company updated its name as *Turner* and has become a part of Warner Bros. Discovery (WBD).

Chapter Summary

Though communication technologies are exponentially enhanced with new devices, software, and interfaces, *interpersonal relationships* still matter greatly for business success. Research for this book shows that relationships are needed for maintaining existing business, generating new business, and sustaining brand loyalty. Chapter 1 debuts *Gao's six-step communication strategy for relationship development* in business, intercultural, interpersonal, and organizational contexts. The six-step strategy indicates that relationship building starts from the *self* with humility and reaches out to the *other* with respect. Like cultivating an apple tree, business relationships grow along a natural Taoist way: progressing from proper I-Thou stand, to selection, observation, caring, strategic patience, and eventually to closing deals.

CASE STUDY 1.1

"What's in It for Me?"

Fundraising with the CFO for Asia-Pacific,
The Coca-Cola Company

Birds were chirping on a sunny day in mid-March 2013. Our non-profit business educational SAUPO[3] conference promoting partnership between Asia and the United States was about to be held in a month, but we still did not have sufficient funding. I was scheduled to have lunch with Mr. Q, the CFO for Asia-Pacific at The Coca-Cola Company. This lunch meeting at a local restaurant, was arranged by my friend Mr. Li, whom I met at a conference in San Francisco in 2008, when I was a speaker. I had talked with Mr. Li for several years about this idea, and finally, he arranged a lunch appointment for me to meet with Mr. Q. In my 12 years as a fundraiser, these kinds of lunch meetings usually are set at noon on a weekday in a local restaurant, often at the sponsors' choice, in consideration of their preference for the location and cuisine. The meeting may also happen at a coffee house, most commonly at Starbucks or equivalent. Before the lunch meeting, I had done my *due diligence*, learning about the background of Mr. Q and his group on his company website, Google, LinkedIn, Facebook, and through my connection with Mr. Li. I had thought about ways to introduce my university and my conference. Past meetings have taught me that budgeting 15 to 30 minutes extra time ahead of the meeting yields enormous advantages: (1) Enough time to avoid potential traffic jams and to find a parking spot, especially in a city like Atlanta; (2) To guarantee that I arrive at the restaurant 10 to 15 minutes ahead of schedule so that I can situate myself, put down my

---

[3] *Symposium on ASIA-USA Partnership Opportunities (SAUPO)* is a business and educational conference organized by the Asian Studies Program at Kennesaw State University in Atlanta, Georgia, USA. Founded in 2011, SAUPO is the largest Asia business conference in the USA, facilitating information exchange, personal network building, global visibility, and cross-border transactions. SAUPO has been held in Atlanta, Asia, and online. Dr. May Gao, the author of this book, is the founder, chair, and lead fundraiser for SAUPO, https://conference.kennesaw.edu/saupo/.

name at the reception desk, and study the menu; (3) Possibility of identifying a table suitable for a mutual conversation, as certain spots in some restaurants can be very noisy with background music or people talking; (4) Being late, for whatever reason, not only shows disrespect to the other party, it also may leave an unfavorable first impression in front of any potential sponsors and partners. I have heard this from many companies, "If you are on time, you are late. If you are early, you are on time." That day at 11:50 a.m., I gave my name to the restaurant reception lady, only to find that Mr. Q and Mr. Li were already there at a table. Perhaps I should have arrived 20 minutes earlier?! I quickly walked up to them, shook hands, and sat down.

We started to introduce ourselves. We also talked about how I met with Mr. Li eight years ago. Mr. Q then asked me to tell him a little about my conference. We were interrupted a couple of times, as the waitress asked what food and drinks that we wanted to order. Without wasting any more time, based on my memory of the menu that I reviewed online prior to the lunch, I quickly ordered a chicken salad and a glass of unsweetened tea. Later, I regretted the *Southern Tea* order, as I should have asked for a Coke product, in front of the CFO of The Coca-Cola Company!

I continued with my *prerehearsed speech* that I have given to many potential sponsors. I made the *"ask"* for the sponsorship while showing him our various sponsorship levels: Presidential, Diamond, Platinum, Gold, Silver, Bronze, and so on. Then, Mr. Q suddenly said, "Dr. Gao, you mentioned a lot about how your conference will benefit from a sponsorship with us. Can you please answer this question: What's in it for me? What will The Coca-Cola Company benefit out of supporting your conference?"

This was a wakeup call! I had to brainstorm on the spot, trying to list how we could promote various Coke drinks to our students, faculty, and conference attendees. Of course, a company as huge as Coke does not need our conference to become famous! In 2013, The Coca-Cola Company did business all over the world, except in Cuba and North Korea. Realizing my struggling efforts, Mr. Q smiled and offered to do his best in supporting our conference. He said The Coca-Cola Company believed in giving back to the communities, and perhaps they could provide the soft drinks for our conference as the in-kind support. A couple of weeks later, a local Coke bottling company agreed to supply our conference with free soft drinks, given the condition that we would not accept soft drinks from any competing soft drink company. I consider Mr. Q as my *First Teacher for Fundraising*. I learned the importance of addressing these questions for fundraising:

- What do they need?
- What do they want?
- What are their aspirations?
- How can we assist them to solve their problems?
- How can we help them to achieve their goals?

Discussion Questions for Readers

1. While doing fundraising or growing any business, why and how should we address this quintessential question for the client: "What's in it for me?"
2. How can we conduct due diligence about an individual, a group, a company before, during and after our meeting with them?
3. How could Dr. Gao have planned better for this meeting?

Introduction

Nowadays, many people can meet, work, shop, and entertain via hand-held smartphones. The contemporary eLife style of *holding the world in my hand* evolves from the advancement of communication technologies, changing needs in lifestyles, and complex circumstances like the COVID-19 pandemic. People are buying books, electronics, furniture, clothes, houses, and even groceries online. U.S. online grocery sales grew 22 percent in 2019 and surged about 40 percent in 2020, propelled by COVID-19 lockdowns (Redman 2020). *Insider Intelligence* reported that in 2022, Walmart Inc. was the number one retailer in digital grocery, followed by Amazon and Kroger. It is predicted that digital grocery will account for over $243 billion in the United States by 2025 (Yuen 2022).

To search for an answer, we Google. To meet with someone, we Zoom. To go somewhere, we Uber. These brands have become verbs, and we have become netizens.[4] Some people are spending so much time on smartphones that *offline* is considered the new luxury. Can smartphones generate smart communication? As we are always looking at them, touching them, listening to them, and getting frustrated without them, are smartphones becoming our new *life partners*? Are interpersonal relationships still important for business if we don't need to, or otherwise are not able to meet in person? Do relationships still matter in the Digital Age?[5]

Value in Learning About the Other

This chapter's case study of my fundraising encounter with Mr. Q shows that it is critical to find out ways to help *the other* achieve their goals. The relational others may be donors, customers, clients, and business partners. The research data for this book reveal that finding out *the needs and wants of the relational other* remains a pivotal challenge for business and non-profit organizations. *To address the quintessential question from the clients*

---

[4] The term *netizen* is a portmanteau of the two English words *Internet* and *citizen*. A netizen is someone actively involved in online communities for work and life.

[5] *The Digital Age* is a time in human history when incredible amount of information is widely available to people through computers, the Internet and new media, enhanced by handheld smartphones, tablets, and other devices.

about "what's in it for me," we must conduct thorough due diligence before the meeting, listen actively with full presence during the meeting, and follow up artfully after the meeting.

Fundraising is tough in the nonprofit sector. Thousands of schools, churches, and organizations in the community approach the same donors. Nonprofit activists are often more sophisticated in creating programs than in communicating to the philanthropists regarding the impact of such programs (Foster, Kim, and Christiansen 2009). Starting and maintaining a business is not easy. Scores of large, medium, and small businesses fail every year. Take small businesses as an example. The U.S. Small Business Administration (SBA) defines a *small business* as a company with 500 or fewer employees, which categorizes many companies as *small business* even though they seem large. In 2017, these small businesses hired over 47.1 percent of the working population in the United States. About 6.5 million small businesses are launched every year, but only a fraction enjoys long-term success (National Business Capital and Services 2020). In 2019, the failure rate of small businesses was around 90 percent. Research concludes 21.5 percent of startups fail in the first year, 30 percent in the second year, 50 percent in the fifth year, and 70 percent in their tenth year (Bryant 2020). Six main reasons contribute to these failures (Bryant 2020), which can be grouped into "problems with self-positioning" or "lack of knowledge about the other."

- *Self #1: Lack of expertise.* Too many entrepreneurs start their business because they need a job. However, without proper business skills and marketable expertise, these entrepreneurs are destined to struggle.
- *Self #2: Wrong market.* Too many people try to start a business targeting everyone as their market. Based on the strength of the entrepreneurs, try to focus on a small niche market and offer your value-added solutions.
- *Self #3: Cashflow shortage.* Cashflow is the lifeblood of a business. When a company does not have enough cash to pay bills, it is hard to survive.

- *Other #4: Not offering what the customers want.* Too many companies go into the market thinking they have a great service/product to offer, but they fail to realize that nobody or not enough customers want that service/product.
- *Other #5: Win–lose relationship.* Many businesses dissolve because the relationship does not work: One party has the *win position*, while the other party has the *lose position.* Creating a *win–win–win* business plan that lays out duties and benefits of all partners and maintaining two-way communication may help to reduce conflicts and build trust.
- *Other #6: Ineffective marketing.* Large numbers of companies spend thousands of dollars fumbling through one-way marketing campaigns via TV, radio, mail flyers, robocalls[6], and social media. Such one-way communication does not invite the establishment of trust-based relationships with customers and clients.

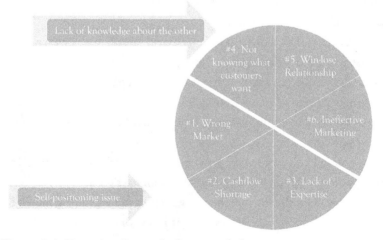

Figure 1.1 Six main reasons for business failures

---

[6] *Robocalls in the United States* are phone calls made by a computer to people's cell phones, which often give recorded messages to the recipients or lead to salespersons pitching on business and political campaigns. Data show that most people would not pick up *spam risk* calls, or they hang up in the first few seconds.

Relationships Matter for Business

On the *American Express* Website (2020), it is stated that a company's growth depends on strong business development strategies, such as *relationship building*, market expansion, and brand awareness campaigns. Business development helps a business expand and improve its sales, revenues, product offerings, talent, customer service, and brand awareness. Whether cultivating new talents, networking with prospective partners, or courting potential customers, relationship-building is an integral piece of the business development process.

All 20 entrepreneurs in various industries interviewed for this book stressed the importance of building relationships for business. Rick Cole, formerly Senior Vice President at Turner Broadcasting System, said that "business is about relationships. Individuals connect with other individuals based on trust." Wendy Lu, a partner at international accounting firm Aprio, pointed out that "relationships are what drives business." Wendy said Aprio partners carefully build and maintain relationships before any business dealings. Cultivating relationships is the main part of the company's daily business operations.

Lucy Lu is the CEO/Founder of aiLegal, an Atlanta-based law firm. She strives for excellence in providing client-focused legal service. She says, "if you do your job right for the clients, money follows your way, and more clients will chase you around." Among her client pool, about 70 to 80 percent are from *word-of-mouth* referrals from existing clients. The rest of the business comes from referrals from other lawyers, Google search, or independent search. Service industries such as accounting, law firms, consulting, and banking rely heavily on relationships.

Can we do business with someone without a relationship? Would it be possible in certain retail businesses? Not really. Brands attract customers to retail stores. People visit certain grocery stores physically or virtually because they have a *relationship* with that brand, such as Publix, Kroger, Trader Joe's, Aldi, or Winn-Dixie. A *brand* stands for quality, predictability, familiarity, and price. A brand helps to maintain a trust-based relationship between consumers and their grocery stores. Some grocery stores offer memberships, coupons, discounts, and loyalty cards, such as a *Kroger Plus Shopper's card* or *CVS ExtraCare Card*, to manage these relationships. Such loyalty cards can collect *big data* for Kroger and CVS to understand the needs and wants of customers.

Relationships matter, even for contactless Internet sales. Amazon Prime is a paid membership program that gives users access to additional services, such as one- or two-day free deliveries, and free subscription to Amazon music and videos. In 2022, Amazon Prime had more than 200 million subscribers worldwide, doubling its 100 million membership total in 2018 (Maglio 2022). Long-term relationships build brand trust, generate repeat business, and expand market share.

In the high-tech sphere, for online streaming, you may think of companies like Netflix and Spotify. Bilibili, with over 172 million monthly active users, is a leading online entertainment platform in China. Bilibili has built a loyal online community rooted in relationships among Gen Z users in China. *Official users* have to pass a rigorous 100-question entrance exam called *barrage comments* (弹幕) (Graziani 2019). With such a relationship-based loyal customer pool, the company is projected to soar in profits.

Doing business starts from establishing brands and building relationships. *A brand is a communication tool that signifies what a company's culture is, what values it holds, and what qualities it represents.* Marcy Sperry, founder of Vivid IP law firm, stresses that we live or die by our brands, and people want to do business with those they know, respect, and trust. Jessica Cork serves as the Vice President for Community Engagement and Corporate Communications at YKK Corporation of America. As one of the world's top manufacturers for zippers, Ms. Cork says the YKK brand is the thread that connects millions of consumers with the company. Whether you are selling a product or a service, eventually, people are buying a combination of your product and service. Service is done by people, and people are relational beings. Relationships matter for business, even in the Digital Age.

Win–Win–Win: A New Paradigm for Business Relationships

This book advocates a dynamic *win–win–win* paradigm for building business relationships. Almost all 20 entrepreneurs interviewed for this book referred to the prominence of the win–win–win standpoint when building relationships with potential business partners, including clients, customers, suppliers, and consultants. *For a relationship to be sustainable, every party in a relationship needs to enjoy certain benefits from the relationship, be it financial or in-kind gains. A win–win–win perspective requires us to identify winning points for all parties involved in the business process, not just for ourselves.*

Stephen Covey (2015) advocates seven habits for highly effective people. One of these habits is to think win–win. Covey states that win–win is a total philosophy of human interaction, which helps us to avoid the mindset of *lack of abundance* or *zero sum game*. He points out that win–win is a much more desirable result than *win/lose, lose/lose,* or *no deal.* Win–win is a belief in the *Third Way*, not your way, or my way. Through mutual dialogue, relationship partners will experience win–win as a better way, a higher way, and a more profitable way. Win–win is a heartfelt *frame of mind* that constantly seeks mutual benefit in all human interactions.

The win–win–win paradigm proposed by this book goes above and beyond Covey's two-party win–win framework. In relationship cultivation, caring about all partners and players in the business process produces winning results in a sustainable manner. Everyone needs to win, including suppliers, clients, assistants, liaisons, consultants, and all persons involved in the relationship process. The new win–win–win paradigm intends to provide *added value* for all parties involved in business transactions. In a win–win–win relationship, all players in a network of relationships feel good about the decisions, and they are therefore committed to the action plans for winning results. When asked about ways of building relationships for business success, Brad Taylor, former brand strategist at The Coca-Cola Company, presented the triple-win concept: "It's about win-win-win! In my case, it should be a win for my company, a win for my clients, and a win for our shared consumers." The Coca-Cola Company desires to pop up as *the beverage of choice* for communities across the globe. Mr. Taylor argues that facing constant competition, it is imperative for the company to continue staying atop in the beverage market. Mr. Taylor stresses the importance to find out the needs of the consumers and the goals of business partners so that everyone is a winner when doing business with The Coca-Cola Company.

We may not realize that we often take an *economic view* to evaluate relationships. The *social penetration theory* (Taylor and Altman 1987) applies an economic framework in balancing rewards and costs in relationships. *Rewards* are any solid asset or in-kind resources to which a person can attach value, such as money, support, information, connections, prestige, affection, recognition, or comfort. *Costs* are items that individuals find draining and undesirable, such as money, time, efforts, sacrifices, energy, anger, stress, technological difficulties, and damage to one's reputation. Like the business sense of *return on investment (ROI)*, relationship development follows the pattern that "greater the ratio of rewards to costs, the more rapid the penetration process" (Taylor and Altman 1987, 264). We may calculate the ROI of each relationship and envision the next step: to continue, to hold, or to suspend certain relationships. Thus, for any relationship to be developed, we need to make sure that every party involved in a relationship *gains* in some way: money, gifts, information, reputation, recognition, support, bonding, unique experiences, or extra value. In other words, in the win–win–win paradigm, we want to make sure every party involved in a relationship wins, including the self, the other, and everyone in between.

How can we be a win–win–win player in business? By *listening* and *observing*! Most global business leaders and entrepreneurs I interviewed highlighted *listening* as the key tool to identify and satisfy needs of the others. They also emphasized the quality of being trustworthy, transparent, and respectful. These were some of the recurring themes in the interviews. Cultivating, maintaining, and strengthening relationships leads to business success. The interview data indicate that when business partners, clients, and consumers recognize that you are genuinely interested in helping them accomplish their goals, you are on the right track to achieve your goals, facilitated by trust-based mutual relationships. *Give them what they want, and in turn, they will reward you with what you want!*

Introducing *Gao's Six-Step Communication Strategy*

A relationship is essentially a mutual commitment between two human beings: the *self* and the *other*. Being able to manage the *self* in relation to the needs and wants of the *other* is an important aspect of every human

Figure 1.2 *Gao's six-step communication strategy for relationship development*

relationship. Setting up *humility for the self* and *respect for the other* launches the sustainable posture for rewarding relationships. This book presents *Gao's six-step communication strategy for relationship development* that leads from proper posture, to selection, observation, caring, strategic patience, and results. *Gao's six-step communication strategy for relationship development* was synthesized from the research data through 12-year participant observation as a fundraiser and in-depth interviews with 20 entrepreneurs.

Step 1: Keeping the proper I-Thou posture. Just like learning a new sport or a new instrument, maintaining a proper posture is the first step. To cultivate a relationship, one needs to demonstrate humility for the self and respect for the other. Being humble does not mean weakness. Taoism classic *Tao Te Ching* states that "the highest virtue is like water" as water flows to the lowest point. The ocean being enormous because it is at the lowest point, and therefore, rivers are attracted to it (Laozi 471 BCE). Laozi teaches us that if one is humble, standing on a lower ground, then more people want to be your friends, choose to follow you, and do business with you. Humility is a virtue in many cultures. Taoism classic *I Ching* revealed that among the 64 possibilities (64卦) of life situations, *humility* (谦卦) scenario is a *forever winning* strategy (Zeng 2013). Being humble helps us to cultivate a confident and caring self-concept when one tries to form a relationship with the other.

"All real living is meeting" (Buber 1970, 124). "To live means to participate in dialogue" (Bakhtin 1981, 292–293). The dialogue theory demonstrates the *twofold* relationship between the self and the other. Martin Buber distinguishes two types of relationships, the I-It and the I-Thou. In an I-It relationship, the *self* treats the *other* as an object, and the attitude of *looking down upon* may be practiced. In an I-Thou relationship, the *self* views the *other* as a whole person, and respect and empathy are experienced. *Humility for the self* and *respect for the other* are two sides of the proper posture for a productive relationship. Chapter 3 discusses the advantages of humility for the self and respect for the other, as well as ways to achieve these goals.

Step 2: Selecting potential partners. Relationships, be it personal or business, are not something that happen overnight. Relationships grow in a process of *back and forth* communication between the self and other. Relationships grow through interactions at restaurants, coffee shops, conferences, business trips, meetings, phone calls and texts, and social media interactions. Cultivating a relationship takes time, effort, money, emotions, and patience. Taylor and Altman (1987) expressed "the economic view of relationship development" in their social penetration theory. Indeed, one must be selective in choosing the *other* as a potential investment for a mutual relationship. The interview at AT&T for this book indicates that when selecting new business partners, calculated risks are considered based on the size of the potential business. Doing business with smaller companies has allowed AT&T to be *disruptive* in cost reduction and innovation. Potential partners must share core values and prove themselves to be dependable and loyal to one another. The business performance track record of a potential partner is essential information in the selection process. To conserve time, money, effort, and other resources, selection is a necessary step for a company to *weed out* potentially unproductive, costly, and toxic partners. The selection criteria for a potential business partner may include compatibility in business, values, organizational culture, leadership personality, speed and rhythm of operation, and methods of communication. In addition to being selective in relationship building, companies need to include a *Safety Net Clause*[7] in their contracts for such partnerships.

Step 3: Observing partners for their needs and wants. According to biologists, one major difference between humans and animals is that people can stand up and walk with our two feet. Such status enables us

---

[7] *Safety Net Clause*: Every commercial project or transaction carries risks of liability. The Safety Net Clause is intended to provide solution to complications in the context that would otherwise impede or hurt a project. A well-drafted *Safety Net Clause* shall be included in commercial contracts, especially for global business when a company has to confront different languages, cultures, and legal systems.

to look up for what the heaven intends to tell us, while animals can only look forward and downward. To observe is a unique quality of humans, and we shall take full advantage of this capacity. Observation has been a method of discovery for millennia. Astrologists in ancient China were assigned to observe and decode phenomena in nature so that they could guide the emperors to rule the country. *I Ching* expert Dr. Zeng Shiqiang states that there are three major constituents in the world from the Taoism perspective: The Heaven (天), The Earth (地), and Mankind (人) (Zeng 2013). Though the Heaven and the Earth do not speak any human language, they *show* (天垂象,见吉凶), rather than *tell* us what's coming: earthquakes, forest fires, hurricanes, drought, and pandemics. As the dominating intelligence on earth, humans are expected to utilize our capacity of *observation*, to interpret what the nature and the society are showing. *Through observation, we can find out what clients need and want, how they behave and communicate, and what they have done in the past.* Regarding communication channels, people have different preferences. Some people prefer to meet face-to-face, some like to talk on the phone, others enjoy texting, and many are active on social media, such as Facebook, LinkedIn, Twitter, Instagram, WhatsApp, and TikTok. One needs to get on the same platform with the relational other in order to communicate on the same (digital) page. Robert Striar, President of M Style Marketing, says that there is so much data out there that you can research on your potential business partners to your best ability. Beyond Googling and surfing the social media, data-based platforms such as *PitchBook*[8] offer valuable business data, with a suite of software applications.

Step 4: Caring for the relationship. For a plant to thrive, a gardener must study and observe what it needs, then provide it with proper care at the right time: sunshine, water, and soil. There are many obstacles when a gardener cultivates an apple tree, such as bad weather (flood, drought, wind, etc.), pests (bugs, squirrels, etc.), or lack of pollinators (bees, butterflies, ants, etc.). Similarly, there are trials and tribulations while one

---

[8] *PitchBook Data, Inc.* is a SaaS company that delivers data, research, and technology covering the private capital markets, including venture capital, private equity, and mergers and acquisitions transactions. It is based in Seattle, Washington, with regional offices worldwide. https://pitchbook.com.

cultivates relationships for business: improper timing, cultural differences, linguistic barriers, political, legal, and accounting disparities, lack of interpersonal chemistry, and integrity issues. To overcome obstacles, one may use *dialogue* as a method of inviting *mutual self-disclosure* to build trust. One must care about the needs of the relational other at every stage, just like studying the needs of a plant. *Caring about someone* in Chinese characters (关心) literally means "locking up the other's heart with love." One can strive to be sensitive to the relational other's needs and wants while providing value-added assistance, products, and services.

Step 5: Strategic patience for relationship fruits. Let nature take its course! Strategic patience is necessary for harvesting deals from business relationships. Laozi advised us over 2,500 years ago: "Simplicity, patience, compassion. Simple in actions and thoughts, you return to the source of being. Patient with both friends and enemies, you accord with the way things are. Compassionate toward yourself, you reconcile all beings in the world" (Laozi, *Tao Te Ching* 471 BCE). Just like a plant growing through the four seasons, it takes time and a process to cultivate a relationship. Laozi stated, "To rule a large country is like cooking a small fish (治大国若烹小鲜)." After making a fish dinner, all one needs to do is to let the fish be cooked. If one stirs the fish too much, the fish may come apart, and the meal may be damaged. In other words, one shall not micromanage or disturb the growth of relationships. When cultivating business relationships, one needs to remember not to bother partners and customers with too many emails, phone calls, or text messages to rush deals. There is a season for every business. How patient should we wait for a relationship to yield results? While letting nature take its course, we can artfully nurture and prune the relationship, and harvest the fruits at the proper time. You reap what you sow, even in relationships.

Step 6: Closing deals yielded from the relationship. Business deals are basically the fruits of relationships. Companies and nonprofit organizations may enjoy *relationship fruits* and close business deals when they are ripe. Relationships take time to grow, and the environment constantly changes. Communication strategies to push the winners across the finish line includes setting realistic and flexible goals, being honest with the business partners, and harvesting deals at the right time. Chapter 2 debuts *Gao's relationship tree metaphor* for business relationships.

CHAPTER 2

About This Book

Provenance, Research, and Results

Quotations to Ponder

It's critical to build relationships at all levels of the organization. There should be relationships at the very top. There should be relationships with users, buyers, evaluators, and gatekeepers.

—Brad Taylor, former Brand Strategist
The Coca-Cola Company

Early on, I learned that real estate is a relationship business and you must invest in the most valuable tangible asset: your network of connections.

—DeAnn Golden, President and CEO
Berkshire Hathaway HomeServices Georgia Properties

When I mentioned that I wanted to establish a new company, my classmate chipped in as a partner. We already have a pre-existing relationship. We know each other's working styles.

—Lucy Lu, CEO/Founder
aiLegal

Cold calls have not worked well with me. Lots of times people just don't really understand our business. It's so difficult to clearly articulate a value proposition in two to three minutes. Cold calls therefore become more of a distraction.

—JR Wilson, Vice President for Tower Strategy & Roaming
AT&T

A soft sell through listening is better than a hard sell or a loud sell with too much talking and push.

—Roger Neuenschwander, former President and CEO

tvsdesign

If you are trying to get started in your career, you can recognize the key people in your organization and what's going on in the business. You go forward by joining that pool of peers and gaining that network of understanding.

—David Kirk, President and CEO

Murata Electronics North America

A winning strategy for YKK has been growing business with a startup mentality. Our business partners opened doors and realized it was wonderful doing business with us. We have to make sure that we don't become the non-responsive complacent supplier.

—Alex Gregory, former President and CEO

YKK Corporation of America

Everybody gives away their personality if you listen. Listening does not mean that you are 100% quiet. You give people reassurances. You nod and you say, 'Sure, I understand.'

—Eddy Perez, Cofounder and CEO

Equity Prime Mortgage

Chapter Summary

This chapter reveals the necessity and sophistication of relationship cultivation. The *Day One* startup mentality has been practiced by many multinational corporations such as Amazon, The Coca-Cola Company, and YKK Corporation of America. This chapter states the provenance, research methods, and findings for this book. Holism serves as the overarching paradigm for this book, covering the systems theory from the West, Taoism from the East, and gardening in nature. This chapter explains the mixed-method approach that generated the data for this book: 12-year participant observation as a fundraiser, semistructured in-depth interviews with 20 entrepreneurs, and autoethnography from field work. The triangulation of research data gives rise to *Gao's Relationship Tree Metaphor* to be introduced in this chapter.

CASE STUDY 2.1

The Coca-Cola Company: A *Startup Business*

In summer 1999, after the first year of graduate study for my master's degree in Mass Communication at Brigham Young University in Provo, Utah, I returned to Hefei to see my family. Hefei is the capital city of Anhui Province in East China, with eight million people, about 300 miles northwest of Shanghai. Walking among the hustle and bustle of cars, motorbikes, bicycles, and people with kids passing by, I smelled home-town restaurants. Separated by different façades of windows and doors, they share a common look: store names engraved with the red and white *Coca-Cola* logo. I asked the owner of a hole-in-the-wall type of store, where he got such a fancy store name inscription board. He proudly said The Coca-Cola Company made the board and provided the commercial cooler, in exchange for his partnership to sell Coke products. Coke prod-ucts taste better while chilled. He also uses this commercial cooler to sell other drinks and ice-cream snacks. Value for value! *Providing extra value* for business partners is appreciated, no matter how small they are.

Years later, I found a professor job in Atlanta. I was privileged to cul-tivate relationships with movers and shakers of The Coca-Cola Company, headquartered in Atlanta. The company was listed as the sixth best global brand in the 2020 Interbrand ranking (Interbrand website 2020), Brad Taylor, a former brand strategist of The Coca-Cola Company illus-trates that maintaining a *startup* mentality motivates its business to stay relevant. My hometown Hefei's example demonstrates how the company supports local communities for win–win–win results, a win for the com-pany, a win for the vendor, and a win for consumers. The Coca-Cola Company has the resources to provide commercial coolers and to design and manufacture fancy store signages for vendors.

New soft drinks emerge daily, people's tastes change, and cultural trends shift. Founded in 1892, being a beverage company with over 130 years of history, The Coca-Cola Company strives to reinvent itself, for *a share of people's stomachs.* Mr. Taylor says since there are many bever-age alternatives out there, it is critical that Coca-Cola maintains a dom-inant presence in every local community by building relationships, just like a startup company. First, a company can connect with customers by being *locally relevant*. The Coca-Cola Company is big and famous; is it still necessary to participate in local events, such as trade fairs, community gatherings, conferences, and seminars? Mr. Taylor asserts that it is vital to participate in these events. Business is local. While the "Coca-Cola" brand enjoys high brand awareness, the company does not want to take that status for granted. Second, the company supports local communities by being *culturally sensitive*. Mr. Taylor says The Coca-Cola Company does not want to be perceived as a giant global brand. The company tries to demonstrate that it is sensitive to the cultures of the customers, no matter where they are. Third, the company *builds partnerships* with local bottling franchises. The company views it as critical to work with local bottling partners, who are independent franchises of The Coca-Cola Company. These bottling partners make it possible for Coke drinks to be sold in 207 countries.

Getting to know more about the customers is a major mission of The Coca-Cola Company. Such research on the needs and wants of the customers are reflected in marketing programs that further drive relevance. For example, many contemporary consumers are health conscious, and may not want drinks with sugar content. Mr. Taylor says the company owns over 500 soft drink brands, and close to 50 percent of those brands do not contain sugar.

Reflection Questions From This Case

1. Why should all companies maintain a startup mentality, regardless of size?
2. How can a company stay relevant to the diverse local communities it serves?
3. How can you execute the *value for value* proposition in your business?

Day One Startup Business Mentality

As illustrated in the case of The Coca-Cola Company in Hefei, China, companies benefit from being relevant to local customers with a startup mentality. Through engaging with local consumers and partners, The Coca-Cola Company reinvents itself and stays competitive in the global marketplace. Jeff Bezos, the founder of Amazon, advocates the *Day One* startup mentality (Salinas 2018). Bezos asks Amazon employees to *delight* the customers, not just to satisfy the customers. For example, Amazon rushes to provide extra values, additional free services, or faster deliveries. To act like a startup, Bezos requires Amazon employees: *(1) to be obsessed with customers; (2) to focus on results over process; (3) to make high-quality decisions quickly ("High Velocity Decision Making"); (4) to embrace external trends promptly.*

Well-established multinational corporations such as The Coca-Cola Company and Amazon know the value of building long-term relationships with customers and partners. They benefit from learning about the needs and wants of the *relational other*: the customers, clients, and business partners. Thus, a company is rewarded with profit by providing value-added solutions to customers' problems and satisfying their needs and wants. Day One mentality drives a company to search for the needs and wants of its customers. This mentality allows a company to avoid complacency by being purpose-driven and relationship-oriented with the customers.

Sears, JCPenney, Xerox, Kodak, Blockbuster, Lehman Brothers, and so on. These formerly well-known companies have either disappeared or gone through serious hardships in the past 20 years. "Why do good companies go bad?" asked Dr. Jagdish Sheth (2021) in his book *The Self-destructive Habits of Good Companies.* Companies can be guided by individuals with big egos and myopic visions. Resting on past laurels, some companies develop self-destructive habits that make them complacent, arrogant, and less competitive. Elon Musk, the CEO of Tesla and SpaceX, stressed the importance for companies to avoid complacency. Musk said a baseball team that has won many times might stop trying hard, and thus not be able to win more championships.

A formerly successful company becoming complacent can be viewed as showing the *Icarus Syndrome* in business. In Greek mythology, Icarus and his father, Daedalus, were imprisoned on an island. To escape, Daedalus created two sets of wings made of wax and feathers. He warned his son not to fly too close to the sun, as the wax would melt. Icarus was so proud of his flight that he went higher and higher. As the wax in his wings melted, he tumbled into the sea and drowned (Beinart 2010). Icarus, who died from lack of humility, can teach every business leader a lesson to avoid complacency. *No matter which business you are in and how the environment changes, you are encouraged to consider your organization as a startup, and search for what your customers need and want from a relational perspective.*

Power of Personal Networks

Connections in personal networks are some of the best resources for business and career development. A good personal network can provide market information, job leads, and business possibilities (Indeed website 2021). Top job search website Indeed highlights the importance of personal networks. Back in 2004, I was enlightened with the critical power of personal networks while working on my doctoral dissertation on job search strategies in the United States. I conducted a survey with 400 foreign-born Chinese people working at professional, technical, and managerial (PTM) positions in Florida. Table 2.1 shows the channels that rewarded positions to job seekers.

Table 2.1 shows that 52.6 percent of respondents found their jobs through personal networks, including relatives (3.8 percent), friends/acquaintances (32.5 percent), and direct employer contacts (16.3 percent). These descriptive data yield the following results. First, the personal network proved to be the most effective among all job-leading channels. In the personal network, one's friends and acquaintances (32.5 percent) are the most likely to provide critical job leading information. When we add the percentage of jobs obtained through relatives (3.8 percent), friends/acquaintances (32.5 percent), and direct contact with the employers (16.2 percent), the survey result then indicated that *52.5 percent* of respondents found their jobs through personal networks. This finding is consistent with Mark Granovetter's findings in the 1970s on job seeking channels (Gao, 2005). By studying the white male workers at PTM job positions in the Newton, Massachusetts area, Granovetter found that 56 percent of

Table 2.1 Critical job leads for foreign-born Chinese in the United States in search of PTM positions (Gao 2005)

		Frequency	Percent	Valid percent	Cumulative percent
Valid	Relative	6	3.4	**3.8**	3.8
	Friend/acquaintance	52	29.4	**32.5**	36.3
	Employer contact	26	14.7	**16.3**	**52.6**
	The Internet	19	10.7	11.9	64.4
	Printed publication	17	9.6	10.6	75.2
	Asked organization	15	8.5	9.4	84.3
	Employment agency	13	7.3	8.1	92.5
	Job fair	5	2.8	3.1	95.6
	Other	7	4.0	4.4	100
	Total	160	90.4	100	
Missing	System	17	9.6		
Total		177	100		

those he chatted with secured their jobs through a personal connection, especially the "weak ties," with whom one does not frequently communicate (Granovetter, 1973). *From the 1970s to the early 2000s, little was changed in the power of personal networks for job search. More than half of jobseekers found jobs through personal networks in the United States.*

Why This Book?

While relationships yield business deals, communication is at the heart of forming such relationships. Eisenberg et al. (2017) state that 70 percent of the *substance* in an organization is communication. Communication, rather than the building, furniture, or devices in an organization, is essential for the survival of an organization. The teleworking experience in the COVID-19 pandemic proves that communication, not a physical office, constitutes the core of an organization. Organizational communication can be divided into two parts: the communication *within* and the communication *between* organizations. Proper communication between organizational delegates, on behalf of their organizations, is vital for the sustainability of an organization to connect with consumers, clients, suppliers, and partners. *Financial capital, human capital, and social capital are considered three critical resources for organizational success* (Fatoki 2011). *Social capital is generated from social relationships and personal networks.*

This book reveals communication strategies for building relationships and expanding personal networks. This book is written for anyone who wants to build productive and mutually beneficial relationships between two individuals, two organizations, and even two countries. All relationships, whether at interpersonal, inter-organizational, or international levels, involves the back-and-forth connection between *self and other.*

Over 12 years ago, I used to wake up at night worrying about these issues: "How can we raise funds to cover the cost of a premier 300-person conference in a five-star hotel? How can we recruit high-profile speakers whom we seem to have no connection with?" In more than a decade of organizing and fundraising for the Symposium on ASIA-USA Partnership Opportunities (SAUPO), a nonprofit educational conference, I have met with numerous compassionate business executives, creative entrepreneurs, and impactful thought leaders. I have struggled with trials and tribulations in fundraising, even encountering rejections and humiliations. I kept fieldnotes and searched for recurring themes in fundraising and business development.

Business deals and sponsorships are gained by satisfying existing clients and recruiting new clients. However, communication may break down, trust is often lacking, and misunderstandings are omnipresent in business. Business authors such as McMakin and Fletcher (2018) shout out for more research-based books in entrepreneurship, rainmaking,

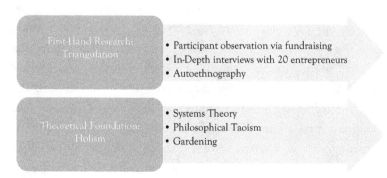

First-Hand Research: Triangulation
- Participant observation via fundraising
- In-Depth interviews with 20 entrepreneurs
- Autoethnography

Theoretical Foundation: Holism
- Systems Theory
- Philosophical Taoism
- Gardening

Figure 2.1 Mixed-method approach for this book

business communication, and relationship building. In their book *How Clients Buy: A Practical Guide to Business Development for Consulting and Professional Services*, McMakin and Fletcher (2018) wrote: "Attention Scholars… Jump in. The water's warm" (p. 12).

This book draws inspiration from three theoretical streams in the realm of holism: modern systems theory from the West, ancient philosophical Taoism from the East, and gardening practiced by all people of the world. Moreover, the author conducted first-hand research in participant observation, autoethnography, and in-depth interviews.

Holism: Source of Inspirations

Chapter 1 presented the dynamic paradigm of doing business for win–win–win results, in order to benefit everyone involved in the business process. This new paradigm is supported by *holism*, the theoretical foundation of this book. The term *holism* was coined by Jan Smuts in his 1926 book *Holism and Evolution* (Poynton 1987). Holism presents the idea that various physical, biological, and social systems should be viewed as *wholes*, not merely as a collection of parts. In other words, different components of a unit are interconnected by relationships. The whole is greater than the sum of its parts (Auyang 1999). Holism is the common frame that is shared by the modern systems theory of the West and the ancient Taoism Philosophy of the East.

Stream #1: Systems Theory. The systems theory is the interdisciplinary study of systems. A system, whether natural or artificial, is a cohesive assemblage of interdependent parts. A tree, a person, a pet, a company, and a nonprofit organization are all examples of systems. Changing one part of a system may affect other parts or the whole system. An open system is influenced by the environment through its permeable boundaries. Relationships are what holds the parts together (Bertalanffy 1972). The systems theory guides us to understand the interconnectedness of human communication as a whole, rather than looking at just the sender and receiver as parts. Organizational communication scholars are interested in the interaction of people to see how they cocreate organizations. For example, what makes Home Depot different than Lowe's? It's not simply their products or prices. Instead, these two home-improvement mega retail stores have certain *personalities* and ways of functioning that are different from each other. With the systems theory, we may see multiple layers of communication as interconnected chains rather than isolated acts.

Stream #2: Philosophical Taoism. Taoism (道家思想) is a philosophical school of thought originated in China several thousand years ago. Taoism emphasizes living in accordance with Tao (道): *the way*, the law of the universe. Living means to flow with the Tao. Taoism is considered the philosophy of harmony, as it takes a holistic perspective and reveals the beauty of unity between opposite powers. Some major ideas in Taoism include human–nature coexistence (道法自然), harmony of opposite energies (Yin Yang, 阴阳), and action through inaction (Wu Wei, 无为). Taoist beliefs emphasize respecting and protecting nature, all in the pursuit of harmony between human beings and the environment. The central sign in Taoism is the Bagua symbol (八卦图), created by Fuxishi (伏羲氏) about 5,000 years ago (see Figure 2.2). This symbol illustrates Yin and Yang energies accommodate with each other and coexist in harmony in the *whole*. Yin (阴), the darker element, represents the quality of passive, dark, feminine, downward-seeking, and corresponds to the night. Yang (阳), the brighter element, represent the quality of active, light, masculine, and upward-seeking and corresponds to the day. *Yin* quality or *Yang* quality is neither good nor bad. They just exist together in harmony. Philosophical Taoism is the foundation of traditional Chinese medicine. The perfect equilibrium in yin–yang balance is the indication of good health. Therefore, the diagnosis on the balance

Figure 2.2 The dynamic interplay of Yin and Yang in the Taoism Taiji symbol

of yin and yang energies in the human body leads to the prescription of treatment with Chinese herbal medicine and acupuncture.

This book highlights wisdom from three ancient Chinese Taoism books: *I Ching* (The Book of Changes, 《易经》), *Tao Te Ching* (《道德经》), and *The Yellow Emperor's Classic of Internal Medicine* (《黄帝内经》). First, The book of *I Ching* (易经), also known as *Book of Changes*, was first written over 5,000 years ago by Fuxishi (伏羲氏), then interpreted by King Wen of Chou Jichang (周文王姬昌), later explained by Confucius (孔子) in *Chou I* (周易). I Ching was written in both Bagua symbols and texts. As the *book of origin* (群经之首) for Taoism and many other Chinese classic thoughts, *I Ching* is a must read. Second, *Tao Te Ching* (道德经), written by Laozi (also known as Lao Tzu, 老子, sixth century BCE), is the *cornerstone* of Taoism. *Tao Te Ching* is the second most translated book in the world, after only the Bible. The key idea from Laozi is the meaning of the omnipresent Tao and how we can be happy by living in harmony with the Tao in nature. *Tao Te Ching* is a book of *linguistic diamonds* that shines wisdom on relationship building. Third, compiled by a group of scholars in sixth century BCE or earlier, *The Yellow Emperor's Classic of Internal Medicine* (*Huangdi Neijing*, 黄帝内经) is foundational for Chinese herbal medicine. Chinese herbal medical doctors treat the whole patient rather than just the symptoms of a disease.

Stream #3: Inspirations From Gardening: For millennia, people of all cultures have practiced gardening for produce and relaxation. A gardener cultivates plants for food, drinks, materials, medicine, comfort, and decoration. The word *horticulture* comes from the Latin *hortus* for *garden* and *cultura* for *cultivation* (Arteca 2015). In gardens, plants are *selected* and *cultivated* purposely for their foliage, flowers, fruits, and roots. To achieve the desired yields, a gardener must *study* the plant, *observe* its character, and satisfy its *needs* in different seasons with proper sunshine, water, and soil, and be *patient* to wait for the yields. Soil nutrition, irrigation, positioning for sunshine, timing, and luck contribute to the quality and quantity of harvests. Gardening involves the active participation of a gardener in the process of seeding, growing, and harvesting, just like cultivating a business relationship.

Mixed-Method Approach for Research

This book is the result of multimethod qualitative research that crystalizes data from 12-year participant observation and auto-ethnography as a fundraiser for SAUPO conference, and in-depth interviews with 20 entrepreneurs. The insights, expertise, and experiences for business relationship development by the interviewees are triangulated in the mixed-methods design (Creswell 2009). The aim of this type of qualitative research is to describe multiple ways in which entrepreneurs generate rich meaning in business development. Triangulation is used for data analysis to synthesize the results of research projects in different methods, based on different theories. First, this research practiced *theory triangulation* by involving both Western and Eastern theoretical schemes in the interpretation of business relationship development. Second, the research adopted *methodological triangulation*, by gathering data via in-depth interviews, participant observation, and autoethnography. Such triangulation provides a more detailed and enriched picture of the situation due to different data collected and multiple theoretical lenses adopted. Twelve years of participant observation as a fundraiser helped to generate the six-step communication strategy for relationship development, while the 20 in-depth interviews facilitated to validate and interpret the six steps.

Research Method #1: Participant Observation as a Fundraiser. As a fundraiser for a nonprofit educational conference since 2010, I collected field notes through participant observation. It is common that sometimes participant observation arises from an ongoing working situation. The researcher in this position acquires an in-depth and first-hand insight into a real-world setting. Participant observation involves the researcher watching participants in their natural environment. In some cases, participants may not know they are being studied, as the researcher fully immerses his or herself as a member in the community. The methodology of participant observation focuses on the meanings of human existence as seen from *the standpoint of insiders* (Jorgensen 1989). The *here* and *now* of everyday life is important to the methodology of participant observation. The aim of this research is to gain an intimate familiarity with global business entrepreneurs and their practices. However (1972) mentions four stages in most participant observation research: (1) getting to know the people and establishing rapport; (2) immersing oneself in the field; (3) recording data and observations; and (4) synthesizing data gathered. Through participant observation, it is possible to describe what goes on, who are involved, when and why things happen the way they do.

My 12-year participant observation as a fundraiser inspired the six-step relationship cultivation flowchart shown in Chapter 1, as well as the interview guide for the in-depth interviews with the entrepreneurs. Going to the community and *asking* for money from potential donors, I learned first-hand the challenges, mysteries, and miracles of fundraising. During all the global conferences that I chaired from 2011 to 2022, I recorded about 80 to 100 pages of fieldnotes for each conference. Therefore, a total of about 1,000 pages of fieldnotes were collected.

Participant observation also includes taking notes while interacting with my students. Most of my graduate and undergraduate students are members in the millennial generation (also called Gen Y, born 1981–1995) and Generation Z (or Gen Z, born 1996–2010). They are the two younger generations in or entering the workforce and marketplace. Each generation grew up in their unique environment with signature events and technological innovations. Different generations' unique preference in media and communication will be synthesized in Chapter 8 on digital transformation in relationship building.

Research Method #2: In-Depth Interviews with 20 Entrepreneurs. "The phenomenon dictates the method, including even the type of participants" (Hycner 1999, 156). Since we want to uncover the communication strategies adopted in the marketplace, I interviewed 20 global entrepreneurs from April 5, 2019 to July 6, 2022. Researchers have stressed that the number of participants should be determined based on the purpose of the research. Seidman (2006) recommends *sufficiency* and *saturation* as the two criteria for deciding the number of participants. Sufficiency refers to the amount and range of participants needed to reflect the population, while saturation of information refers to the point where the data collection no longer reveals new information. Twenty entrepreneurs from different industries proved to be the *point of saturation* in the sampling for this study. Saturation is a point in qualitative research where the researcher has exhausted all possible themes that the data suggest. It means that any additional interviews will not bring in new data. These qualitative in-depth interviews show us the insiders' stories about relationships, business, fundraising, and entrepreneurs. From April 5, 2019 to July 6, 2022, I completed semistructured in-depth interviews with 20 global business leaders, with each about 75 minutes. During the interviews, 20 entrepreneurs and leaders in the private sector shared their experiences and insights about business and relationships, generating 1,875 minutes of MP3 files and 200,000+ words in transcripts. Patterns and themes in the interview transcripts were searched, analyzed, and summarized in this book. Certain quotations from the interviews are so profound that I highlight these words of wisdom at the beginning of each chapter as *Quotations to Ponder.*

Research Method #3: Autoethnography. At the beginning of each chapter, I composed one or two case studies, mostly based on situations I experienced in organizing SAUPO or stories I heard during the interviews. I write these case studies as narratives in the method of *autoethnography*, aiming at providing vivid details of texts and contexts. I believe autoethnography brings readers closer to these business cases. In general, autoethnography involves self-observation and reflexive investigation in the context of ethnographic field work and writing. Caroline Ellis, (2004) a founder of this research method, defines autoethnography as "research, writing, story, and method that connect the autobiographical and personal to the cultural, social, and political" (xix).

Gao's Relationship Tree Metaphor

Holism inspires us to look at a system as a living organism (Morgan 1998). An interpersonal business relationship can be viewed as a living organism, adapting to the ever-changing environment. In the time of social distancing due to the COVID-19 pandemic, many people have adopted a new hobby: gardening. I enjoy planting flowers and vegetables, while being one with nature. I learned to be better at gardening by observing what the plants want and need, and by learning from my mistakes. Timing of planting, exposure to sunshine, amount of irrigation, type of soil, and a

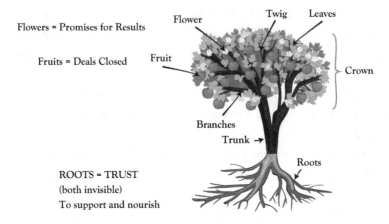

Nutrition for tree via Roots = Relationship Building Communication
Tree (Relationship) Positioning matters for sunshine, water and nutrients.
It might take years for a tree (relationship) to produce fruits (deals).

Figure 2.3 Gao's Relationship Tree Metaphor

little bit of luck are just some key elements that contribute to the desired results. Sunshine, water, soil, and timing. These ingredients enable a seed to germinate and grow into a mature plant, potentially yielding fruits, or vegetables for you.

Through pondering upon the success and failures in the gardening experience, I apply lessons learned into business relationship cultivation. I would like to use an apple tree to form a *Relationship Tree Metaphor*. After an apple seed is planted into soil, the root is the first organ that grows out of the seed. The root system of the apple tree is underground and has two major functions. First, the root system anchors and supports the plant in the soil. Second, the root system absorbs water, oxygen, and other substances from the soil, and transports these nutrients to the stem and the rest of the plant. The root supports a tree, much like *trust* sustains a relationship. Before any relationship even develops, trust must be developed, much like the root is the first part growing out of a seed. Trust is the foundation of all relationships, just like the roots of plants. The size and strength of the roots indicate the size and health of a plant, similar to the fact that *trust* dictates relationship strength. Therefore, *trust* for a relationship is like *root* for a plant, as they are both less visible, yet vital for the existence, health, and growth of the relationship/tree.

Trust supports and nourishes a relationship, just like the root for a tree. After the root germinates, a plant is well on its way to grow. "Human follows the Earth, the Earth follows the Heaven, the Heaven follows Tao, and the Tao follows what is natural" (Laozi, 471 BCE). Ultimately, Human, Earth, Heaven, and the entire universe follow *what is natural*, including relationship building. The next chapter prepares the *relationship gardener* with the proper I-Thou posture: *Humility for the Self and Respect for the Other.*

CHAPTER 3

Between Self and Other

With Humility and Respect

Quotations to Ponder

Having an impeccable reputation will always precede a relationship and confirm who you are. It's important to make a great first impression, tell the truth, be genuine, and be transparent.

—DeAnn Golden, President and CEO
Berkshire Hathaway HomeServices Georgia Properties

I think humility has to be instinctive. Life humbles a person.

—Alex Gregory, former President and CEO
YKK Corporation of America

Treat everybody with respect, including all on the totem poles. Involve them. Share both good and bad news with them.

—Roger Neuenschwander, former President and CEO
tvsdesign

You have to listen. If you think you are the smartest person in the room, number one, you are wrong. Number two, you just lost an opportunity to get a piece of gold out of others.

—Rick Cole, former Senior Vice President
Turner Broadcasting System

People want to do business with those they like. I must build relationships so that my customers like me and like my company. You can get people to like you by listening to them, and by demonstrating to them that you can deliver value to them.

—Brad Taylor, former Brand Strategist
The Coca-Cola Company

Everything is a relationship game. Every social media platform is a relationship platform.

—Eddy Perez, Cofounder and CEO
Equity Prime Mortgage

Knowing others is intelligence; knowing yourself is true wisdom. Mastering others is strength; mastering yourself is true power.

—Laozi, Author
Tao Te Ching

Chapter Summary

This chapter defines and explains concepts like *humility*, *respect*, *I-Thou*, *hearing*, and *listening*. Based on Gao's six-step communication strategy for relationship building, this chapter elaborates on the proper positioning of *self* and *other*, toward a mutually beneficial, trusted relationship. A mutual self and other relationship shall be grounded with humility for the self and respect for the other. By adopting a humble attitude for ourselves and treating others with respect, we can listen with empathy. The I-Thou dialogic posture invites authenticity, vulnerability, affirmation, and mutuality in a trust-based relationship. The stance of humility for the self is strongly supported by the winning *Qian* (謙, *humility*) motif in the book of *I Ching*. Further, this chapter outlines strategies for designing the everlasting first impression, including e-profiles at social media sites, nonverbal and verbal messages at first meetings. This chapter presents communication strategies for people to skillfully practice and embody humility for the self and respect for the other. The chapter also underscores the importance of proper communication strategies with relational names and first impressions.

CASE STUDY 3.1

Mr. Smith's Meeting with the CEO on the First Day of His Job

Steve Johnson is the president and CEO of a multinational manufacturing firm. He is known to be a humble leader, always very respectful and considerate of others. Ten years ago, the firm's human resources (HR) department hired Robert Smith as a new mid-level manager. On his first day at the corporate headquarters, Robert walked to the end of the hallway, and stepped inside the office of the CEO, who liked to keep his door open for the employees. The CEO Mr. Johnson had not met with Robert yet. As soon as Robert walked inside the CEO's office, Mr. Johnson looked up. Robert said to Mr. Johnson loudly and jokingly, "So, what do we pay you to do?" Confronted with this question, Mr. Johnson was a bit shocked and then smiled. He thought, "This is not a very nice hello. It was perhaps his way of being funny, but it was not very thoughtful and sensitive." Over the next few months, Robert worked with Mr. Johnson closely together on some projects. Although Mr. Johnson's impression of Robert got better, the negative first impression never left his mind after many years.

In psychology, a first impression is the event when one person first encounters another person and forms a mental image of that person. Impression accuracy varies depending on the observer and the target being observed. *First impressions have long-lasting impacts. We do not get a second chance to build the first impressions.* Therefore, it is beneficial to *design* a first impression for important encounters, including studying the background of those whom we are meeting with, dressing for success, and being aware of our nonverbal messages.

Discussion Questions for Readers

1. How could have Mr. Smith acted differently to make a good first impression with the CEO?
2. How often do you rely on your first impression of people to make judgments? What types of messages stand out the most?
3. How can we practice and embody humility in relationships?

CASE STUDY 3.2

It's Essential to Treat Others with Respect

Sonny Patel is the director of information technology (IT) at a global software firm. In 1995, he started his career in IT programing, fresh out of an engineering university in India. One day, he attended a networking event in Bangalore (i.e., Bengaluru), the capital of global outsourcing industries. Presenting his newly made business cards with both hands and a smile with his mouth and eyes, Mr. Patel tried to meet with the vice president (VP) of a well-known company. The VP said "hi," but he did not accept Mr. Patel's business card and did not shake his hand. Instead, the VP walked away, saying he was going to get some more drinks. Mr. Patel felt disrespected and hurt. Today, out of hard work and experience, Mr. Patel has been promoted to the director of IT at a global software firm. Mr. Patel reminds himself never to repeat the same mistake made by that VP. We need to respect a person for his/her full potential, even if the person just started his/her career. The person will grow, the maturity may accumulate, and he/she might be rewarded with a different job title, but the need for dignity of a person stays the same.

Discussion Questions for Readers

1. Why is respect important in cultivating business relationships?
2. How can we maintain respect toward others regardless of their credentials?
3. Do we need to be humble to respect the other person? Why?

Introducing *Organizational Delegates*

Businesses need to connect with other companies and organizations in the communities to generate, sustain, and grow revenues. In practice, organizations connect with each other through their employees. Inter-organizational relationships are indeed executed at the interpersonal level. Individuals function as organizational delegates, representing their respective organizations in certain authority, capacity, and power. Organizational delegates stand for their organizations based on tasks at hand, such as public relations (PR), marketing, negotiation, supply chain management, charity, education, and fundraising. By building interpersonal relationships between two organizational delegates, the two companies and organizations work together.

Depending on the task, organizational delegates can be the president or CEO, any member in the leadership, management, or sales teams, or employees at different levels of the organizational chart. Rick Cole, former Senior VP at Turner Broadcasting System, states that "business is about relationships." Spending time in building interpersonal relationships enables us to get to know "the person behind the position." Jessica Cork, the VP for Community Engagement and Corporate Communications at YKK Corporation of America, emphasizes authenticity in relationships. She says part of authenticity is getting to understand the whole person, beyond their work selves. *Because it is impossible to establish trust between two positions, a trust-based relationship can only be*

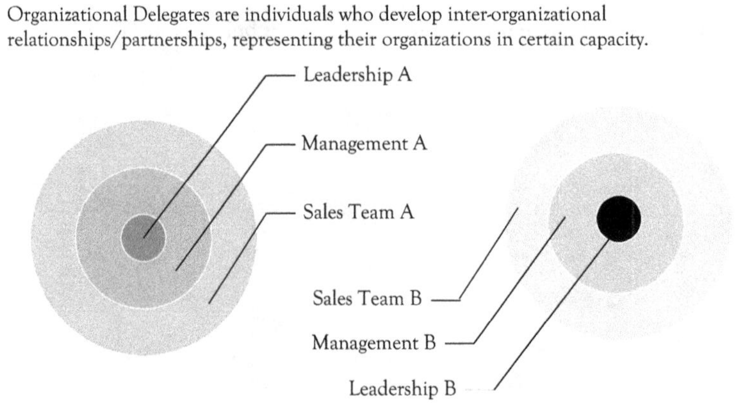

Organizational Delegates are individuals who develop inter-organizational relationships/partnerships, representing their organizations in certain capacity.

Leadership A

Management A

Sales Team A

Sales Team B

Management B

Leadership B

Figure 3.1 Gao's organizational delegates model

built between two persons. Once two organizational delegates establish trust with each other, two organizations have a chance to grow a partnership.

The trust-based relationships between organizational delegates are viewed as social capital by companies. Thus, it is imperative and profitable for organizations to *inherit* these relationships before the organizational delegates retire or leave the companies and organizations. Often, we see that individuals in two different companies develop a relationship with each other for business deals between the two companies. If either organizational delegates retires or leaves, this inter-organizational relationship is interrupted or terminated, leading to change, disruption, or reduction in business deals. These business relationships shall be systematically and sensitively passed down as a kind of *relational inheritance*. David Kirk, president and CEO of Murata Electronics North America shares, "It takes many years to build that deep relationship. When we make some changes, we continue to carry on that relationship." To cultivate win–win–win type of relationships between two organizational delegates, this book advocates I-Thou relationships.

I-Thou Relationships with Mutuality

This book intends to highlight the immense value of *active listening* in relationship building. Interview data show active listening skill is essential for due diligence and business development. For effective communication, active listening involves four steps: (1) to listen to verbal messages; (2) to observe nonverbal messages and the context (the face expressions, body language, room arrangement, time, atmosphere, etc.); (3) to understand the true *meaning* of verbal and nonverbal messages from the speakers' perspectives; and (4) to provide feedback and ask for clarifications. *Active listening skill is not taught enough in schools. In the United States, K-12 and college students are usually being taught how to speak and debate. Class participation grades often reflect how great students talk, but not so much on how effective they listen.* In a culture of debate for political elections, students view debate as the dominant form of communication. The ultimate purpose of debate is to defeat the other, which is not conducive for collaboration at work and for business. On the contrary, dialogue embraces active listening, mutual respect, and collaboration.

I-It (Belittle, Disrespect)   I-Thou (Empathy, Respect)

Figure 3.2 The I-It versus I-Thou relational attitude

Dialogue is at the heart of two-way communication. In contrast to monologue, debate, or *two TV sets talking at each other*-type of conversations, dialogue embraces mutual understanding, constructs common ground, and therefore allows for win–win–win business relationships. An I-Thou relationship asks us to respect the other with empathy and present the self with humility and confidence. Like setting up the proper posture for golf or tennis, adopting the I-Thou relationship is the starting point for Gao's six-step communication strategy for business development, introduced in Chapter 1.

The dialogue theory inspires the I-Thou relationships advocated by this book for business success. Martin Buber (1970) teaches us that there are two modalities in self–other relationships: *I-It* and *I-Thou*. The I-It modality treats the other as an object or less than a human being, while the I-Thou modality values the other as an equal human being, affirming his/her past, present, and potential. In an I-It relationship, the attitude of *looking down upon* and sympathy may be practiced. In an I-Thou Relationship, the *I* respects the other, seeks to understand the other from his/her perspective. For Buber (1970), the fundamental human existence is the dialogue that takes place in the *sphere of the between*. Buber was inspired by his experience in translating the Bible, while maintaining a dialogue with God, the *Eternal Thou*.

David Bohm (1996) states the term *communication* is based on the Latin word *commun,* which means *to communicate* or *to make something common*. The term *dialogue* comes from the Greek word *dialogos*. Logos means *the word*, and *dia* means *through*, not *two*. Bohm explains that in a dialogue, nobody tries to win points over others. Rather, all participants gain. Bakhtin (1984) advocates that we participate in dialogues with open mind and open heart. Participating in conversations with an I-Thou perspective can be a game changer in relationship building. Valuing the other as *Thou* instead of objectifying the other as *It* changes the dynamics and energy we put in conversations.

In an I-Thou relationship, the *I* affirms the other as a whole person with active listening. In an effort of lowering oneself with humility and elevating the other with respect, one may have a new discovery about the other and oneself. In an I-Thou relationship, the *I* respects and listens to the other, which opens doors for a possible mutually beneficial relationship. In an I-Thou relationship, the humanness in the *I* is fully present when communicating with the other, whether in person or online. There is no room for a narcissistic ego in an I-Thou relationship. The awareness of one's ego can become an obstacle to dialogue and hinders the possibility of the productive "dialogic moments" (Katriel 2004) when new meaning is cocreated by the self and other.

A popular example of an I-Thou relationship may be illustrated in the *Undercover Boss*[1] television show. In each episode, a top executive leaves the comfort of his/her office and secretly takes on low-level jobs within the company. This show utilizes hidden cameras to provide an authentic view of their journeys as they are immersed in the daily operations. In the process of these undercover missions, the leaders learn more about the company, their employees, and themselves. Many executives become better leaders through such a humbling experience.

Humility for the Self

Using a standard *interview guide*, I asked the 20 entrepreneurs the same set of questions about the secrets for business relationship building. Should

---

[1] *Undercover Boss* is an American reality television series, based on the British series of the same name and produced by Studio Lambert in both countries. Each episode depicts an upper manager going undercover as an entry-level employee to discover issues in the company. The first season consisted of nine episodes produced in 2009 and first aired on February 7, 2010, CBS.

the self be proud or humble when approaching the other for a business relationship? All entrepreneurs replied: The *self* shall be humble, and we should approach the other with respect. Such an attitude is consistent with the perspective for an I-Thou relationship. In life or at work, someone may appear to have a proud or even an arrogant attitude. However, being proud or arrogant may shut doors for new business relationships. On the contrary, being humble provides the self with opportunities to listen and observe the other. By finding out what the customer wants and needs, we can connect with them to form business relationships. As a result, we are rewarded for making value-added products, services, and solutions to satisfy their wants and needs. Being humble does not mean that we are not confident about ourselves. Being humble reflects self-confidence.

Being humble applies to companies of all sizes. Brad Taylor, former brand strategist at The Coca-Cola Company, states that companies should stay humble and be locally relevant. Mr. Taylor shares that there was a period at The Coca-Cola Company when much business was lost due to a high level of arrogance. Mr. Taylor emphasizes that nothing will humble you faster than losing business! The company now desires to hire those who represent themselves in a confident yet humble way, someone who demonstrates a sense of curiosity and a willingness to learn about the customers.

There is a delicate balance between self-confidence and genuine humility. Being humble does not mean we behave in a timid or fearful manner. In fact, being humble requires self-confidence and assertiveness, supported by a strong self-concept. For example, if you are trying to sell, you need to display confidence to match your messages. We should be proud of who we are and live with a sense of gratitude and appreciation. Being truly self-confident means recognizing that you may not be the brightest, quickest, or most articulate team member, but that you are nevertheless comfortable with who you are.

Master Nan Huaijin (南怀瑾), a contemporary I Ching expert, teaches us that all six strokes of the 15th motif *Humility* (*Qian* 谦卦) demonstrate lucky tendencies. There is simply no unlucky stroke in the motif of *humility*. The symbol for humility shows a *flat ground with mountains hidden underneath*, indicating humility established upon substance, confidence, and credibility (Qiyuange Website 2020). *Humility* can be

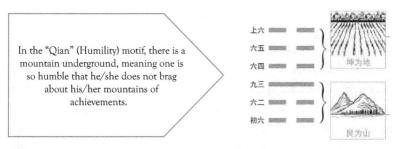

In the "Qian" (Humility) motif, there is a mountain underground, meaning one is so humble that he/she does not brag about his/her mountains of achievements.

Figure 3.3 The ever-winning Qian *(humility) motif based on the book of* I Ching

used as a winning strategy in all situations. A humble person tends to keep a low profile, listen to others, and learn from others for continuous self-improvement.

Laozi, the author of *Tao Te Ching*, describes the highest virtue for a person is to be like water (上善若水). Humility is an inherent virtue of water, as water always flows to the lowest point in its vicinity. All rivers flow to the sea because the ocean stays much lower than rivers. Laozi suggests that if you want to govern the people, you must position yourself lower to serve them. If you want to lead the people, you must learn to follow them. Servant leadership is a leadership philosophy in which the goal of the leader is to serve. A servant leader shares power, puts the needs of the employees first and helps them to develop and perform at their highest potential (Sendjaya and Sarros 2002). If a leader strives to maintain the virtue of humility, this leader is one step closer to practice servant leadership, which will be further demonstrated in Chapter 9 of this book.

In negotiation and diplomacy, people are often advised *to negotiate from a position of strength*. As a result, we see actions of arrogance and aggression. People may have a misunderstanding with this phrase. From the Taoist perspective, equipped with substance, strength, and integrity, one may speak from humility in search of common ground with the other, for a mutually beneficial relationship. It is human nature that everyone wants to be a winner, and nobody desires to be a loser. The best strategy for solving conflicts in interpersonal, interorganizational, and international contexts is to search for win–win–win solutions for all parties involved from a relationship perspective.

Respect for the Other

Respect for the other goes hand in hand with humility for the self in an I-Thou relationship. Eddy Perez, cofounder and CEO of Equity Prime Mortgage, stated in his interview, "There is nothing more important in life than respect because everybody wants to be loved, and respect is the ultimate sign of love." *Respect allows listening, mindfulness, understanding, and gaining of knowledge. Eventually, respect facilitates mutual liking, the bridge to business relationships.* Brad Taylor, former brand strategist of The Coca-Cola Company, says that people want to do business with those they like and respect. If we want someone to respect us, then we better figure out a way to respect them. Mr. Taylor shares, "If you're a likable person, and you're smiling with your eyes and your mouth, you generally are going to make a good first impression. If you want to get business, do more listening than talking."

The dialogic I-Thou relationship requires transparency and authenticity between the self and other. Being transparent, vulnerable, and authentic requires open communication, including keeping each other informed of both good and bad news. When it comes to business or life in general, we like to hear and tell good news. Good news usually means business is going well, everyone is healthy, and life continues as usual. However, bad news happens. For example, there is a delay in production, a mistake in communication, a disaster at work, a loss in an election, an earthquake, or a pandemic. All entrepreneurs I interviewed for this book stress that honestly sharing bad news can strengthen credibility and boost mutual respect in relationship building. Some of the entrepreneurs say that sometimes maybe the best thing you can do is to say, "Look, I don't think I'll be able to help you at this time." By being transparent about a challenging situation, we allow for collective input for problem-solving and gain trust from relationship partners. Relationships may grow stronger even in difficult times. Delivering bad news in an authentic way is a sign of respect for the other.

How do we demonstrate respect for the other? Laozi says, "a thousand miles journey starts from the first step" (千里之行，始于足下). Showing respect starts with details, such as being punctual, providing feedback in various communication channels, following up on your promises, and showing appreciation. You need to respect who people are and what challenges they have. The *I* may show respect to the *Thou* by listening, by not wasting their time, and by delivering what is promised. Here are some strategies to demonstrate respect:

- Send out handwritten *thank you cards* to show appreciation.
- Write customized notes on *happy birthday cards* to accent personal touch.
- Say *we* instead of *I* more to highlight the team spirit and relationship.
- Be punctual, or slightly early for business meetings.
- Smile with both your eyes and your mouth.
- Use proper nonverbal messages and dress code when meeting people.
- Listen with full presence and full attention.

The Everlasting First Impressions

First impressions matter. You do not get a second chance to make a first impression. A first impression is the event when the *self* encounters the *other* for the first time and forms a mental image of the other. The first impression forms an important database that greatly influences how we see the other. It takes just one-tenth of a second for us to judge someone with a first impression (Willis and Todorov 2006). Initial encounters are emotionally concentrated events that can be overwhelming. We walk away from these events with a head-to-toe photographic image that never seems to entirely fade. In this *snap time*, your observers form an opinion about you based on your facial expressions, body language, mannerisms, outfit, smell, and interactions (Knight 2016). Our ability to present and read first impressions drives the quality of our personal and professional lives (Wood 2012). Ensuring that people see the best of us from the beginning will improve and expand our networks.

Watzlawick declares "one cannot *not* communicate." Humans are always communicating in front of an observer, despite whether that message is intended (Watzlawick, Beavin, and Jackson 1967). Much of our daily communication is conducted subconsciously and automatically.

Even when you think you are *not* sending any messages, the nonverbal messages, the silence, and the inaction may present certain messages to an observer. The axis of time and space combined is imprinted in the snapshot of first impressions. Chronotope, coined by Bakhtin, literally means time and space united. Mikhail Bakhtin (1981) underscores the intrinsic connectedness of temporal and spatial relationships. I believe the concept of chronotope can be applied to relationship building. Choosing proper time and space for the acts in relationship development can be critical for success. We may therefore intentionally choreograph the time, location, and image of first impressions.

Marcy Sperry, the founder of Vivid IP law firm, stressed the importance of professional appearance, due diligence, being early, and following up. She said that whether people admit it or not, they expect you to come across as polished, professional, and sophisticated. She would rather show up dressed in a suit and have everybody else wearing jeans than show up under-dressed. Being early opens doors for us to make good first impressions and to network for business. At business meetings or events, it is critical to show up early because that is where some of the most important networking takes place. If you get there right on time, the program may be about to start, and the place is probably really, really crowded. Conversely, if you get there early, you can scope out the room and have more intimate conversations with some of the players who have also arrived early. It is valuable to do some research on event speakers ahead of time and then specifically target two to three speakers you want to connect to your network. You can think ahead of time about what subject matter would be relevant to them so that you may engage with them in meaningful conversations. You may send them a LinkedIn invitation afterward to follow up. In proper time, you may invite them out for coffee or lunch and continue to develop the relationship. What Marcy Sperry did not recommend is to hand out lots of business cards and shake a 100 people's hands, because it is almost impossible to foster relationships with all these people. We must be selective as our time and energy are limited. To establish good first impressions when communicating with Asian people, we need to pay attention to the exchange of business cards and gifts. Respectfully handling business cards with both hands and giving proper gifts to your Asian business partners frame you in a friendly light for first impressions. Here are more tips:

- Do research about the other and his/her company before the meeting.
- Dress the part for a professional look.
- Arrive early.
- Show warmth.
- Be a likable person.
- Maintain eye contact (although in China, Saudi Arabia or other countries, prolonged direct eye contact between opposite genders are seen as impolite and improper).
- Smile with both your eyes and your mouth.
- Do more listening than talking.
- Show genuine interest in that other person.
- Observe the whole room.
- Focus on a few new contacts at an event.
- Be brief in telling others about you and your company.
- Research on what gifts are proper to people of different cultures.
- Avoid political, religious and sexual topics during conversations.

Names Are Relational and Cultural

Although my cell phone is registered in the National Do Not Call List, I still get calls from numbers not in my caller ID list frequently. Occasionally, I will pick up the calls in case it is an inquiry for my conference. However, if I am greeted with the following questions, it is probably a good idea to hang up. The callers clearly do not have a relationship with me, as they are not addressing me as *May*:

- "Is Mr. Gao there?"
- "Is the head of the household there?"
- "Hello! I would like to talk with you about your car's extended warranty."

Names are relational. Paul Watzlawick states that every communication episode has a content aspect and a relationship aspect. Relational messages can stand alone or be attached to task messages.

The function of the relational message could be to affirm information given by the speaker, to show support to the speaker, to signal to the speaker to continue, or to disqualify someone's message. The relationship message classifies the content message in the capacity of *meta-communication* (Watzlawick, Beavin, and Jackson 1967). Relational messages can make or break the content messages. Relational information occurs in all messages of any contexts. People's names, as symbols of communication, are no exception.

Confucius says in *The Analects*, "If the name is not proper, then it is difficult to communicate. If it is difficult to communicate, then the project cannot be accomplished" (名不正则言不顺，言不顺则事不成). People's names are important symbols for communication. In fact, names are symbols that represent our identities and reputations on paper, in computer systems, on phone calls, and social media platforms. Each of us usually has multiple names: given name (first name), surname (last name, family name), middle name, nickname, pen name, maiden name, married name, legal name, passport name, and preferred name. Sometimes, educational degrees and job titles are also added to our names, such as *Dr., Prof., Honorable, and President.*

Names are also cultural. In Eastern Asian cultures, *surnames* or *family names* appear first, and *given names* appear last. In Chinese, Japanese, Korean, and Vietnamese cultures, surnames are considered more significant than given names. In collectivist cultures, the interest of the group is more important than that of the individual. In the American, European, and Latin cultures, given names appear first in the order of names. Asian Americans, Asian immigrants to the United States, and Asian people with international encounters usually adopt an *English name* for easier communication. Therefore, their names may be reversed to fit into the Western cultural tradition of *first name, last name* order. When we communicate with Asians or Asian Americans, it is imperative to discover which name is the *last name (family name)*, which name is the *first name (given name)*, and which name is their preferred English name. Even though they may have English names on their business cards, many businesspeople from Asia still prefer to be called Mr. Wang, Mr. Choi, Ms. Watanabi, or Mrs. Ho. This is because in most East Asian cultures, for example, given names are reserved for spouses, lovers, and parents.

Because names are relational and cultural, improper name usage may lead to an awkward beginning, a dead end, a failure in business relationship building. When you approach the other, the first most important task is to find out what name he/she prefers to be used when relating with you. Perhaps one's business card shows *Thomas Robert Davis, PhD*, but his preferred name is Tom, Tommy, Rob, Bob, TR, Dr. Davis, Mr. Davis, or Prof. Davis. We need to learn to properly use names to communicate in a relational, sensitive, and respectful way. For example, depending on my relationships and lived experience with the other, I expect them to address me with different names, such as May, Hongmei, Dr. Gao, Gao Hongmei, or others. Finding out what names people prefer to communicate with you is the critical first step in building business relationships. Remembering their preferred names of communication will be the second step in relationship building. Here are some strategies to remember people's names:

- Google this person and find out how his/her name is being used.
- Write down the preferred name on the back of their business cards.
- Use their preferred names immediately while speaking back to them.
- Repeat their names three times back to them during conversation.
- Talk about the meaning and stories of their names.
- Try to remember their names in your fragmented time.
- Take selfies with him/her if appropriate.
- Check their social media pages, and learn about their usage of names: LinkedIn, Facebook, WhatsApp, Instagram, Tik Tok, WeChat, and so on.

Alex Gregory, the former president and CEO of YKK Corporation of America, shares his methods for remembering names. When he goes to YKK Canada for a meeting, there could be 25 managers. At airports or airborne, Mr. Gregory would review the meeting agenda and make a special entry for this meeting on his smartphone. He lists everyone's names

Figure 3.4 Milestones from listening to relationships

and writes a short note about each participant. The next time when he travels to Canada, Mr. Gregory would pull up that list on his smartphone and refresh himself with these names and his notes on them. Mr. Gregory says since he is the guest coming, everyone in the Canada team would remember his name. Therefore, he must work harder to remember their names. By going down that list and working on those names on the trip to Canada, Mr. Gregory says he usually could remember everyone's names before the meeting. People are frequently impressed by that and appreciate his remembering their names. Further, Mr. Gregory reveals that he keeps a daily journal in an Excel file, in which essential information of daily meetings and activities is recorded. When a new year arrives, Mr. Gregory would create a new Excel file by copy and updating the former year's Excel file. People's birthdays, wedding anniversary dates and other key information remain in this new journal file. A couple days before or on people's birthdays and anniversary dates, Mr. Gregory would send them greetings, cards, handwritten notes and gifts. Just in time delivery of relationship cultivation messages! Many employees, customers, and community partners are so impressed by his kindness and attention to details. It takes a long time and much effort for us to develop long-term and deep business relationships with customers: from listening to mutual liking.

Conclusion

Organizations relate with each other through human beings who are the organizational delegates. An interpersonal relationship is essentially a connection between the self and the other in personal, social, business, international, and other contexts. To build win–win–win relationships, this book presents the dialogic I-Thou perspective on relationships. An I-Thou relationship is naturally enriched with mutuality, transparency, collaboration, and trust. The I-Thou relationship, in contrast to the I-It relationship, treats the other as a human being with his/her full potential. Adopting a humble attitude for the self, while treating the other with respect in an I-Thou relationship, the self tends to listen with empathy and therefore understand the other better from his/her perspective. The I-Thou posture for win–win–win business relationship building is supported by the "Humility" motif in the ancient Taoism book of I Ching. Finding out the other's preferred name and intentionally constructing a positive first impression are the first steps in business relationship building. Next, trust needs to be *germinated* for the relationship under our tender care. Chapter 4 unearths the mystery of trust.

CHAPTER 4

Trust

The Root of a Relationship

Quotations to Ponder

Earning trust is a process that usually takes a long time, but trust can be lost in minutes. You always need to treat people with respect, and you need to show genuine interest in people.
— Alex Gregory, former President and CEO
YKK Corporation of America

In Japan, trust is everything! Before any business, you must gain your client's trust first. We don't really do cold calls in Japan, almost every business comes through referrals.
— Masae Okura, Partner
Taylor English Duma LLP

With all the means of social media, to connect with someone is relatively easy. However, to really get to know each other and to grow a mutual relationship, it is not easy. Trust is needed for a productive relationship.
— Glad Cheng, Chairman
China Window Group

Brands are promises to consumers for value delivery, while trust is the glue that holds the relationship between the brands and consumers.
— Brad Taylor, former Brand Strategist
The Coca-Cola Company

*Trust is something that takes a tremendous amount of time and invest-
ment. Trust takes "walking the talk," meaning if I say something, I do
it and I do it consistently.*

—JR Wilson, Vice President for Tower Strategy & Roaming
AT&T

*At the heart of every relationship is trust. You can't have a business
relationship if there's no trust. It would end in disaster.*

—Rick Cole, former Senior Vice President
Turner Broadcasting System

*In a licensed profession, it takes trust to build a relationship. Trust-
worthiness means you back up what you say, and you deliver what
you promise.*

—Roger Neuenschwander, former President and CEO
tvsdesign

*Building trust takes time. You need to make initial good impressions
and to do what you promise over time. Keep the honest communication, even if you have bad news to tell.*

—David Kirk, President and CEO
Murata Electronics North America

Chapter Summary

This chapter illustrates the value of "trust as the root of a relationship." First, this chapter illustrates how to grow trust, nurture trust, and let trust support the relationship. Second, this chapter identifies key *trust intermediaries* in people's personal networks so that one can approach certain individuals to start a potential relationship. Third, this chapter presents specific communication strategies to grow, nurture, maintain, and repair trust for business relationship development. The research data indicate that the trust customers have for a company is symbolized by their relationship with the brand. Online reviews deserve proper attention for brand protection and promotion. The chapter suggests specific communication strategies to create and strengthen trust. For example, business developers may reach out to trust intermediaries among *sensei* professionals or *centers of influence (COIs)* to be connected to a potential business partner.

CASE STUDY 4.1

Boeing 737 Max: Sacrificing Trust to Save Cost?

On December 23, 2019, Boeing fired its CEO Dennis Muilenburg and replaced him with its Chairman David Calhoun. The Boeing Company, commonly known as Boeing, is an American multinational corporation that designs, produces, and sells airplanes, rockets, satellites, missiles, and telecommunication equipment. Since October 2018, Boeing has been struggling to regain the trust of regulators, customers, and the public in the wake of two fatal crashes of its Boeing 737 MAX. The two crashes—in Indonesia in October 2018 and in Ethiopia in March 2019—claimed 346 lives. The Boeing 737 MAX passenger airliner was grounded world-wide between March 2019 and December 2020 for over 20 months, the longest such action in aviation history. Boeing has overhauled the plane's design and software, and paid billions of dollars to try and move past the incidents (Cohn 2022). In November 2020, the U.S. Federal Aviation Administration (FAA) announced that it had cleared the 737 MAX to return to service. Airlines around the world slowly returned this aircraft to service in 2021, though they remained grounded in some countries until 2022, most notably in China (Lee and Che 2022).

As one of the biggest crises in its more than 100-year history, Boeing suffered broken trust with the public. The board determined that a change in leadership was necessary to restore confidence in the company moving forward, and that "we will proceed with a renewed commitment to full transparency, including effective and proactive communications with the FAA, other global regulators and our customers," CFO Greg Smith, who became interim CEO, said in an announcement (Josephs 2019).

Software defects have been blamed for Boeing 737 MAX crashes in Indonesia and Ethiopia. A software system called the Maneuver Characteristics Augmentation System (MCAS) was designed imperfectly due to cost-saving measures (Dawson 2019). MCAS software was developed at a time Boeing was laying off experienced engineers and pressing suppliers to cut costs. Increasingly, the iconic American plane-maker and its sub-contractors have relied on temporary workers making as little as $9 an hour to develop and test software in places such as India. Sara Nelson, president of the Association of Flight Attendants, representing over 50,000 cabin crew members, called Muilenburg's resignation *long overdue* and blamed the planes' failures partially on the pressure for Boeing to deliver excessive returns to investors. "Safety must always come first," said Nelson (Robison 2019). In 2020 and 2021, the global COVID-19 pandemic immensely disrupted global travels and further strained the sales of Boeing airplanes. *Trust is damaged with the Boeing brand in the global market, due to cost-saving measures offsetting airplane quality. Is it worthwhile to generate long-term deficit in trust and sales while saving production cost in the short term?*

Discussion Questions for Readers

1. In which ways do you think a brand stands for quality, consistency, and integrity? How is brand related to consumer trust for its products and services?
2. What happens when companies jump on the bandwagon of saving money through outsourcing jobs, such as the designing of key software, to developing countries?
3. In which ways can Boeing repair its public image and regain the trust from global regulators and customers?

CASE STUDY 4.2

Finding Clients via Cold Calls or Warm Leads?[1]

In September 2019, one of my colleagues, Dr. Jason Baker, thought about inviting Erica Tanaka, a prominent Japanese American anchorwoman, to come for a campus event. Dr. Baker said perhaps Ms. Tanaka could moderate a panel about U.S.–Japan relations on campus in October 2019, with some outstanding panelists. He Googled Ms. Tanaka and found her email address and cell phone number online. Dr. Baker dialed her number at our meeting and even got her on the phone on the second try. After a few sentences of introducing each other, Ms. Tanaka asked him to send her an email introduction. He emailed her the same afternoon and followed up with another enthusiastic email the next week. There was never any response from Ms. Tanaka. I was thinking about what went wrong in this instance. My colleague was being proactive by Googling and cold calling, which seems to be a common practice these days.

When I mentioned this story to my friend Masae Okura, a senior Japanese lawyer in the United States, she laughed and shared her stories. Several years ago, Ms. Okura was invited to join an American law firm. As soon as she joined this firm, a partner said, "Okay, Masae, give me a list of all your Japanese companies." Okura asked, "What are you going to do with my list?" "We're going to Google your list, look for the company names, figure out the contact persons and their in-house counsels. Then we are going to call them," the partner replied. Astonished, Ms. Okura said, "No, stop, don't do that! You are embarrassing me. If you want to talk to some company, let me know. I will talk to someone in that company and try to get you to the right person. I'm going to lose my entire client network if you just Google and cold call them." Ms. Okura said most of her clients have been with her for years. They are her friends through tons of experiences together, for better or for worse.

Ms. Okura shared another story about the power of trust intermediaries in Japanese culture. She attends a U.S.–Japan business conference

---

[1] All names of people and companies in this case are pseudonyms, except the name of Ms. Masae Okura.

every year. A couple of years ago, she was preparing for her trip to Japan. She wanted to fully utilize her time in Japan to visit some existing business partners and connect with some new contacts. She made a lot of appointments with her existing clients. In addition, she wanted to set up meetings with some banks and people she had not met before. First, she called one of her current clients in Atlanta. She said, "I know you use XYZ bank; do you know someone there on the Japan side?" Her client in Atlanta approached a member in his network, who then contacted the bank's representatives (reps). Finally, the official New York rep for XYZ bank contacted colleagues in Japan. It took a couple of weeks for Ms. Okura to set up these meetings. These efforts bring solid results. By the time she arrived at XYZ bank in Japan, there were eight people waiting for her, ready to talk business. The Japanese side of the bank heard about her law firm through all the mid-level persons they trust. Ms. Okura felt the meeting went perfectly, even though she had never met them before. If she had just Googled the bank in Japan, and called them, "Hello, I am so and so, and I sincerely want a meeting." They may say, "Well, we're busy, thank you!" *Warm leads by trust intermediaries are much more effective than cold calls for business relationship development, in almost all cultures of the world.*

Discussion Questions for Readers

1. Have you ever used Google search and made cold calls for business? If so, what were the results?
2. How would you react if someone cold calls you for business? Why?
3. Who are the trust intermediaries in your networks that may lead you to new business?

Introduction

Googling on the Internet and making cold calls may be an appealing option for some to find new clients and business partners. While this type of online search is helpful in learning about the business partners you want to reach out to, securing a response from these partners may be difficult. Li Wong, publisher and CEO of *Georgia Asian Times*, shares that based on his experience of working in and with various industries, cold calls rarely work, as they are inherently un-sophisticated and can leave an unfavorable impression in the target relationship. Mr. Li advises that one needs to put in *personal face time* for relationship building, starting from growing and nurturing trust. *Trust matters. Long-Term clients are secured with trust-based friendships that take years to grow.* Taoism classic text *I Ching* underscores the importance of trust: "A person gains help from others or the Heaven because of trust" ("人之所助者，信也").

The ABC of Trust:
Ability, Benevolence, and Core Values

Trust seems to be such a common term, frequently taken for granted. People often say, "Trust me on this one!" "I don't trust him." "She is not to be trusted." "This company is very trustworthy." "A name you can trust!" "In God We Trust." Trust is used in many slogans of mass media agencies in the United States:

- CNN: The Most Trusted Name in News[2]
- Fox News: Most Watched, Most Trusted[3]
- *The Wall Street Journal*: Trust your source. Trust your decisions. (Roush, 2021)

---

[2] CNN tagline. "The Most Trusted Name in News" is prominently displayed on CNN website, www.cnn.com/services/trusted/ (accessed January 7, 2021).

[3] Fox News current motto is "Most Watched, Most Trusted" since 2017. M.M. Grynbaum. 2017. *Fox News Drops 'Fair and Balanced' Motto* (New York Times), www.nytimes.com/2017/06/14/business/media/fox-news-fair-and-balanced.html (accessed July 7, 2021).

Despite being prevalent in slogans, trust is at an all-time low. In general, public trust in mass media has drastically declined. Many people view them as *fake news*. A recent global study by *Ipsos* shows that respondents have high trust for doctors, nurses, and engineers, but low trust for corporate executives, politicians, journalists, and government officials (Chadwick 2021). A survey conducted among 2,382 U.S. residents by CBS News in March 2021 found one-third of unvaccinated people did not trust the science behind the vaccines, and they would never get vaccinated against COVID-19 (Fearnow 2021).

Stephen Covey asserts that trust is the most overlooked, misunderstood, and underutilized asset to enable business performance (Covey and Merrill 2006). Work gets done with and through people, and trust is the foundation of any interpersonal relationship. Companies must make genuine efforts to build, strengthen, repair and restore trust at all times. In *Webster's Dictionary* (2021), *trust*, as a noun, is defined as assured reliance and confidence on the character, ability, strength, or truth of someone or something. Synonyms for trust are "confidence, faith, belief, and reliance." Trust as a verb is defined as "believe in the reliability, truth, ability, or strength of." The antonym of trust as a verb is "distrust, mistrust, and suspect." Trust is our willingness to be vulnerable with or to take risks with Party B *(person, company, organization, government)* based on our perception of Party B. There are three drivers for positive perceptions that lead to our trust for Party B which I summarize as ABC.

The ABC of Trust: Ability + Benevolence + Core Values

- *Ability:* Is Party B capable of delivering what is promised? Has Party B done this before successfully? Is Party B's ability valued by peers? Party B's abilities should be reflected in his/her reputation established on past achievements.
- *Benevolence:* Does Party B care about me? Is Party B kind to me? Do I feel like I can connect with Party B? Caring about the other inherently means Party B letting go of self-ego. Does Party B really have my best interest at heart?
- *Core values:* Does Party B act according to a set of admirable core values? Do I agree with this set of values, principles, and

beliefs? Should I risk my money, time, efforts, energy, life, wealth, health, reputation, and career to be in a relationship with Party B?

Trust, the Root of a Relationship

Many companies depend on rainmakers to grow their business. Rainmakers are those who generate income for a business or organization by brokering deals or attracting clients or funds. Rainmakers McMakin and Fletcher (2018) state, "credence goods are sold on trust" (p. 30). The word *credence* comes from the Latin term *credere*, a verb that means *to believe* or *to trust*. Credence is related to words like *creditor*, someone who trusts you, and *credibility*, a quality assigned to someone worthy of trust (McMakin and Fletcher 2018). Consulting, medical, legal, financial, accounting, IT, educational, mechanical, and other professional services are considered providers of credence goods. All entrepreneurs and business leaders I interviewed emphasize the critical importance of trust for relationships. They shared their stories and strategies about gaining trust, building trust, losing trust, and repairing trust. In this book, I compare *trust* for a relationship as a *root* for a tree.

First, roots and trust are both *hidden* from human eyes. Looking around, you may see many tall, green, and healthy trees. However, you normally do not see their roots. In fact, however large a tree is, its root system extends underground deep and wide, mirroring its height and size. Invisible and intangible, trust is an abstract concept. The mantra of "seeing is believing" tends to make us think that roots and trust do not exist. However, although we cannot *see* trust, we know trust exists, just like we know roots live under a tree.

Second, the root system *anchors* the tree in the soil. A tree cannot stand still if it has no roots to situate it down to earth. Roots have the enormous task of securing the plant in the ground through wind, rain, snow, and storms. Imagine the force of a hurricane blowing through a huge tree, then you know the incredible strength of the roots keeping the tree grounded, stable, and alive. Similarly, trust anchors a relationship in its context and communities. Trust keeps a relationship standing by anchoring it to the rich ground of mutual care and shared memories.

Third, the root system *nourishes* the tree by absorbing water, oxygen, and minerals from the soil, and transporting these elements to the rest of the tree. Without the root, the trunk and leaves will wither or die from malnutrition. The root is where the tree eats and drinks. Trust absorbs nutrients for a relationship, just like the root of a tree. A relationship develops based on the strength of trust.

Fourth, a root is usually the first part of the plant to emerge when a seed germinates. When a seed germinates, the primary root, or radicle grows downward into the soil, anchoring the seedling. Secondary roots grow laterally from it to form a taproot system. Like roots, trust is the first part to be built for a relationship. Before we do any business, it is better to connect with each other and build mutual trust. Business partners will benefit from creating shared memories such as enjoying meals, coffee, karaoke, trips, concerts, sporting events, birthday parties, or other activities together to build and strengthen trust. Shared memories store the nutrient for a long-term relationship, withstanding potential storms of changes and conflicts in business.

Finally, trust and roots are both *fragile*. The root of a 100-year old tree can be cut instantly by chainsaws. Beautifully green but for a short time, most Christmas trees we buy from stores do not come with roots. Depending on the variety, it can take 7 to 12 years for a Christmas tree to grow to six feet. Trust is similar to a root in the vulnerability aspect. Alex Gregory, the former president and CEO of YKK Corporation of America, emphasized that "trust takes years to build up, yet it can be lost in minutes." David Kirk, president and CEO of Murata Electronics North America, agrees that building trust takes time and we should protect and treasure the mutual trust we have with others. Mr. Kirk says the best way to build trust is to deliver what you promise. Do what you say you are going to do and do it again!

Brands and Trust

"You cannot ask for trust. You have to earn trust," states Jeff Bezos, the founder of Amazon, who says that the most valuable intellectual property for Amazon is its brand, which stands for trust. In *Fortune*'s 2020 rankings of the World's Most Admired Companies, Amazon brand came in second place (Apple was number one). Bezos states,

> we are grateful that customers notice the hard work we do on their behalf, and that they reward us with their trust. Working to earn and keep that trust is the single biggest driver of Amazon's Day One culture (Aten 2020).

Brad Taylor, former brand strategist for The Coca-Cola Company, says that brands are promises companies make to customers, and trust is the glue that holds customers in relationships with the brands. If a brand keeps breaking promises and does not consistently deliver the value, then a customer would have no reason to stay in a relationship with this brand. Once a trust-based relationship is established between a brand and its customers, the customers would rather pay more for a brand, because they perceive an enhanced value in this brand that no competitor can provide. When facing competition, *brand* is the winning card. Stan Wang, president of Tenfunder, a global investment company from China, elaborates that brand （品牌）encompasses three levels of trust in *quality*（品质）, *integrity* （品格）, and *style* （品味）, which stands for *promises, benevolence,* and *beauty.*

Public trust can be lost in a brand if the promise of quality and value is broken. In April 2020, Chipotle Mexican Grill, Inc. agreed to pay a $25 million dollars fine to resolve criminal charges that tainted food served at this fast-food chain sickened more than 1,100 people in the United

Figure 4.1 What does a BRAND represent?

States from 2015 to 2018. Chipotle was charged with serving adulterated food that caused outbreaks of norovirus, including diarrhea, vomiting, abdominal cramps, and food poisoning. Consumer trust in the Chipotle brand was damaged. "This settlement represents an acknowledgment of how seriously Chipotle takes food safety every day and is an opportunity to definitively turn the page on past events," stated Brian Niccol, chairman and CEO of Chipotle (Ortiz 2020). Chipotle tries hard to repair the damaged trust in its brand. To repair and restore such broken trust in its brand might take years and millions of dollars.

Trust Intermediaries

Instead of contacting new companies through Googling and cold calling, approaching a trust intermediary may be the solution to build new business relationships. Trust intermediaries can be family members, friends, neighbors, colleagues, partners, classmates, or anyone who trusts you. Trust intermediaries can also be members of the knowledge-based service sectors, such as bankers, lawyers, accountants, consultants, and professors, who are called *sensei* (先生) in Japanese culture or Centers of Influence (COIs) in the American culture. Conferences, events, activities, and gatherings organized by COIs offer business networks potentially rich in trust intermediaries for designated industries and sectors. Trust intermediaries seal the trust between two new parties who want to establish relationships, both to connect and to assist with trust.

Many businesses grow through word-of-mouth referrals. Lucy Lu, the founder of aiLegal, says most of her business comes from word-of-mouth: "The most powerful tool in marketing is endorsement from your existing clients who trust you." *Word-of-mouth* or *viva voce* is the sharing of information from one person to another via casual formats. Word-of-mouth implies trusted information when one person passes it to another. Word-of-mouth can be a powerful recommendation and even advantageous for advertising, as this type of rich information comes from trust-based third parties.

Companies often hire athletes, movie, TV, and Internet stars as trust intermediaries to promote their products and services. As these stars usually have a large pool of followers who trust them, they are poised to act as brand/company spokespersons. In June 2016, Actor Tom Selleck, who plays the role of NYC Police Commissioner Frank Reagan in the

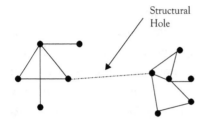

- All around us, there are many structural holes when examining people's personal networks.

- Finding and "filling" such structural holes can be strategic steps in connecting two potentially mutually-benefiting networks.

Figure 4.2 **Structural holes** *between networks*

television series *Blue Bloods*, became the newest celebrity spokesman for American Advisors Group (AAG), a national reverse mortgage lender. An iconic figure in American television for the past four decades, Selleck inspires credibility and trust, even though he is asking people to sell out their houses. AAG said in a statement, "Our research reinforced the wide-spread recognition and respect that Tom Selleck has garnered among Americans and crosses generations. We believe he is the best candidate for the job" (Branson 2019). Further, Internet stars are recognized for their power of influence in the smartphone age. Internet influencers, opinion leaders, reality TV show hosts, food, gardening, and travel *vloggers*[4] have gained millions in sponsorships thanks to their popularity with trusted followers via social media platforms at YouTube, Instagram, TikTok, Facebook, Weibo, and others.

Typically, the trust intermediaries are the critical links between your business and the networks you would like to reach out to. For example, you want to expand your business to your clients' friends, to your colleagues' families, or to the Internet influencers' followers. These potential trust intermediaries are the *structural holes* to be filled. *Structural hole* is a concept in social network research originally developed by Ronald Burt (1995). A structural hole is "a separation between non-redundant contacts, those contacts who can give one access to new networks" (Burt 1995). Individuals hold certain positional advantages/disadvantages in social networks. A structural hole is a gap between two individuals in two different

---

[4] *Vlogger*: A vlogger is a person who regularly posts short videos to a video blog site, shared at social media platforms such as TikTok, YouTube, Facebook, Weibo, and Instagram. A vlog or *video log* is a form of blog that combines embedded video with supporting text, images, and other metadata.

networks, with possible complementary values to each other. Here are some samples of digital *trust intermediaries*:

- Contacts in Facebook
- Connections at LinkedIn: a digital personal network and online resume
- Google reviews
- Yelp reviews
- TripAdvisor reviews
- Reviews of VRBO, Airbnb, hotels, and so on.
- Reality show hosts
- Travel and food vloggers
- Influencer blogsites

Repairing Damaged Trust

Trust repair is a delicate process in relationship building, just like keeping the health of the root of a tree. If you overirrigate, the soil's pH is unbalanced, or there are pest activities around your tree, your tree's roots may be damaged. You might want to limit the water, balance the pH, and reduce pest activities around your tree. Sometimes, the root damage is beyond repair. The root is dead. For certain plants, they can be propagated from stem cuttings to grow a second generation of the plants. First, you take some healthy stem cuttings; then, you place them in water or a growing medium until they develop roots. After the roots are developed with good care and luck, you place the rooted cuttings into pots or the ground. However, it takes a few years and tons of care for the stem cutting to grow into the same size as the mother plant.

On April 20, 2010, one of British Petroleum (BP)'s Deepwater Horizon oil rigs exploded in the Gulf of Mexico, killing 11 workers, and causing one of the worst environmental disasters in U.S. history. For 87 days, oil and methane gas spewed from an uncapped wellhead in the Gulf. It was estimated that 4.2 million barrels of oil spilled into the Gulf. Public trust in BP brand was damaged. Many customers refused to visit BP gas stations. BP's bill for compensation, penalties, and clean-ups topped $65 billion. BP chairman Carl-Henric Svanberg called every BP board member every day for 100 days to keep them informed and solicit views. From that process came the decision to oust CEO Tony Hayward, who caused offense by telling reporters he wanted his *life back*. Measures were taken to rebrand BP as an American company that cares about local fishermen in the Gulf, instead of an aloof *British Petroleum*. BP's chairman tried hard to keep the communication going. "After any crisis, it is vital to have the right voice out there immediately and transparently, to tell the company's story about what it knows and what it doesn't know so far," says Michael Watkins, professor of leadership and organizational change (Ward 2018). To keep the trust of your customers, it is imperative to keep the promises and be honest. Trust begins to erode when people make commitments that they are unable to keep, advertently or inadvertently.

Stella Ting-Toomey elaborates on how people from various cultures manage rapport and disagreements differently with the face negotiation theory. *Face* or self-image is a universal phenomenon that pervades across cultures. In conflicts, one's face is threatened; thus, the person tends to try to save or restore his or her face. *Face,* as a metaphor for self-image, is originated from two Chinese concepts: *Lian* （脸） and *Mianzi* （面子） (Ting-Toomey and Kurogi 1998). *Lian* is the internal moral face that involves shame, integrity, debasement, and identity issues, while *mianzi* is the external social face that involves social recognition, position, authority, influence, and power. Erving Goffman (1959) links Chinese concept of *lian* and *mianzi* to Western concepts of *identity* and *ego*. People of all cultures are very sensitive and proud about their identities, self-images, and reputations. We need to be mindful and sensitive in recognizing (giving face) and protecting (saving face) their reputations to keep and strengthen trust. Publicly criticizing someone hurts one's face and therefore damages trust. Here are some strategies in protecting and repairing trust:

- Maintain a willingness to work on the relationship.
- Adopt active listening.
- Show respect and gratitude.
- Reflect and learn from the experience.
- Practice forgiveness. Give others another chance.
- Avoid dwelling on the past and focus on the future.

- Create new memories and reignite the connection.
- Keep communicating about the progress and your expectations, needs, and wants.
- Be respectful and considerate of each other and give face to each other.
- Avoid face-to-face conflicts and employ constructive dialogues.
- When a crisis happens, immediately communicate to stakeholders, and try to gain their trust back.

Conclusion

Trust is not built in one event. It takes a process. JR Wilson, vice president at AT&T states, "Trust takes a tremendous amount of time and investment." Mr. Wilson says once a month, he would call all his major business contacts just to say hi and ask how they were doing in business and in life. Ms. DeAnn Golden, president and CEO of Berkshire Hathaway HomeServices Georgia Properties, advocates a *surge* method of client communication, like surges of ocean waves. Each of her associates is encouraged to engage with their clients regularly, regardless of whether the clients have expressed a wish to buy or sell houses. The phone calls will cover topics of weather, friendship, family events, things going on in the industry, the housing market, and interest rates. Controversial topics on politics and religion are to be avoided. Both Mr. Wilson and Ms. Golden say after these casual friendship phone calls, new business is often generated as a bonus. Here are some tips:

- Tell the truth.
- Be authentic.
- Walk the talk.
- Keep the communication going.
- Show genuine care about the other.
- Deliver what you promise repeatedly.
- Keep the quality of your product and service in a consistent manner.
- Be professional.

- Respond to online reviews timely to keep trust with your customers.
- Keep rituals to build trust and relationships, such as making phone calls or social media chats with your clients regularly.

What is the most critical asset in your organization? Is it your product, your services, your employees, or your brand? Oldfield (2017) believes the *center of gravity* is the *trust* that clients and customers have for your organization (p. v). For a business, trust is the strongest insurance against competitive disruption, the antidote to consumer indifference, and the best path to continued growth. Without trust, credibility is lost, reputation can be threatened, brand is damaged, and the relationship dies. We shall protect trust like we protect our eyes so that the relationship can grow strong and healthy. If you feel the trust is damaged, you may want to immediately repair the trust via I-Thou dialogue so that the hurricane of misunderstanding will not damage the trust even further. Trust, being the root of the relationships of your selection, is worth investment in time, effort, and emotion. The next chapter elaborates on strategies of the relationship selection process.

CHAPTER 5

Selecting Business Partners

Quotations to Ponder

As always, place the best interest of your clients above everything else.
—DeAnn Golden, President and CEO
Berkshire Hathaway HomeServices Georgia Properties

We would go to some industry events, but more than likely we would be going to specific customer's supplier day events. We try to build a very, very deep relationship with them.
—David Kirk, President and CEO
Murata Electronics North America

Business is more relationship-oriented than some people realize. I don't care if it's a product or a service. Those relationships must be sustainable.
—Alex Gregory, former President and CEO
YKK Corporation of America

What you never want to do is get into a relationship that has no value for you or the other person, because you will fail inevitably and usually with dire consequences.
—Rick Cole, former Senior Vice President
Turner Broadcasting System

When we come to USA for business partners, we let them find us. As they approach us, we observe them, and decide whether they are whom we are looking for. It goes both ways.
—Glad Cheng, Chairman
China Window Group

Before we accept new clients, we go through a new client screening procedure. There is a checklist we must fill out. This is the full company background check.

—Wendy Lu, Partner

Aprio

Try to create value and incentives for business partners and customers. When you find success, repeat it. When you find failure, be honest and direct, and don't repeat the same mistake.

—JR Wilson, Vice President for Tower Strategy & Roaming

AT&T

Chapter Summary

Where do we find potential business partners? Can the process of selecting business partners and clients be compared to dating? Highlighting the power of personal networks for business partner selection, this chapter presents paths that lead to partner selection, ranging from due diligence research, to trust intermediaries, to COIs, to complimentary lunch-and-learns. Research data show the business relationship selection process is a two-way street. While one selects his/her business partner, the other party also observes and decides whether to choose this relationship. This chapter displays three standards used by most entrepreneurs in business partner selection: *trust, yield, and compatibility.*

CASE STUDY 5.1

From *Free Dating* to *Forced Marriages*: tvsdesign in Global Business

Founded in 1968 by Thompson, Ventulett, and Stainback, tvsdesign[1] is a global architectural design firm headquartered in Atlanta, Georgia, with branch offices in Chicago, Dubai, and Shanghai. With nearly 350 employees, the firm has shaped Atlanta's skyline by designing the CNN Center, the Georgia Aquarium, the Omni Hotel, the Georgia Dome, the AT&T Promenade, and the Mercedes-Benz Stadium. Beyond Atlanta, the firm designed the Washington, D.C. Convention Center, the Nanjing International Expo Center, and the Vision Tower in Dubai (tvsdesign website 2021). Their projects range from skyscrapers to city districts, to convention/expo centers and sports facilities (*Architect Magazine* 2021). In 2002, tvsdesign was presented the *Architecture Firm Award* by the American Institute of Architects (Dorton 2019).

Developing business relationships overseas is not an easy task, where global entrepreneurs are confronted with different languages, cultures, histories, religions, traditions, laws, and ways of doing business. Roger Neuenschwander served as the president of tvsdesign from 1994 until his retirement in 2016. Mr. Neuenschwander started at tvsdesign as a young intern in 1973. During 43 years at the firm, he witnessed and oversaw much of its expansion. During his more than 50 trips to China, together with his director in China, Mr. Neuenschwander met with numerous government officials, prospective partners, and Chinese architects. No matter where they are, he and his team try to build relationships first, without a project in mind. He prefers to go slow for developing long-term relationships. Once selected, these relationships are carefully managed.

Mr. Neuenschwander adopts the *3-R-Rule* to select business partners globally: *references, reputation, and research*. First, he and his team check references with people who had worked with this person/company

---

[1] The company name *tvsdesign*, usually written in lowercase letters, is a combination of the first letters of its founders last names *Thompson, Ventulett, and Stainback* plus the word *design*.

before, asking them what it was like in day-to-day interactions. Second, they assess the reputation of the potential partner. In architecture or any industry, the network of core movers and shakers is relatively small. Mr. Neuenschwander stresses that the key to identifying a good business partner is "whether we are compatible, whether we have similar goals and objectives, and whether we approach business in a similar way." He and his team would do intensive due diligence and reference checks, as well as just walking around in foreign cities and observing how people live their lives.

Mr. Neuenschwander shared his frustration in a global market: "We had experienced forced mergers. Sometimes we were not in complete control in the selection process. We were asked to partner with less experienced, but good people." Foreign governments may have preferences about partnerships, diversities, and community participation. In Dubai, sometimes his firm had to partner with people who do not have the *fire power* in skillsets or industry reputation. The partner's sole condition was to get some profit out of it. Mr. Neuenschwander's firm always signs contracts around a safety net. If the partner starts to miss deadlines, give defective drawings, or not meet quality standards, tvsdesign has the right to take over the business as the prime architect. Mr. Neuenschwander says, "Last thing we need is to have our company caught up in legal dynamics because of a forced marriage. We show the partner that this is good for both of our interests."

Questions for the Readers

1. Why and how should businesses conduct due diligence and experience ways of life in foreign markets?
2. Do you think the 3Rs (references, reputation, and research) are good tools in assessing the qualifications of a potential business partner at home and abroad? Why?
3. What would you do if you were forced to work with a business partner in a foreign country?

Introduction

A *business partner* can be any entity (an individual or organization) in a business venture in any capacity such as a collaborator, supplier, investor, client, customer, or sponsor. Business partnership requires mutual respect, understanding, and reciprocal benefits. Dating is a process of romantic relationships practiced in many modern societies around the world. In dating, two individuals meet with each other to assess the other's suitability as a prospective life partner, with the possible union in marriage. The rituals and practices of dating allow two individuals to explore whether they are compatible with each other in personalities, backgrounds, status, habits, abilities, hobbies, goals, and values. Each side comes with his/her own standards of selection in this two-way selection process. Some entrepreneurs compare the selection process of business partners to *dating*. Indeed, courting business partners resembles dating in many ways. First, you try to make yourself *visible* by attending events, activities, meetings, and social gatherings, and letting people know you are looking for a business partner. Second, partner selection is a two-way street. While you select the other party, they are observing you and making decisions about whether to collaborate with you. In some traditional societies, dating is not practiced or allowed. Instead, they have arranged marriages or forced marriages. Similarly, in international settings, American companies may be asked to form joint ventures with certain groups designated by local governments. Finally, the success of business partnership depends on the caring efforts from both sides and fate of compatibility, similar to the longevity of a marriage.

Business partnerships allow entrepreneurs to enjoy complementary skill sets, share costs, and partake in risks. Unfortunately, about 70 percent of business partnerships fail (Ward 2020), mainly due to lacking trust and deteriorating relationships (Local Government Chronicle 2008). Partners often underestimate the time and resources it takes to select, establish, and develop strong relationships. Rick Cole, former Senior Vice President at Turner Broadcasting System, shares that usually 10 to 20 percent of clients generate 90 percent of the problems. Like social relationships, business relationships can become toxic. These harmful business relationships drain entrepreneurs mentally, physically, emotionally, and financially.

By carefully selecting business partners, we can focus our money, energy, effort, time, emotions, time, and other limited resources on a few promising candidates for relationship cultivation.

Business Partner Selection Process

Research for this book shows four steps in business partner selection process: due diligence, visibility, two-way selection, and mutual commitment.

In 2012, Xi Jinping, then vice president of the People's Republic of China, visited Muscatine, Iowa, aside from his state trip to the United States, invited by U.S. President Barack Obama. Mr. Xi went to Iowa to meet with some *old friends*, with whom he stayed in 1985 when he and his colleagues were studying modern agriculture as China's next generation of young leaders. Inspired by Chinese media coverage of this story, Glad Cheng, a shrewd investor from China decided to visit Muscatine Iowa. Glad Cheng had never been to the United States. In 2013, following Mr. Xi's footsteps, Mr. Cheng arrived at the small town of Muscatine, Iowa, on the bank of the Mississippi River. Mr. Cheng purchased the house where Mr. Xi stayed in 1985, and transformed the modest property into the *Sino-U.S. Friendship House.*[2] Mr. Cheng was impressed with the beauty of the landscape and the warmth of the local people. He decided to invite his children and wife to study and live in Iowa. As a newcomer in Iowa, Mr. Cheng took his time to search for business partners in the United States. Mr. Cheng followed a four-step approach for business partner selection: *due diligence, visibility, two-way selection,* and *mutual commitment.*

Figure 5.1 Business partner selection process

---

[2] *Sino-U.S. Friendship House*: Located in Muscatine, Iowa, this is the house where Chinese President Xi Jinping stayed when he visited Muscatine in 1985 as a young delegation member from China. Photos and other memorabilia about President Xi's trips to Iowa are preserved and displayed here. Learn more at www .meetmuscatine.com/434/Sino-US-Friendship-House.

*First step: **Due diligence.*** *The first stride for business development is to conduct due diligence about the target market and identify major players in the industries.* Due diligence is the comprehensive study that one conducts about potential business partners, through online searches, reference checks, market research, legal, and financial analysis. The Internet makes searching for potential clients possible with a few clicks, via Google, social media searches, and news reports. However, *Googling* someone may not provide correct, dynamic, or updated information. Many multinational corporations hire market research firms and intercultural consultants for this type of background checks. For buyers and investors, their attorneys, accountants, or financial advisors usually review the target company's assets, liabilities, structures, operations, and key business relationships. Wendy Lu, a partner at Aprio, shares that her firm has a *Client Acceptance/ Retention Committee* that oversees the strict process of new client acceptance, following a *New Client Screening Checklist*. Ms. Lu's firm subscribes to LexisNexis[3] and other databases for this kind of background checks. She also verifies prospective clients' background in SEC Filings and other platforms. In the United States, SEC Filings are regulatory documents that companies and issuers of securities must submit to the Securities and Exchange Commission (SEC) on a regular basis. The purpose of such filings is to provide transparency and information to investors, analysts, and regulators. Mr. Cheng studied about the background of some key business leaders in Iowa.

*Second step: **Visibility.*** *Seeing is believing. Showing up matters.* If you are not visible, people may not think of you when opportunities arrive. It is vital for businesses to enhance visibility and stay on the radar screens of potential partners, clients, and customers. Radar screens include people's smartphone screens, social media platforms, TV and radio, conferences and events, and community gatherings. Jessica Cork, vice president at YKK Corporation of America, underscores volunteerism and speaking

---

[3] *LexisNexis* is a corporation that sells data mining platforms through online portals, computer-assisted legal research (CALR), and information about vast swaths of consumers around the world. As of 2006, the company had the world's largest electronic database for legal and public records-related information: www .lexisnexis.com/en-us/gateway.page.

engagements as natural means to shine on radar screens. Being an intro-
vert, walking around at an event and passing out business cards is difficult
for her. Instead, she enjoys volunteer work and taking on leadership roles
in nonprofits and industry organizations. While volunteering or speaking at events by Japan–America Society of Georgia, International Cherry
Blossom Festival, World Affairs Council, and universities, Ms. Cork
meets with potential partners interested in her work at YKK. Staying on
clients' radar screens through complementary lunch-and-learns has been
a successful partner recruiting tool for Marcy Sperry, founder of Vivid IP.
Ms. Sperry would approach current and future clients and provide them
with free lunch-and-learns on a legal topic of their choice, such as trade-
marks or entertainment law. After presentations, Ms. Sperry usually would
walk away with either additional business from an existing client or signing the prospect into an official new client. Ms. Sperry asks her employees
to regularly follow up with current and past clients so that Vivid IP stays
on their radar screens. Mr. Cheng sponsored several large Chinese New
Year galas, cultural exchange events and conferences in Iowa, Chicago and
Atlanta areas to gain visibility in the communities.

   Third step: Two-way selection. Mr. V is a car mechanic in business
for about 25 years at the same location in Atlanta. His business grows
mostly via word-of-mouth. Occasionally, there are walk-in customers.
Through first impressions from handshakes, eye contact, and conversations, Mr. V selects his customers. When he feels certain customers may
become problem accounts, Mr. V gives a car repair price quote so high
that they will likely not accept. Mr. V conserves his time and energy by
selecting customers for car repairs. Mr. V's story conveys that business
relationship selection is a two-way street. Lucy Lu, the founder of aiLegal,
says that clients are very smart. Through their own Google and independent searches, clients evaluate a law firm's qualifications. Glad Cheng,
Chairman of China Window Group, shares his story about such two-way
selection. Through attending local and national gatherings, and hosting
Chinese cultural events, Mr. Cheng, the Sino–U.S. Friendship House,
and his investment company became visible on local, national, international news reports and social media platforms. Like a patient fisherman,
Mr. Cheng waits for qualified admirers to take the bait. Mr. Cheng says:
"We do not look for business partners. Instead, we let them find us."

Nagendra Roy is the CEO of AanseaCore, a global management consulting and information technology (IT) company. Mr. Roy says that in the IT industry, feedback for two-way selection is often categorized into three types: reaction, reply, and response. The *reaction, reply, response* concepts in IT mirrors Karl Weick's (1969) notions of *Act, Interact, and Double Interact* for *the infrastructure of organizing*. Weick views the *double interact loop* as the solid building blocks of every organization, because this loop embodies the valuable two-way communication (response, feedback, and follow-up) in relationships.

Scenario #1: Reaction (Act): A sends B an email, B does not send any message back. B uses silence to show his/her reaction. The attempt of relationship building is ignored. This feedback is negative for relationship development.

Scenario #2: Reply (Interact): If A sends B an email, B replies: "Hey, I am busy, and I won't be able to talk to you until next year." This means no business relationship for now.

Scenario #3: Response (Double Interact): If A sends B an email, B gives this type of response: "Hey, I am busy, but let's have a conversation on the phone in 15–20 minutes. Then if things go well, we can plan for a coffee or lunch together." This feedback is positive toward a potential relationship. If you don't see this type of response, it's hard to start a relationship, because you don't have a back-and-forth connection.

Fourth step: Mutual commitment. After a possible partner is identified through two-way selection, it takes months or years for both parties to observe and engage with each other in a meaningful way. Eventually, *business dating* might lead to commitment for partnerships, investment projects, joint ventures, or mergers and acquisitions (M&A). Commitment is when two partners formally establish partnerships through *symbolic moments*, by signing letters of intent (LOIs), memorandums of understanding (MOUs), Purchasing Orders (POs), agreements, contracts, or joint announcements. Such symbolic moments in business relationship development can be compared to engagements or weddings in interpersonal relationships. Mr. Cheng met many potential business partners in the past few years in the United States, and he has committed to a few joint investment projects in education and real estate in both the United States and China.

Trust Intermediaries Lead to Business Partners

Where do we find new business partners and clients? Research data indicate entrepreneurs find business partners and clients mostly through personal networks! Despite the rise of modern communication technologies, the Internet and social media, interpersonal referrals dominate business development, just like in the old days. Atlanta-based *aiLegal* is a law firm that covers client-focused services in immigration, business, employment, and litigation. Its founder Lucy Lu believes that "if you do your job right, money follows your way, and clients are going to chase you around." She says among her client pool, about 70 to 80 percent are from *word-of-mouth* referrals by existing clients. An additional 10 percent are recommenced by other lawyers. Only about 10 percent of clients are walk in customers who find her firm from independent searches via Google, Baidu, or other platforms. Global business leaders and entrepreneurs shared their common paths for partner selection: referrals from family, friends, former colleagues, existing clients, and COIs, all of which are trust intermediaries. *Known and trusted by both parties who are strangers to each other, a trust intermediary is a third-party with the capacity to connect the two parties for win–win–win opportunities.* Trust intermediaries for business development can be categorized as advocates, COIs, and allies.

1. *Advocates (family and friends):* They are mostly family, friends, colleagues, or existing clients. They often refer business prospects without requesting benefits for themselves, simply because they trust you and hope you prosper. These are *low-hanging fruit* for someone who wants to develop new business relationships. Marcy Sperry, the founder of Vivid IP law firm, says that when she launched the firm, she relied on clients she had developed over years of practicing law at other firms. David Kirk, president and CEO of Murata Electronics North America, says "We would go to some industry events, but more than likely, we would be going to specific customer's supplier day events. We try to build a very, very deep relationship with them. Our CEO and president Tsuneo Murata and our head of sales would meet with them. We try to have a complete engagement with that new customer. We don't want to wait until there is suddenly a delivery problem to develop this relationship."

2. **Centers of Influence (COIs):** COIs are the most common trust intermediaries, who make casual referral arrangements in noncompeting businesses. COIs are individuals who are *hubs* in networks enriched with trust-based relationships, valuable for business referrals. COIs are well-connected and highly respected influencers, members, and leaders of their groups, industries, and communities. They are professionals who come into regular contact with your potential clients. Potential clients tend to follow the advice of these COIs, and they are willing to give new business partners a chance. When approached properly, COIs can boost your credibility and expand your business. Building a reliable network of COIs is one of the best ways to engage with new prospects. For example, when buying a home, one needs a realtor and many service providers: loan agents, home inspectors, bankers, lawyers, and handyman services. The realtor, who has the homeowner's trust, can make recommendations for these players in the home purchase process. The realtor is a COI in this case. For a financial advisor, the COIs may include CPAs, bankers, attorneys, mortgage professionals, event planners, and others. These service providers often reciprocate the favor of referrals to benefit from each other's client networks. Getting to know key COIs in target markets provides possibilities for referrals for new business development. Entrepreneurs meet with COIs regularly for business development.

3. **Allies (channel partners, brokers, and agents):** Companies often form strategic alliances to generate business leads for each other. These are reciprocal referral arrangements, and sometimes include revenue sharing. If two law firms keep referring business to each other, it is probably a good idea to formalize a casual COI practice and transform the partnership into an alliance: *channel partners*. A channel partner is a company that partners with another company or organization to market and sell products or services. Channel partners may be upstream or downstream distributors, vendors, retailers, consultants, collaborators, and *value-added resellers* (VARs). Wendy Lu, a partner at Aprio accounting firm, says she also recruits new clients through channel partners, which include other accounting firms, law firms, and business consulting companies. Establishing

alliances not only ensures client quality, but also enhances business development sustainability.

As trust-based relationships take much effort and time to build up, trust intermediaries select their endorsements carefully. If they recommend someone who does a shoddy job, it reflects poorly on their judgment and reputation, and hurts their relationships with either or both parties. The recommendation by trust intermediaries shall be appreciated with ultimate respect. The process of building relationships with trust intermediaries can be divided into four stages:

1. *Make a list of "trust intermediaries" who can help your grow market share.* After due diligence, make a short list of professionals that you want to approach to help expand your business in the target market(s).
2. *Start the communication.* When you make the first communication (email, call, and social media app), you may want to position it this way: "I want to understand your business and see if we can partner together for win-win-win results." Through listening, you gain insight into the type of clients and market they work in. You can think about ways to partner and deliver value.
3. *Keep in touch.* Try to connect with them on social media and follow up with online and in-person engagement. With continued communication at formal and informal meetings, you get to know their needs and wants, gain their trust, and become friends with them.
4. *Follow up after the introduction.* When trust intermediaries give you an introduction, make sure to thank them. After you meet with the new clients, ensure you keep them informed as you go along your process. After the first couple of introductions, they will let you fly solo. Even then, ensure you keep them in the loop.

Relationship Selection Standards

It seems that most entrepreneurs develop new business partners and clients through trust intermediaries in their personal networks. Three levels of selection standards are utilized by entrepreneurs to test for *trust, yield,* and *compatibility*. First, the *trust standard* evaluates potential partners on

Figure 5.2 Three levels of standards for business partner selection

their *ability, benevolence,* and *core values,* the ABCs of trust. Second, the *yield standard* assesses the potential partner's prospect of contributing to the relationship with an economic view, regarding whether a relationship will yield fruit and close deals. Third, the *compatibility standard* studies the potential partner's personality, work manners, life habits, and communication styles, and finds out if the *self* and the *other* are compatible in the daily operations of business.

Level 1: Trust standard. Trust is the root of a relationship. Without trust, credibility is lost, reputation can be threatened, the brand is damaged, and relationships die. Here are three fundamental questions we ask to find out whether we can trust someone: *(1) Ability:* Does he/she possess the ability to complete the tasks the way I want? *(2) Benevolence:* Does he/she have my best interest at heart? *(3) Core values (integrity):* Does he/she demonstrate admirable values, integrity, and accountability from my perspective? First, the potential partner needs to have all the qualifications in education, experience, resources, and capabilities for the jobs to be done. Second, the potential partner shall care about us and our interests. Third, the potential partner needs to share our values. Usually, partnerships fail because the partners are not in alignment regarding the values and/or goals of the organization (Ward 2020).

JR Wilson, vice president at AT&T, states that it is important to get to know potential partners on a personal level so that we can choose to work with people we respect, based on their abilities, personalities, and integrity. Sometimes we lose respect for them, and we will have to react professionally. Before diving into any business, evaluating the track record and matching core values of business partners are basic steps by many multinational corporations. Alex Gregory, former President and CEO of YKK Corporation of America, states that potential partners must share core values and prove themselves to be dependable and loyal to one another. Alignment in core values is also practiced by many nonprofit organizations in fundraising. Wade Edwards had worked as a fundraising specialist for two decades at nonprofit organizations, such as UNICEF[4] and Habitat for Humanity International. Mr. Edwards says nonprofit organizations screen donors and make sure there is alignment between the donor's reputation, industry, and core values with nonprofit brands. At UNICEF, he was prohibited to accept donations from companies that are in the industry or business of firearms, because conflicts and wars are often the cause of emergency situations for children.

Level 2: Yield standard. The yield standard strives to answer these question: "Will this relationship yield positive results for me?" and "Is it worthwhile for me to stay in this relationship?" Return on investment (ROI) is a financial ratio used to calculate the benefits investors will receive in relation to their investment cost. ROI is commonly measured as the net income divided by the total capital cost of the investment. The higher the ratio, the greater the benefit earned (Corporate Finance Institute 2021). The social exchange theory (Blau 1964) states that humans weigh relationships with the other on a reward/cost scale. If the interaction has been satisfactory, then that person is viewed favorably, and the relationship is likely to be selected and continued. If an interaction has been costly, stressful, or toxic, then the relationship may be paused or discontinued. The cost in a relationship can be monetary, or in-kind, such as effort, time, emotions, stress, reputation, and others. In general,

---

[4] *UNICEF*, also known as the United Nations (UN) Children's Fund, is a UN agency responsible for providing humanitarian and developmental aid to children worldwide. UNICEF is the successor of the United Nations International Children's Emergency Fund (UNICEF), created in 1946. UNICEF relies on voluntary contributions from governments and private donors. Its total income as of 2018 was $5.2 billion, of which two-thirds came from governments of various countries and one-third from private donations. www.unicef.org.

people choose to maximize rewards and minimize costs in their relationships (Altman and Taylor 1973). For example, you might not want to
invite a friend with *alligator arms*[5] for lunch, as he always expects others to
pay for his meals. For communication channels, you might prefer to communicate via social media apps, such as Facebook Messenger, LinkedIn
Message, WhatsApp, GroupMe, WeChat (for Chinese), KakaoTalk
(for Korean), or Line (for Japanese), but when an acquaintance keeps
emailing you, texting you or calling you, even after office hours, the
communication *cost* seems too high to select this person for a business relationship. Such communication disconnects break relationships.

Business profit basically rests on two pillars: *increase in sales* and
reduction in cost. Multinational corporations give priority to cost reduction. JR Wilson, vice president at AT&T, states that when he meets with
vendors, the top criterion is whether a vendor can save costs for AT&T.
Mr. Wilson says, *"I love cost savings. They are sometimes more powerful than
growing top line. Every dollar you save goes right to your profit margin, the
bottom line."* Rick Cole, former Senior Vice President of Turner Broadcasting System, agrees with this approach. Mr. Cole says that his goal is to
cut costs while vendors want to increase their revenue, which seems to be
an impossible contradiction. To make both parties happy, vendors need to
provide efficient solutions for a company like Turner Broadcasting System
or AT&T. Mr. Cole suggests vendors look at technological investments,
process innovation, and automation to drive efficiencies in their own
organizations, and then pass those cost savings to Turner Broadcasting
System. Mr. Cole says, "I will give them the next part of the business so
they can do the same again. Their revenues can increase over time and my
internal costs can decrease." Just providing the cheapest product or service
will not win trust and contracts. Vendors offering cost-saving solutions
will be selected, building upon their solid reputations, successful track
records, and compatible ways of doing business.

Entrepreneurs create win–win–win partnerships so that everyone
involved gains from the relationships. Brad Taylor shares how Home

---

[5] *Alligator Arms* refers to someone who pretends to reach for wallet at a meal with
friends but always gets to it a little too late. People use this phrase to describe a
cheap friend.

Depot was persuaded to have refreshment stands at their checkout lines over a decade ago. When customers go to Home Depot, their goal is not to buy beverages. However, when customers wait at the checkout line on a hot day, seeing the cooler filled with ice-cold beverages, *impulse purchase* becomes possible. Research shows that roughly 40 to 50 percent of all purchases carried out by 18- to 64-year-old people in the United States are the result of impulse purchases (Tighe 2020). It is profitable to make your product and service *impulse purchase worthy*, and present them in accessible ways to your target customers. Mr. Taylor says that The Coca-Cola Company has *mined* the landscape for opportunities of impulse purchases. This strategy has opened doors for many partnerships that normally never would have existed. Coca-Cola's bottling partners provide free commercial coolers. Home Depot buys the beverages at wholesale price and sells them at the checkout lines. Guided by the measurement of profit per square footage, Home Depot identified that selling Coca-Cola beverages is more profitable than selling other items. This is a win for Coca-Cola, a win for Home Depot, and a win for the customers.

Level 3: Compatibility standard. Potential business partners need to match up in work style, speed, and rhythm of business operation, social media adoption, and even personal chemistry. Lucy Lu, founder of aiLegal, says that for partners, she prefers to choose someone with a pre-existing relationship with her. When she mentioned that she wanted to establish a new firm, her classmate from Harvard Law School immediately volunteered to become the chief technology officer (CTO). She says they know each other's communication styles and work ethics. She knows that he would deliver quality work on a timely basis. Contrasting personalities can amplify differences in viewpoints and lead to resentment and conflicts. Mr. Gregory, former President and CEO of YKK Corporation of America, says, "Sometimes the chemistry doesn't work, and you have to be sensitive to that." Incompatibility of personalities can happen at the working relationship level. The managing director of an accounting firm conducting an audit may not be a pleasant person, which can be a problem for both the accounting firm and the client.

Beyond the standards for trust, yield, and compatibility, one needs some good luck to find the perfect business partner. Glad Cheng, chairman of China Window Group, states that finding and securing proper business partners relies partially on karma.[6] He says, "You may find many people talk a big game, which makes it sound like you can collaborate with them, but it is very rare you can collaborate with them in reality." Roger Neuenschwander, the former President at tvsdesign says, "My business has very high standards. We want someone who is financially stable, experienced, committed to the community, and attentive to the customers. We ask: Do they act like us?" We also need to be aware of shortfalls in arranged or forced marriages, and lack of information in due diligence. While tvsdesign has a *safety net* for their interest, Aprio charges retainer fees[7] with a new client to eliminate their risk in the partnership. Jeff Weiner, CEO of LinkedIn from 2009 to 2020, was asked about what competitive advantage a jobseeker might have when a few candidates look similar on paper. Weiner (2020) responded:

Connection! There are certain people whom I have the privilege to not only meet, but then ultimately work with. Within a few minutes of our interview, I felt I have known them for years. They felt very familiar in certain ways. I think we shared a value system, a sense of purpose, and a sense of humor. All of these things help people to forge strong connections, which can be incredibly valuable when you are working at a company together and trying to traverse the ups and the downs.

Conclusion

Selecting a business partner or client can be compared to the process of dating, marriage or arranged marriages. An entrepreneur may spend more time with a business partner for work than with his/her spouse for life. One's time and energy is limited, it makes sense that entrepreneurs should

---

[6] *Karma* is a concept originated from Hinduism and Buddhism. Karma indicates that the sum of a person's actions in this and previous states of existence affects his/her fate and opportunities in future existences.

[7] *Retainer fee*: A retainer fee is an amount of money paid upfront to secure the services of a consultant, accountant, freelancer, lawyer, or other service professionals.

be selective in deciding with whom to work. The relationship selection process is a two-way street. While one selects his/her business partner, the other party observes and decides whether to choose and accept this relationship. Highlighting the power of personal networks for business partner selection, this chapter presents various types of trust intermediaries that lead to partner selection advocates, COIs, and allies. The process for selecting business partners progresses from due diligence to visibility, two-way selection, and mutual commitment. This chapter displayed three standards used by entrepreneurs in business partner selection: trust, yield, and compatibility. When compatible and mutually beneficial relationships are formed between organizational delegates, more business may be generated, and more deals may be closed for organizations. The next chapter introduces methods to observe the selected business partners and find out what they want to make the relationships successful and fruitful. Equipped with relationship selection standards, we are ready to secure promising business partners. We then observe them to find out what they want.

CHAPTER 6

Relationship Cultivation Strategies

Quotations to Ponder

Observe! Present yourself in such a way, so that they understand it's not just about you. While speaking, be more concerned with how they are receiving your message.

—Nagendra Roy, CEO
AanseaCore

Why is listening more important than talking? Because how can you truly communicate with someone if you are not listening to them first? Seek first to understand, then be understood.

—Brad Taylor, former Brand Strategist
The Coca-Cola Company

Once you get your foot in the door, you have to stay there. You can only stay there by being dependable, reliable, and committed.

—Robert Striar, President
M Style Marketing

Be interested, instead of interesting! Get to know them first. Ask what's happening in their lives, and usually people open up to you. Listen until your ears bleed.

—Eddy Perez, Cofounder and CEO
Equity Prime Mortgage

Active listening is vital! Communicating early, sharing information, being transparent, those things build trust.

—Alex Gregory, former President and CEO
YKK Corporation of America

You need to have the product that they are interested in, and you have to arouse an eager want in them for your product by your presentation.

—Cathy Garces, former Sales Executive

Emirates Airlines; Japan Airlines

Kindness in words creates confidence. Kindness in thinking creates profoundness. Kindness in giving creates love.

—Laozi, Author

Tao Te Ching

Chapter Summary

This chapter presents specific strategies for observing business partners while building relationships. From a win–win–win standpoint, "knowing what the other wants" is essential for business relationship cultivation. Research data for this book shows that entrepreneurs use a plethora of bonding experiences to create *shared memories*. This chapter suggests the relationship cultivation plan of LOVE, which is the acronym of listening, observation, value proposition, and empathy. Entrepreneurs interviewed for this book stress that listening is of maximum significance for relationship observation, because listening is the most direct way through which to find out what the other party wants and needs. This chapter advises on various methods of active listening, including conducting due diligence, reading body language, asking consequential questions, and genuinely caring about the other party. This chapter recommends the *full presence* of the self in a relationship, whether in physical meetings, virtual meetings, phone calls, or using various apps.

CASE STUDY 6.1

Client-Focused Active Listening

Robert Striar is the president of M Style Marketing, a New York-based marketing consulting firm with clients in the United States and Europe. Mr. Striar accepted my interview through a phone call in April 2020. In late January 2020, seeing how the pandemic was spreading from China to Europe and the Americas, Mr. Striar asked his employees to work from home. Mr. Striar said, "You have to pay attention to what's going on in the lives of our employees and customers, and respect that." During the pandemic, Mr. Striar completed some free work for his clients due to their reduced marketing budgets. He believes this type of goodwill facilitates the growth of business relationships. Mr. Striar stresses the importance of active listening in business. *More than hearing, active listening searches for both verbal and nonverbal messages and combines text with its context in communication. Active listening aims for the meaning intended by the speaker and considers the emotional tones of the speaker at the time of communication.*

One morning a few years ago, he was driving into Manhattan of New York City from his home in New Jersey. While going down the Westside Highway, someone called him and said, "Rob, I need to speak to you." This call was from Mr. T, one of his major clients. Sensing a serious problem, Mr. Striar answered, "I can't answer this right now. Can you give me two hours?" Mr. T responded, "Yeah, I'll give you two hours." Mr. Striar called his office, canceled the rest of the day, drove to New York's La Guardia airport, and booked himself a seat on the next Delta flight from New York to Boston. Within two hours, Mr. Striar was sitting in Mr. T's office. Mr. T was shocked. "How did you get here so quickly?" Mr. Striar responded, "Let's go to the conference room with your eighteen-member staff and look at every question you have." It turned out to be a three-hour productive meeting. Mr. T said, "I don't know how to thank you." Mr. Striar replied, "You don't need to thank me. You are my client. This is my responsibility." As they walked out, Mr. T said, "You know you just got your new contract right here." To grow business relationships, you need to listen to clients for meanings and emotions, then follow up with cost-effective solutions at the right time.

CASE STUDY 6.2

Observing Customers via Big Data for
Smart Manufacturing

One method of observing millions of customers for their needs and wants is to collect and analyze *big data*. Big data is an innovative approach that systematically collects, analyzes, and extracts information from data sets too large or complex to be dealt with by traditional data-processing software. Big data was originally associated with the six Vs: *volume, variety, velocity, value, veracity, and variability* (Jain 2016). Big data can be applied to business by using mathematical analysis, optimization, inductive statistics, and concepts from nonlinear system identification to infer laws and patterns from large sets of data (Billings 2013). Although the term *big data* was coined in the 1990s, only recently the application of big data in industries has become a reality.

After helping millions of Chinese and foreign retailers modernize their operations online, Alibaba Group Holding Ltd. applies big data to textile manufacturing. In China, the garment industry was valued at 2.2 trillion yuan ($328 billion) in 2019 based on Euromonitor International data. Alibaba said that one in four of all clothing items purchased in China was shipped via its e-commerce platforms, granting Alibaba rich data for garment design and production. Alibaba also uses these data to centralize textile material procurement to reduce costs. *Xunxi* (迅犀, *Fast Rhino*) is a three-story facility that houses Alibaba's pilot project of garment production and distribution with big data. Artificial intelligence (AI), robotic arms, 3D printing, and other in-house technologies are implemented at the Xunxi factory prototype.

It usually takes three months for apparel companies to bring a new design from the runway to stores, but Alibaba claims it can cut lead time by 75 percent. With the help of AI, designers can review simulated rendering effects on *digital fabrics* via their computer screens, rather than going through a *real* process to dye the fabric. Garment workers at the factory have high-tech assistants, such as AI-enabled cutting machines and Internet-connected sewing devices, that help fine-tune their work. Items for each piece of custom-designed clothes are transferred between workstations via complex conveyor belts, controlled by AI powered computers. In this digital model, clothes for men, women, and children are being made simultaneously on the same production line, based on online orders. As the entire workflow is recorded digitally, factory management can track the progress remotely on computers or smartphones. The data and technology deployed at the Xunxi factory enable entrepreneurs to decide on the merchandise in two weeks, instead of 90 days. Big data allows Alibaba to find out what the customers need and want, and therefore catch up with the latest trends in fashion and accessories, reduce the need to accumulate inventory, and increase profit. Xunxi was one of ten factories highlighted by the World Economic Forum in 2020 as adopting *The Fourth Industrial Revolution technologies*. Daniel Zhang, the CEO of Alibaba said, "Large-scale standard manufacturing is being transformed to flexible small-scale productions" (Liu and Wei 2020). Alibaba's goal is to become a one-stop provider for garment merchants on its *Taobao, Tmall*, and *AliExpress*[1] online marketplaces. In the textile or other industries, it is a new trend to transform from the assembly line type of mass production of the industrial age to *digital customization* of the digital age. Companies can complete just-in-time manufacturing, inventory, and delivery with the adoption of proper technologies and management.

Discussion Questions for Readers

1. Why should we observe the actions and behaviors of clients and customers?
2. How can we effectively observe clients and customers for business growth?
3. How can a company transform itself to join the wave of *smart and just-in-time manufacturing?*

---

[1] *Taobao* (淘宝), *Tmall* (天猫), *and AliExpress* (全球速卖通) are various digital shopping platforms and apps owned by the Alibaba Group Holding Limited, commonly known as *Alibaba* (阿里巴巴). Founded in 1999 in Hangzhou, China, by the legendary Jack Ma (马云), Alibaba provides C2C, B2B, and B2B sales services via Web portals for customers all over the world.

Introduction

In the summer, when the sky turns dark and trees shake violently from the wind, we know a thunderstorm might follow. The 5,000-year-old Taoism classics text *I Ching* proclaims, "the sky shows phenomena" (天垂象). *The sky never talks, the sky shows. A wise person observes a phenomenon and figures out the mechanism that leads to this phenomenon.* Legend has it that in 1665, a young Isaac Newton returned to his childhood orchard when he observed an apple falling from a tree. Why do apples always fall straight to the ground, rather than sideways or upward? This *aha moment* inspired the recognition of the law of universal gravitation (Nix 2018).

Plants do not talk. Plants communicate via nonverbal messages. If a rose bush does not blossom, it probably is asking for more sunshine, less irrigation, or aphid protection. Experienced gardeners *listen* to and *observe* the plants, *interpret* their nonverbal messages, and *discover* what they need. Give the plants what they need, and the plants will likely reciprocate with what you want: flowers, fruits, and vegetables.

Although knowledge about the other is essential for business relationship cultivation, relational partners do not always clearly tell us what they need and want. Mr. Brad Taylor, former brand strategist of The Coca-Cola Company underscores that "people want to do business with those they like." With a startup mentality, Mr. Taylor strives to build relationships with his customers so that they like him and like his company. The Coca-Cola Company pays attention to the *likability* of its organizational delegates to their customers. According to *Webster's Dictionary*, being *likable (also likeable)* means to be *pleasant, friendly, and easy to like.* Synonyms of *likability* include *attractiveness, delightfulness, enjoyableness, civility, politeness, thoughtfulness, cheerfulness, kindness, comity, and pleasantness.* Mr. Taylor says that businesspeople become likable to their clients through *listening* and demonstrating to them with the promise of *delivering extra value.*

With active listening, one understands where the other person is coming from and what he/she is looking for. As a result, one can present an attractive value proposition. Active listening and careful observation facilitate healthy growth of business relationships. This chapter presents a fourfold *LOVE strategy* for business relationship cultivation: *listening, observation, value proposition, empathy.*

Cultivating Relationships: The LOVE Model

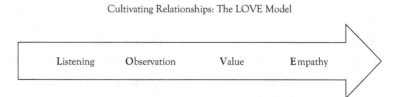

Figure 6.1 Relational cultivation process: the LOVE model

LOVE Model Part #1: Listen for the Intended Meaning

Research data collected for this book show that active listening is of maximum significance for relationship cultivation because listening is the most direct way to find out what the others need and want. Active listening requires *full presence* of the self in a relationship, whether at face-to-face meetings, video conferences, phone calls, or social media platforms. Ernest Hemingway once said, "A human being needs two years to learn to speak, and sixty years to learn to be silent." A Chinese proverb goes, "Eloquence is silver, but silence is golden.(沉默是金)" Listening is a top relationship cultivation strategy. Successful entrepreneurs know it well. "Listen, listen, listen! This is how you get *gold* out of the other person," stressed Rick Cole, former Senior Vice President of Turner Broadcasting System. Ms. Cathy Garces, a former sales executive for Emirates Airlines, says business is gained "by listening and not wasting their time, and by delivering what you promised."

Active listening requires discipline. An effective listener seeks to understand the *intended meaning* of the speaker, manifested by the words uttered, vocal variations, body language, and the context. The total message of communication includes three Vs: *verbal, vocal,* and *visual.* First, the verbal message (V_1) presents what is said, written, or published. An email, a text message, a newspaper report, or a company guideline document are examples of V_1. Second, the vocal information (V_2) reveals how the message is said, such as the vocal variations and emotional tones. Third, the visual appearance (V_3) covers eye contact, facial expressions, body movements, dress code, time, and space. While V_1 is the *message released* by the speaker, V_2 and V_3 serve as the *metamessage* or *paralanguage* that defines, revises, modifies and sometimes contradicts the message expressed in V_1.

Total Message = V_1 (Verbal) + V_2 (Vocal) + V_3 (Visual)

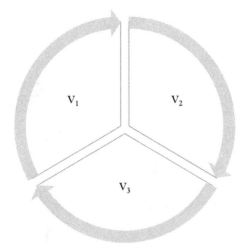

Figure 6.2 The three Vs of a message

To grasp the intended meaning of the total message from the speaker, one needs to listen to all three Vs in communication: the verbal, the vocal, and the visual. Drastically different from hearing, listening is a trained skill that requires participation of the ears, the eyes, the mind, and the heart. Sometimes, nothing is spoken ($V_1 = 0$), but the speaker's body language tells it all. Other times, there is just no response to your message, which may be the result of no interest, lack of attention or technical blockage. Silence, whether by accident or on purpose, shall be understood with care.

Meaning resides in people, not words. Each of us probably has a different interpretation and experience of the same word. Humans communicate with abstract symbols, complicated by sophistication in languages, dialects, accents, and personal voices. Miscommunication frequently happens because people have different understandings and perspectives on the meaning of the same word. The semiotic triangle of Richards and Ogden (1923), also known as the triangle of meaning, indicates how linguistic symbols (words) relate to the objects they represent. When a speaker uses a *word* (symbol) to communicate, he/she usually does not explain and describe the intended meaning (connotations) of this word. The listener, being another human being with different life experiences and reference points, often understands the same *word* (symbol) differently from the speaker. I often joke with my

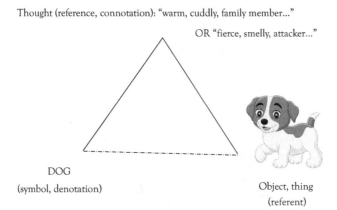

Thought (reference, connotation): "warm, cuddly, family member..."

OR "fierce, smelly, attacker..."

DOG
(symbol, denotation)

Object, thing
(referent)

Figure 6.3 The semiotic triangle

students that I as the speaker saying the same words in class, but the students listen differently and each earning a different grade. It is normal that the listener may misunderstand the speaker. For example, Andrew likes dogs; therefore, when Andrew talks about dogs, he may automatically assume that everyone likes dogs. Among the listeners, Emma was once attacked by a dog in her childhood; therefore, Emma fears dogs. If Andrew gives a dog to Emma, that gift may not be appreciated. Active listening embodies five complicated processes of hearing, observing, understanding, thinking, and seeking clarification. To become effective communicators, we need to make an effort to listen for the intended meaning.

Meaning is the essence of communication, not words. Pearson and Nelson (2000) define communication as "the process of understanding and sharing meaning" (p. 6). In the Chinese language, the word *meaning* is written as the Chinese character 意 (pronounced as *yi*). The top part of this Chinese character is 音 (*sound*, pronounced as *yin*), and the bottom part is 心 (*heart*, pronounced as *xin*). The etymology of the Chinese character for *meaning* demonstrates that "meaning is the sound from the heart."

Miscommunication is common, and misunderstanding is costly for business. Personal and professional relationships suffer when such misunderstanding happens frequently. The key is to listen with one's full presence and to identify the intended meaning of the speaker. Good listening makes the communication accurate and more efficient. Today, there are numerous social media platforms for us to post our opinions. They are mostly one-way communication where we *talk* but hardly listen. Lack of listening creates a cacophony of thoughts in our heads. Here are some tips to improve active listening skills:

- Stop talking (the letters for *listen* and *silent* are the same).
- Pay attention and show interest: Give the speaker your undivided attention.
- Listen with your full presence, in person or online.
- Acknowledge the message with your body language (gesture, eye contact, nodding) to show that you are engaged.
- Learn to take notes.
- Empathize with the speaker; Affirm with the speaker, Ask questions.
- Listen to understand.
- Defer judgment.
- Respond appropriately.
- Ask for clarification.
- Paraphrase the other person's statements with your own words and ask for feedback.
- Know it is therapeutic for others to talk.
- Ask the right questions at the proper time.

LOVE Model Part #2: Observe Key Players

An organization could have hundreds or thousands of people working there, each in a different role. Whom should we observe and listen to? *When a delegate from Organization A goes out to sell a product/service or to seek sponsorship with Organization B, it is critical to find out the decision-makers of Organization B.* Brad Taylor shares that in The Coca-Cola Company, these key decision makers are named as *economic buyers*. To close deals, Mr. Taylor wants to build relationships at all levels of the organization with the economic buyers, procurement personnel, evaluators, and gatekeepers.

How do you find out who is the decision maker? First, *studying the organizational chart* provides the starting point. Robert Striar, the president of M Style Marketing, takes a *top-down approach*. Mr. Striar will study the organizational chart and go as high up on the organizational chart as he can. He would contact executives who are at the CEO, COO, and CMO levels. Mr. Striar then tries to connect with account executives and procurement managers who control budgets and other decision procedures.

Second, forming an alliance with *internal champions* yields valuable information and shortcuts. In *Sunzi Military Tactics*, the critical function of *spy* (间, pronounced as *jian*) is mentioned in multiple chapters (Sunzi, 5th century BC). A spy is sometimes called an *undercover agent* or *secret agent*, hired by a state or a company to obtain valuable information about enemy countries or competitors. For business relationship development, it is beneficial to identify, recruit, and unite with internal champions. Wade Edwards prefers to take a *bottom-up approach* by allying with internal champions to raise funds for nonprofit organizations. When he was working for UNICEF in Japan, he would often get in the door by working with junior-level staff and have them champion the ideas upward. Mr. Edwards says,

> Going bottom up can be very successful. You first start the engagement and relationship with junior staff members who are working with the marketing, product development, or advertising teams. They understand where there may be a linkage to work together, and then they become internal champions to introduce UNICEF to some of the senior managers or C suite-level individuals.

The bottom-up approach can be a longer process, but Mr. Edwards thinks it makes for a much more interesting relationship because the internal champions can weed through the internal politics and reach out to the decision makers.

Third, culture matters in international companies regarding who the economic buyers are. Global entrepreneurs I interviewed shared that for Chinese companies, usually the economic buyer is the CEO. For American companies, sometimes it is the middle managers. Stan Wang, President of the Tenfunder Investment Group, reveals that decision makers in Chinese companies usually are quiet. They are often older, more experienced individuals with unique charisma. You may detect certain individuals being decision makers simply because of the way they conduct themselves and how the people around them react and follow them.

Do we need to observe business partners' family situations? Regarding whether we need to observe the potential partner's family life, there is a spectrum of answers. Many American business leaders say that we need to pay attention to their family lives, but only do so if they are open to it. In China, entrepreneurs care very much about the partner's family background. Glad Cheng, the chairman of China Window Group, says, "If you cannot manage your family, how can you manage your business?" Mr. Cheng says business partners are like extended family members, and thus, they need to be observed thoroughly.

For more than 30 years, Cathy Garces has worked as a sales executive for Emirates Airlines, Concorde Hotels, Japan Airlines, and Air Canada. Ms. Garces shares her roadmap to "hunt down the economic buyers." Via due diligence, it is important to find out which part of the company is managing the travel business. She says some companies manage their travel out of procurement, while others by finance or human resource (HR) departments. If HR is managing travel, the top priority will most likely be travelers' comfort, whereas if finance is handling it, the goal will be cost reduction. If procurement is managing travel, usually there is a blend of the two. Ms. Garces has experienced her share of drilling down through emails and phone calls. She says most of the times, she does not get a response on the phone and leaves voicemail messages. If she is lucky enough to get an email response, she follows up with an email response for a lead-in that makes them want to read the rest. She asks for 15 to 20 minutes to explore whether the two sides have an opportunity to help one another. Just like in hunting, Ms. Garces does not let her targets out of sight. She stresses the importance of *following up. After a sales appointment and conversations, if one does not follow up, it is for nothing.*

LOVE Model Part #3: Value Propositions

When we cultivate relationships for sales and fundraising, we must present an attractive value proposition. JR Wilson, a vice president at AT&T, acknowledges that there are a gazillion companies approaching him for business with AT&T. Willing to *disrupt the business* by partnering with smaller companies, Mr. Wilson asks the newcomers to lay out who they are, what their value propositions are, and how they can help AT&T to reduce cost and increase sales.

The success of firms in the marketplace is linked to the value they provide to customers. Companies are encouraged to invest resources in market research, allowing them to gain deeper customer insights and, thus, improve value propositions. Creating a value proposition is an essential component of the business relationship cultivation strategy. Kaplan and Norton (2004) state, "Satisfying customers is the source of sustainable value creation" (p. 10). *A value proposition is a statement that identifies clear and measurable benefits a buyer gains when purchasing a product or service. A value proposition is a promise of value to be delivered, communicated, and acknowledged from one party to the other.* This value proposition leads to a competitive advantage when a buyer picks your product or service over other competitors.

The value proposition can include *both professional and personal values.* Professional value means that they would benefit financially or gain reputation by partnering with you. Personal value could be you presenting meaningful gifts, providing helpful information about local school districts, helping them to settle down in your city, or inviting them to your golf club. Brad Taylor, former brand strategist of The Coca-Cola Company, provides this value proposition to his business partner, "If you sell Coke products, not only you can make more money, but also you will be given vouchers to watch Olympic Games onsite!" Mr. Taylor rewards business partners with VIP tickets gained by The Coca-Cola Company being an official sponsor for the Olympic Games. Consumers and clients are always looking for the best possible deals. The value proposition is the promise that the business will give the consumer or client the best possible value. DeAnn Golden, the president and CEO of Berkshire Hathaway HomeServices Georgia Properties, encourages all real estate agents to hone their skills, be laser-focused on client experiences, and be diligent in keeping in touch with these clients before, during, and after transactions. Ms. Golden says that "placing the best interest of clients above everything else" is a commitment grounded in the Code of Ethics for the National Association of REALTORS®.[2]

---

[2] *The National Association of REALTORS (NAR)* is America's largest trade association, representing 1.5 million members. NAR membership is composed of residential and commercial brokers, salespeople, property managers, appraisers, and counselors engaged in the real estate industry. The term REALTOR is a registered mark that identifies a real estate professional who is an NAR member subscribing to its strict code of ethics.

Good value proposition is reflected in consistent and timely customer service. Jessica Cork, vice president at YKK Corporation of America, shared a negative and positive example of customer service. Ms. Cork was experiencing troubles and headaches with Vender F. However, one day, she received a gigantic box of peaches from Vender F's headquarters. She wrote back to her contact at Vendor F company to thank him, and he responded, "What peaches?" Ms. Cork assumed that she was listed in a database, and something triggered the PR person to send every single vendor in that list a box of peaches, while her contact at the company had no idea of these peach gifts. Ms. Cork thought, "I like peaches, but what I really need is good customer service. Help me solve the real problem at work, please!" Authenticity matters. Treating each customer as unique, and getting to know his/her needs at all times enhance customer service. Ms. Cork considers Uberflip, a content experience platform and software company, an ideal business partner known for its *caring* customer service. Unlike many companies that vanish after subscriptions are secured, Mr. M from Uberflip sets up monthly conference calls with his client companies. Mr. M asks if Ms. Cork has experienced any issues and questions while using Uberflip software. Sometimes, Mr. M would introduce new technologies that he thinks might be beneficial for YKK Corporation of America. There is never any unreasonable additional charges. Ms. Cork enjoys the conversations and learning experiences of these calls and meetings. She treasures such a long-term business partner who desires to make her business better. She considers Uberflip a *giver* of technologies and customer services, instead of a *taker*. *Ms. Cork recommends that we become givers in relationships, always providing extra value to the other. Nobody wants to maintain a one-sided relationship where the other person only contacts us when he/she needs something.*

LOVE Model Part #4: Empathy

"Put yourself in someone else's shoes." This idiom teaches us empathy, which means understanding and entering into another's feelings. Empathy is one's capacity to understand or feel what another person is experiencing from within their frame of reference. Empathy is fundamentally different from sympathy. In empathy, the *self* views the *other* on an equal basis and tries to understand the other from the respectful I-Thou perspective. In sympathy, the *self* maintains the I-It perspective while looking down upon the *other*.

Empathy asks us to think from the perspective of the other: the clients, customers, and business partners. The empathetic view is a strategy endorsed by most business leaders and entrepreneurs. Robert Striar, president of M Style Marketing, says, "I think there's an element of empathy in listening and paying attention. You need to respect who people are and what challenges they have." JR Wilson, a vice president at AT&T, strives to view a partnership from *the other side*. Mr. Wilson mentioned that he tried to view a deal or an opportunity from the perspective of the client. This allowed him to fully appreciate the challenges of the client and adjust accordingly. There are conflicts and varying interests in business. Everyone wants to do what is best for his/her company. *Looking at what business partners need from their perspectives can help one figure out the best course forward.*

In relationship building, small talk is anything but small. Small talk can produce big results. Small talk is an informal type of discourse that does not cover any functional topics of conversation or any transactions that need to be addressed. In essence, it is polite conversation about unimportant things. The phenomenon of small talk was initially studied by Malinowski (1923), who coined the term *phatic communication* to describe this communication concept. Small talk is a bonding ritual. The ability to conduct and participate in small talk is a sophisticated social skill. Small talk helps people to explore each other's backgrounds, interests, personalities, and communication styles. Small talk may cover topics about one's hometown, hair styles, hobbies, families, and travel stories. Through small talk, we observe the other, listen to the other, and find out what the other cares about. Alex Gregory, former president and CEO of YKK Corporation of America, weighs in on small talk, "You need to pay attention to what people like to talk about, because obviously those things are very important to them."

"Spending time together" can be in meetings, meals, coffee, tea, wine and dine, golfing, karaoke, family gatherings, and sports events. Entrepreneurs interviewed for this book are familiar with most of these bonding experiences, which not only serve as opportunities for observation, but also function as occasions to create *shared memories* that nourish the relationships.

Glad Cheng, the chairman of China Window Group, acknowledges that these are important activities for relationship cultivation. Informal meetings help relational partners to facilitate mutual self-disclosure, find common ground, and establish trust. Roger Neuenschwander, former president of tvsdesign, shared, "Business relationships become personal relationships and friendships, through day-to-day activities."

Bonding experience creates shared memories, which are essential building blocks for a long-lasting relationship between two organizational delegates. Wade Edwards was once a fundraising director for Habitat for Humanity International, a global nonprofit organization headquartered in Atlanta. Mr. Edwards thinks these bonding activities allow one to observe how people live and how one can contribute to their lives where appropriate. Mr. Edwards says,

> I think bonding experiences are crucial and it really does allow the next level of trust to be built. But it needs to be done in a transparent way. It gets a little tricky to navigate and find the right way to bond together outside of a nine-to-five or an office experience.

Are *wine'n'dine* necessary or overrated? Roger Neuenschwander, former president of tvsdesign, says that some American and foreign clients expect wine'n'dine after they become long-term customers. Ms. Masae Okura, a Japanese lawyer, shares a story about her acquaintance Mr. Marek. Mr. Marek had been courting a Japanese company for a few months to close a business deal. The Japanese team seemed happy with his presentations and his products. One day, they invited him for dinner at a local restaurant. After everyone were seated, the CEO of the Japanese company asked what alcoholic drink to order for him. Mr. Marek said, "Sorry, I don't drink." Right at that moment, everyone's faces changed from *smiley* to *frozen*. The deal never happened for Mr. Marek after that.

Stan Wang is the president of Tenfunder Investment Group, and he invests in real estate in China, Australia, Germany, and the United States. Mr. Wang stresses that one needs to keep *bonding experiences* in a simple way, because too much *wine'n'dine* may have a negative impact on relationship building. Contrary to popular belief, Mr. Wang says that in China, potential business partners are usually very direct about what they want. They want your strength and resources. Mr. Gregory, former President and CEO at YKK Corporation of America says, "Alcohol is dangerous. Bad things can happen. We have very strict policies about driving our company cars under the influence of alcohol."

Conclusion

From a win–win–win standpoint, knowing what the business partner wants is essential for business relationship cultivation. Communication is the basic building block for relationship cultivation. In Latin, the root for the word *communication* is *communicare*, which means to share, or to make common. An experienced entrepreneur listens and understands the other, then presents a value proposition that satisfies the common interests of both parties. Cissna and Anderson (1994) explain, "Dialogue implies more than a simple back and forth messages in interaction. It points to a particular process and quality of communication in which participants *meet* which allows changing and being changed" (p. 10).

Common practices in relationship observation, such as meetings, wine'n'dine, golfing, entertainment, and sports offer valuable occasions for mutual observation. *Bonding experiences in creating shared memories are necessary, but the actual practice can be flexible based on needs, timing, and cultural preferences.* This chapter introduced a fourfold business relationship cultivation LOVE strategy: listening for intended meaning, observing key players, value proposition, and empathy for the other. From a win–win–win standpoint, *knowing what the other wants* is essential for business relationship cultivation. Listening is of maximum significance for relationship observation because listening is the most direct way through which to find out what the other party wants. One needs to maintain the *full presence* of the self in a relationship, whether in physical meetings, virtual meetings, phone calls, or using various apps. The next chapter talks about closing business deals by overcoming obstacles.

CHAPTER 7

Overcoming Obstacles to Close Deals

Quotations to Ponder

Don't ever categorize all business relationships as equal. You have to observe and be aware of what type of relationship it is, and never let it come out of that category, unless it is ready to.

—Rick Cole, former Senior Vice President
Turner Broadcasting System

You must have patience for business relationships. If you have ten initiatives and two are working, focus on the two, while caring about the others.

—DeAnn Golden, President and CEO
Berkshire Hathaway HomeServices Georgia Properties

Putting timelines to business is risky because most people quit three feet before they hit gold. You need to keep fostering it.

—Eddy Perez, Cofounder and CEO
Equity Prime Mortgage

Deliver on your promises. Never embarrass your partners. Never do the blame game.

—Roger Neuenschwander, former President and CEO
tvsdesign

It doesn't matter how good friends we are in business, if the timing is not right, nothing is happening.

—Nagendra Roy, CEO
AanseaCore

Not being able to deliver what the client needs is the biggest obstacle to closing deals.

—Cathy Garces, former Sales Executive
Emirates Airlines; Japan Airlines

You had better understand the cultural norms. Obviously, you can't be an expert in every culture. At the end of the day, we humans want the same things. We want to grow, to be happy and to have a better life for our children.

—Rick Cole, former Senior Vice President
Turner Broadcasting System

Nature does not hurry, yet everything is accomplished. By letting go, it all gets done.

—Laozi, Author
Tao Te Ching

Chapter Summary

What are the obstacles in relationship building? How do we overcome obstacles and care for the growth of business relationships? This chapter synthesizes five obstacles in relationship growth: culture, language, attitude, structure, and haste (CLASH). After we overcome obstacles on the road of relationship growth, how can we harvest deals when they are ripe? Research for this book underscores four winning mindsets to close deals: goal-oriented, opportunity-driven, learning about relationships, and deal-closing (GOLD). Go for the GOLD, close the deals! It shall be noted that deal-closing is the beginning of a new chapter in business relationship development.

CASE STUDY 7.1

Approaching Women in Hijabs: Investment Bankers From Kuwait

Lucy Lu is the founder of Atlanta-based aiLegal law firm. One time, Lucy was in a training program for business at Harvard University in Boston. At the end of the training, the organizer hosted a social event. Talking and laughing, people were drinking wine and eating snacks. Lucy mingled with a few classmates and walked around the room. Suddenly, she noticed a few Arabic women wearing hijabs in a corner, no snacks, no drinking, sitting far away from all the people networking. No one made any effort to approach them. Lucy felt awful about the situation. She said to herself, "If they belong to the same program, we should talk to each other. We cannot be hosting one event, but ending up with two different worlds here." Ms. Lu gently approached them and asked, "Why are you not participating in the social event?" They said, "We are Arabic. Being Muslim, we cannot really drink wine. We cannot be too close to men, either." Lucy smiled. She started some casual chit-chat with these ladies in hijabs. It turned out that these Arabic women came from a large investment bank in Kuwait. From there, they built up a trust-based relationship. Since then, Ms. Lu has been doing business with them for many years. In today's global business, one needs to be culturally sensitive and compassionate. With an open mind, one can care about people in various surroundings. With compassion, Ms. Lu was concerned about these few Arabic women who were left alone in a party, never even thinking that perhaps they were businesswomen. Kindness wins!

Discussion Questions for Readers

1. Have you ever made cultural mistakes in business? If so, how can you improve?
2. How would you approach a group of businesspeople in different cultural attire?
3. What cultural obstacles prevent us from developing a mutually beneficial business relationship with potential customers?

CASE STUDY 7.2
U.S.–China Differences in Business Hospitality

Confucius said in *Analects*: "When there are friends visiting from afar, isn't that the happiest time?" (子曰：有朋自远方来，不亦乐呼？). Over 5,000 years of history brews an aged culture of hospitality in China. Most people in China love to entertain guests, especially when they learn you are from far away cities and countries. In 2013, Glad Cheng, chairman of China Window Group, preserved the *U.S.–China Friendship House*, to commemorate the happy memories of Chinese President Xi Jinping's visit to Iowa in 1985 and 2012. In 2014, Glad Cheng invited his new American friends from Iowa to his hometown in Zhejiang province, East China. These American friends range from local government officials, bankers, and investors, to consultants, all hoping to develop business relationships in China. During the one-week trip, they were picked up at the airport, invited to three fancy meals per day and postdinner entertainment, all paid for by Mr. Cheng and his Chinese business partners. The American visitors were treated warmly as friends in the Chinese way. It shall be noted that in the Chinese culture or many cultures around the world, such friendship display implies mutuality and reciprocity. Quid pro quo! In other words, these Chinese businessmen expect themselves to be treated with similar hospitality when they travel to the United States.

A year later in 2015, Mr. Cheng and his Chinese business partners made a return visit to Iowa. Instead of hospitality, Mr. Cheng said they were *treated with politeness*. Other than a few official meetings at the city hall and the economic development office, they were left alone. No meals, no entertainment, no friend-like activities. To save face, Mr. Cheng invited his Chinese business partners to local restaurants. There was an obvious disparity in business hospitality between businesspeople from the two cultures. It seems that in China, the *relationship red carpet* was extended, while in the United States, people were restricted by concerns for time and budget.

Chinese delegations sometimes feel uncomfortable, neglected, and abandoned when visiting their business counterparts in the United States. This perception and experience are not helpful with business relationship building in the global context. In China, there is usually a budget for

relationship building, covering meals and entertainment. In public organizations in the United States, taxpayer money cannot be used for food
and beverages.[1] This means government agencies cannot use their tax supported budgets to grow relationships, including entertaining international
guests. Private businesses in the United States typically have some funding
for entertaining clients, though expenditure priorities and reimbursement
procedures differ among organizations. The total cost of meals, taxes, and
tips in upscale restaurants in the United States can be very high. Even if a
U.S. business partner desires to entertain a Chinese delegation at his/her
own expense, the cost to do so at the expected level might be prohibitive.

Even though the financial situations of companies in the two countries are different, *reception equivalency* can be achieved via other means,
such as taking Chinese guests for a house dinner, backyard party,
coffee time, or touring natural, cultural and historical parks in the United
States. Friendship building activities can be cost-effective and innovative,
as long as they serve the purpose of entertaining the international guests,
spending time with them, and creating shared memories. *If you want to
do long-term business with international business partners, you will need to
treat them as friends, and provide innovative hospitality when they visit you
in the United States.*

Discussion Questions for Readers

1. Within your budget restraints, what are the best practices of hosting
   business visitors and clients?
2. How can we achieve equivalency in business hospitality with people
   of other cultures?
3. How can we be innovative in introducing our culture and business
   to international guests?

---

[1] *Organizational funding for relationship building in the United States:* The restric-
tion on the use of taxpayer money for food and drinks is true in public institu-
tions that rely on public funding. Private businesses would not have these same
restrictions. Some public agencies have discretionary funds raised through donations and other means to support relationship building activities.

Introduction

After you select business partners and clients, you work hard to nurture these relationships with active listening and consistent observation. However, after a while, you still have not harvested any business deals, such as signing a contract or being offered a purchase order (PO). What went wrong? What are the obstacles in relationship growth? Improper timing, cultural differences, linguistic barriers, political, legal, and accounting disparities, lack of interpersonal chemistry or integrity issues ... these are just several obstacles mentioned by global business leaders and entrepreneurs. This chapter synthesizes five obstacles in business development: *culture, language, attitude, structure, and haste (CLASH)*. Johnston and Gao (2009) highlight three *I's* that lead to conflict: *interdependence, incompatibility,* and *interaction*. If any of the five obstacles causes incompatibility, there may be conflicts in a business relationship.

Obstacle #1: Culture

Culture plays a critical role in business relationship development. Eating crab legs, lobster heads, and slurping soup in business meetings ... these behaviors may be acceptable in China, Japan, Korea, Vietnam, and other countries, they are considered *unsophisticated* in the United States. Geert Hofstede (1991) states that culture forms lenses through which we view and interpret people and our environment. To have a deeper understanding of one's business partners, it is rudimentary to understand his/her culture. Cultural barriers exist as major obstacles to relationship growth.

Culture shapes communication and communication is culture-bound. On the one hand, people from various cultures assign different meanings to the same word. On the other hand, culture impacts nonverbal communication in facial expression, body language, and how we utilize time,

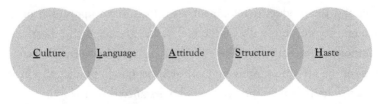

Figure 7.1 Five obstacles against relationship growth: CLASH

space, and silence. Alex Gregory, former president and CEO of YKK Corporation of America, shares a story of cultural differences. Discussing YKK zippers' application in the medical field, Japanese and American doctors met for a brainstorming session. Trained with public speaking skills, American doctors broke the ice. Japanese doctors listened and took some time to think about the ideas. Feeling awkward with the silence, American doctors talked again for a long time. By the end of the meeting, Japanese doctors barely got a word in, as they prefer to listen, think, and then respond. By the time Japanese doctors were ready to give well thought out feedback, the American doctors were talking again.

David Kirk, president of Murata Electronics North America, shares the difference in human resources practices between the United States and Japan. In a Japanese company, at the beginning of the fiscal year on April 1, there may be 500 fresh faces hired. They come with various degrees: bachelor's, master's, or doctoral. Mix and match, each of these newcomers is randomly arranged at a position of finance, engineering, or sales, which may not be directly related to their degrees. They will start with this position and go for an upward cycle of promotion, based on their performance. Japanese companies usually do not have massive salary differences among salespersons, engineers, and finance officers. The salary levels are relatively flat, so leaders can move people around. An employee may be in accounting today, in sales tomorrow, and in engineering five years later. These HR practices help to motivate all employees in different divisions to respect each other and work toward the same goal: the advancement of the company. For Murata Electronics North America, a Japanese company in the United States, it is challenging to adopt this HR practice as is. Mr. Kirk tries to fulfill some of these rotations and cross-trainings early in people's careers. This way, no matter what position employees hold, they learn the rewards and challenges of other positions, and gain a holistic view of the company. I heard that in some American companies, the sales team and the product development team look down upon each other, because they do not totally understand and appreciate each other's contributions to the company. There is also a huge gap between the income levels of the two teams. Sometimes, a salesperson for a product can make more than double than the engineer who designed this product.

Culture is reflected in people's daily thinking, behaviors, and emotions, as well as in behaviors and actions. For instance, paying for meals is conducted differently depending on the cultural context. *Going Dutch* is a dining etiquette practiced in West Europe and North America. Going Dutch indicates that each person is paying for his/her own expenses, rather than any one person paying for the entire group. In other regions around the world, it is uncommon and may be considered rude to have separate bills. In China, after a group meal, it is expected that the bill be paid by the person with the highest social standing or income, or by the host who made the invitation. In the United States, it is a common practice for businesspeople to meet for *lunch*, and one person might pay for some or all diners. Reciprocation of payment is implied for the next lunch.

"This ain't my first rodeo!" Some Americans use this expression to show that they are experienced and prepared for a situation. Recently, a few American employees in a Japanese company invited their colleagues from India to a rodeo show that involves horses, cows, and other livestock. The American employees tried to show their business hospitality by challenging the Indian colleagues to ride a baby cow, not knowing this action was offensive to the Indians who viewed cows as sacred.

Obstacle #2: Language

Tony Bell is a vice president at a bank. One day, a new employee Jennifer knocked at his door and tried to say hi. Looking at the items on his desk, Jennifer shouted: "Wow! You use the old-fashioned calculator. I remember my grandfather had the same kind!" "Well, you certainly make me feel old," Tony responded. "Oh, no. That's not what I mean. Sorry about that." While it may not be Jennifer's intention to make Tony feel old and embarrassed, her interaction did not leave a good first impression. Miscommunication happens. Linguistic barriers are another obstacle for relationship building. To successfully grow business relationships with clients and customers, linguistic barriers need to be overcome with sensitivity. R. D. Laing (1961) wrote in his book *Self and Other*, "self does not experience the experience of the other directly," (p. 19) rather, the self *infers* what the other experiences. *As the self and the other are two human beings with two different experiences, miscommunication is the norm. Language, a tool we use to communicate, can become an obstacle for relationship building.*

The words we use to communicate are strongly influenced by our backgrounds, cultures, experiences, and perspectives. Once upon a time, you were listening to a story told by your friend or colleague from Chinese, Japanese, or Korean culture. Suddenly, you lose track of the people they are talking about. You might interpose and ask, "Wait, is this person a man or a woman?" In Chinese characters, the words for *he, she, it* (他，她，它) sound the same: *Ta*. Therefore, it takes extra efforts for a person growing up in East Asian cultures to correctly use the pronouns *he, she, it* in a conversation. They may randomly mix and match the third person singular pronouns in spoken English. This could create misunderstandings.

The idiom *lost in translation* means that a word or words have lost their meaning, subtlety, and significance when translated from the original language to another. American multinational corporations may have experienced rough starts overseas simply because they did not pay enough attention to *translation equivalency* for brands and corporate communications. Francis et al. (2002) said,

> When a brand is expanded into a foreign market, a careless choice of a new or translated brand name can have negative effects on the product as well as on the company in terms of loss in sales, damage to credibility, and damage to reputation (p. 99).

Transliteration refers to a process of finding a similar meaning and sound, and *transcreation* involves creating a new message that preserves the intent of the source message (Regmi et al. 2010). Translation equivalency aims for translations with same value in both languages, which can be almost impossible to achieve. Companies must take a holistic approach in translating brands and other corporate communications when entering foreign markets.

Obstacle #3: Attitude

We are proud people, no matter what culture we are from. We want to keep our faces whenever possible. If one's face is damaged publicly, it creates obstacles in relationship growth. *Face* reflects one's dignity, prestige, and reputation in the dynamics of social interaction

(Goffman 1959). A person may experience embarrassment or humiliation when the person perceives his/her face as being discredited. The concept of face applies to every individual, entity, and organization in all cultures. In conflicts, one's face is threatened, and thus, the person tends to save or restore his or her face. These communicative behaviors are called *facework* in the *face negotiation theory* (Ting-Toomey and Kurogi 1998). Entrepreneurs have a vested interest in protecting the reputation (saving face) and enhancing the reputation (giving face) for their customers, clients, and business partners. Negligence in relationships produces negative attitudes among clients and business partners. Ms. Jessica Cork, a vice president of YKK Corporation of America, says ignoring the relationship can be a major obstacle for developing long-term relationships. Ms. Cork suggests meeting with the clients and business partners occasionally and making sure to understand the changing dynamics in relationships.

Obstacle #4: Structure

To close deals, one needs to develop relationships with *economic buyers*, sometimes with the assistance of *internal champions*. There are many structural difficulties one may have to deal with before meeting with the economic buyers. To eventually close a deal with the economic buyer, one must successfully maneuver structural barriers in both human and digital gatekeepers.

First, human gatekeepers may include compliance people, evaluators, secretaries, assistants, and organizational teams. To close deals, one must navigate through these people in different roles to build a win–win–win relationship with the decision makers. What's more, sometimes your business contacts leave their job positions through resignations, retirements, or position transfers. The business relationship you built for years could fall through the cracks.

For nonprofit fundraising, structural obstacles may exist in the ambiguity of organizational charts. Wade Edwards used to be a fundraiser for UNICEF and Habitat for Humanity International. Mr. Edwards says that a lot of times, fundraising comes down to where the budget resides and who can make something happen, and junior staff are not necessarily in those positions. Mr. Edwards says usually the corporate social responsibility (CSR)[2] division of Fortune 500 or Fortune 1000 companies are attached to the president's office, the senior management team, or the marketing division. It is usually faster working with the marketing division because they have the ability to re-address some of their budget to work with a nonprofit. People in other parts of the company may not have that flexibility. Mr. Edwards says that understanding the location and budget of the economic buyers constitutes the main part of due diligence in the early stages of engagement.

Second, technologies function as *digital gatekeepers* in relationship building. Digital gatekeepers range from company email system *firewalls* to compatibility of video conference platforms, Internet disruption, or adoption of apps and software. For instance, after a networking event, you try to follow up with Mr. Miller by sending him an email based on his business card. After two weeks, you do not hear anything from Mr. Miller. Other than the possibility that Mr. Miller is not interested in this relationship with you, it could be that Mr. Miller never received your email. Maybe your email was pushed to the *spam email* inbox by his company email firewall system.

The COVID-19 pandemic fueled an explosion in online video conferences via Zoom, Microsoft Teams, Google Meet, and other apps. If one's laptop does not have the latest version of these applications, communication among business partners can be challenging. After a storm, your neighborhood may be out of power, and you cannot communicate with your potential buyers. Not having a presence on various social media platforms poses a digital barrier. For example, if you are not on LinkedIn, you basically do not exist in the professional world. Digital gatekeepers can be as powerful as national firewalls. In China,

---

[2] *Corporate social responsibility (CSR)* is a self-regulating practice that helps a company be socially accountable to itself, its stakeholders, and the public. By practicing CSR, also called corporate citizenship, companies engage with the communities to enhance positive impacts in economic, social, and environmental areas.

Internet users with no VPN[3] cannot access Facebook, Twitter, Google, or YouTube. To overcome this obstacle, Chinese people usually suggest their U.S. partners to use WeChat[4] for communication with them. To do business with any Chinese person or company, you have to download WeChat app and register an account at WeChat. Launched in 2011 by Tencent, WeChat has become the dominate platform of communication for the Chinese people.

Obstacle #5: Haste

Haste makes waste. This common idiom indicates that doing something too quickly causes mistakes that result in the loss of time, effort, materials, and other resources. It takes time and a process for an apple tree to grow, blossom, and yield fruit. In business, we must practice "strategic patience" to allow deals to mature. The word *patience* is often defined as "the capacity to accept or tolerate delays, troubles, or sufferings without getting angry or upset." *Strategic patience* is a method in business relationship cultivation that seeks to wait for the right time to close deals. Be patient and let nature take its course. Robert Striar, president of M Style Marketing, shares, "We have potential clients we've talked to for years. One of my biggest clients is someone I spoke to for four years before they became a client." In the long-term business relationship cultivation process, we keep the conversation going, strengthen the trust, and be ready to close any deals at the right moment. Laozi, the author of *Tao Te Ching*,

---

[3] A *virtual private network (VPN)* is an encrypted connection over the Internet from a device to a network. The encrypted connection helps ensure that sensitive data are safely transmitted. It prevents unauthorized people from eavesdropping on the traffic and allows the user to conduct work remotely. It provides access to resources that may be inaccessible on the public network. VPN technology is widely used in corporate environments (Cisco 2021).

[4] WeChat (pronounced as 'weixin" 微信) is a Chinese instant messaging, social media and mobile payment app, launched by Tencent in 2011. Capable of sending texts, images, voicemails, videos, Microsoft files, and money, as well as hosting phone calls, meetings and conferences, WeChat has become the social media of everything for people in China. Billions of dollars of businesses have been conducted via WeChat.

asks: "Do you have the patience to wait until your mud settles and the water is clear?"

Timing is everything. Confucius said, "timing is the fate" (时也,命也). A popular Chinese saying points to the combined effect of "timing in Heaven, location on Earth, and harmony of the people" (天时、地利、人和), with timing listed as the number one variable to consider. Timing matters for business relationships, just like crops follow the cycle of growing seasons. In business, one needs to find out when people's projects become available in their business lifecycles, who they have as their supervisors, and if they are interested in us as a vendor now. Not paying attention to the timing and tenor of priorities of the economic buyers poses a major obstacle in business. We do have a *deadline culture* in the United States. There are deadlines in everything: projects, contracts, construction, and business deals. However, business relationships cannot be rushed as they follow their own growing seasons and speeds.

The Taoist concept of *wu wei* (无为) reminds us to be strategically patient, letting nature take its course for relationship development. Often misunderstood, wu wei literally means *inexertion, inaction, effortless action*, or *action through inaction* (Slingerland 2007). Without forcing it, wu wei allows things to happen in their natural pace. You may execute some interventions, such as sowing the seeds, moving the rose plant to a sunny spot, or adding some water and fertilizer, but then, you must wait patiently for things to happen. Sinologist Jean Francois Billeter describes wu wei as a state of perfect knowledge on the reality of the situations, efficaciousness, and energy interplay dynamics (Slingerland 2007). Practicing wu wei through strategic patience lets us to be ready when the right moments come. Many times, things will work out better with less intervention. Problems tend to solve themselves in some cases. Sometimes, all we need to do is to take a deep breath, wait, and let things happens.

In April 2020, one month after national and state pandemic shutdowns in the United States, I interviewed Rick Cole, former Senior Vice President at Turner Broadcasting System. During the two-hour phone call, Mr. Cole shared that sensitivity and patience are important for business. He said you have to look at relationships with care and figure out the proper speed for each project. A project might be moving slowly until an external variable makes it go quickly. The pandemic slowed down a lot of business in 2020. Leaders of some companies became frustrated. In these situations, a business manager might say to his/her employees, "These are hard times. We need to reach out to everybody, and we've got to find a way to generate more business." Mr. Cole says companies can ruin relationships with insensitive and aggressive actions. Here is a sample episode:

> Seller: *"We have this contract in the works and need for you to take the necessary steps to close this deal for us."*
> Buyer: *"You know how I am going to finish it? This conversation is over."*

DeAnn Golden, president and CEO of Berkshire Hathaway Home-Services Georgia Properties, says that you cannot force the growth of a relationship. She advices us to keep caring about the relationships based on *business seasons*. In real estate business, Ms. Golden views clients in four growing stages: *A, B, C, D*. The As are the ones generating business now. The Bs have great potential next. The Cs are not ready yet, so you continue to foster that relationship. We may have to *de-select the Ds* as they can be the toxic and draining relationships.

Winning Mindsets to Close Deals: GOLD

Making money is a priority for most companies. Money can only be made when deals are closed. After overcoming obstacles and waiting patiently, how can we harvest deals when they ripen from these relationships? Research for this book underscores four mindsets to win deals: goal-oriented, opportunity-driven, learning about relationships, and deal-closing (GOLD). Go for the GOLD, close the deals!

Winning Mindset #1: Goal-oriented. Persistence, patience, and perspiration build business relationship growth. Being persistent and goal-oriented helps to close deals. Eddy Perez, cofounder and CEO of Equity Prime Mortgage, stresses the power of persistence. He asks his employees to keep fostering the relationships, just like nurturing fruit trees for years. Brad Taylor shared what he learned at The Coca-Cola Company. He said even for Coke, there were times when he did not get any business deals from a client. Mr. Taylor said, "You may be told no, but you want to keep the door to that relationship open, because you never know when a no could become a yes." Mr. Taylor says if the business environment changes,

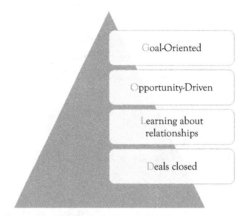

Figure 7.2 Winning mindsets to close deals: GOLD

or if we offer a different set of products and services, the client's answer may be changed to *yes*. Ms. Cathy Garces is a former sales executive for Emirates Airlines and Japan Airlines. Ms. Garces says if a brand does not deliver the service or product that was promised, an obstacle is created for developing future business. Consistent delivery of product and service is the key. The seller must keep his/her promise in providing a *good fit* product or service for the client.

Winning Mindset #2: Opportunity-driven. To close transactions from business relationships, one must maintain an opportunity-driven win–win–win mindset. Rainmakers are usually eager and resourceful to discover opportunities for all parties involved throughout the relationship growth process. If shared opportunities are identified, all parties are likely to strengthen their relationship with each other. JR Wilson, a vice president at AT&T, made it clear to his vendors that seeking shared opportunities is the essence of business. Vendors need to act in the best interest of AT&T every day. If circumstances change that might benefit a vendor in cost reduction for AT&T, the vendor should figure out ways to continue adding value for AT&T, despite what the agreement might state. Given the nature of technology advancements, policy and regulation changes, and disruptions in global supply chains, Mr. Wilson builds a special clause into contracts, stating that the vendor should always seek to act in the best interest of AT&T. If the business environment changes, the parties will agree to collaborate and renegotiate certain clauses in the contract. Otherwise, a termination clause in the contract will be executed by AT&T. The danger of a business relationship being terminated has proven to be a strong incentive for vendors to continue working with AT&T for mutual benefits in a turbulent and changing environment.

Winning Mindset #3: Learning about relationships. In gardening, you reap what you sow. In business, financial success depends on how much you satisfy the ever-changing needs and wants of the customers, clients, and partners. The best customer service is for you to become *a trusted advisor or consultant*, providing the much needed solutions for problems they encounter in work and life. DeAnn Golden, president and CEO of Berkshire Hathaway Home Services Georgia Properties, provides her perspective on learning about clients. She defaults to a customer service method called L-A-S-T: *listen, apologize, satisfy, thank*. In real estate sales, there can be misunderstandings and frustrations among the home buyers, sellers, the real estate associates, inspectors, loan providers, and attorneys. There may be a poor customer service experience by any of these providers. Sometimes a client is frustrated because the real estate associate said it would be easy, when in fact, it is complicated, due to unforeseen circumstances. Ms. Golden says when people are upset, they want to be heard. The associate should *listen* and sincerely *apologize*, "I'm sorry about that. I really wish it hadn't happened." Then the agent should strive to *satisfy*: "What can I do to make it better? How can I fix the issue now?" Finally, be sure to *thank* the clients, keep learning about them, and make them happy. Following the LAST method, Ms. Golden says complicated problems can be fixed properly based on her experience in hundreds of cases. When the time is right, try to close the transaction, which is the win–win–win goal for all! Ms. Golden prefers to rephrase *closing a deal* to *closing a transaction* because this moment of a successful sale is just the *beginning* of a new chapter in a business relationship. The same client might want to refinance the mortgage, buy a second home, buy or rent an investment property, or give a referral in the future. An experienced real estate associate would want to take care of all these needs and wants.

Winning Mindset #4: Deal-closing. The Symposium on ASIA-USA Partnership Opportunities (SAUPO) is the largest Asia business conference in the United States. In January 2013, almost two years after its inauguration, we were preparing to host another SAUPO. To organize an impactful SAUPO conference, we needed to invite influential speakers. Our trust-based personal network has been where we search for these speakers. I turned to Alex Gregory, then president and CEO of YKK Corporation of America, who spoke at SAUPO 2011. Mr. Gregory invited me for lunch at the Georgian Club. As I arrived, I saw another impressive gentleman there: David Kirk, president of Murata Electronics North America. During lunch, I listened to the two leaders, and enjoyed their conversations with each other. When it was my turn, I introduced SAUPO and extended our sincere invitation to David Kirk to be a SAUPO 2013 speaker. Mr. Kirk accepted this invitation with a smile. Mr. Gregory said to me, "May, you are a closer! You closed the deal." This was my first lesson about the importance of closing deals at the right time.

An experienced gardener harvests fruit at the proper time. By picking apples from the apple tree, we enjoy the fruit of labor after a whole year's hard work. Deals are *ripened fruits* on relationship trees. To cover the cost and maintain cash flow, companies and nonprofits need money. Money comes from closing deals. Closing deals allows the value exchange between *product + service* and *cash*, facilitated by the seller and buyer. If one develops a proper value exchange formula, deals can be closed by solving a problem for a client and better his/her work and life. If the perceived value exceeds the market price, people will pay. This is the magic moment when deals are closed.

DeAnn Golden, president and CEO of Berkshire Hathaway HomeServices Georgia Properties, says in the relationship-oriented real estate business, closing a deal is just the moment when a new chapter is opened for the clients and for the agent–client relationship. This entails cultivating a relationship before, during, and most importantly, after a transaction, as well as throughout all the future moves and home services needs of every client. Listening carefully and developing a full understanding of our clients' real estate goals and homeownership dreams deepens the connection and allows us to guide them with empathy, intention, and care. *Closing a deals is helping clients arriving at the finish line and making them successful. When the clients are successful, the company becomes successful.*

However, even if you have cultivated the relationship and convinced the client to close the deal with you, there are many moving parts before the deal can be closed. For example, in purchasing a home, you may need to have all parties involved moving in the same direction: buyer, buyer's agent, seller, seller's agent, mortgage company, title firms, attorneys, inspectors, survey providers, and handymen. In the airline industry, challenges in supply chain management and transportation planning are referred to as the *last mile*. The challenge of last-mile delivery continues to be a massive pain point for logistic companies. In a product's journey from warehouse shelf to the back of a truck, to a customer doorstep, the last mile of delivery is the final step of the process. The last-mile delivery is both the most expensive and time-consuming part of the shipping process (Dolan 2021). In any business, the last mile to close the deal may be the most difficult part, which demands full attention. Here are some tips:

1. Ask for documents to solidify the sale: purchasing orders, sponsorships, contracts, agreements, memorandum of understandings, deposits, membership application, and so on.
2. Do not fear rejection.
3. Engage in conversations.
4. Listen and focus on the customer, not on the deal.
5. Pitch your total solution, not just the product and service.
6. Know your product, but sell its relevance to the client.
7. Find more ways to help the client.
8. Keep growing the relationship with the client by following up after the sale.

Conclusion

Improper timing, cultural differences, linguistic barriers, political, legal, accounting disparities, lack of interpersonal chemistry, and integrity issues ... these are just a few obstacles to relationship building mentioned by global business leaders. "Timing is everything!" Taoism stresses the importance of timing. How do we overcome these obstacles and care for the other so that the relationship can grow? How much patience should we endure to wait for a relationship to yield results? "The course of true love never did run smooth," said Lysander in Shakespeare's (1605) *A Midsummer Night's Dream*. There are many obstacles to overcome for business deals: cultural, linguistic, attitudinal, style, and haste (CLASH).

Who says "money doesn't grow on trees?" Business deals are the *ripened fruit* grown on relationship trees. Start from *the low-hanging fruit*, then observe, care, and wait for other fruits to ripen. For example, you have ten business initiatives, and you know two are currently working. It is practical to work on the two initiatives now, while sensitively fostering the other eight relationships. By closing deals at the proper time, companies make money and nonprofits gain funding. Go for the GOLD!

To close deals, four mentalities are recommended: goal-oriented, opportunity-driven, learning about relationships, and deal-closing mentalities (GOLD). Closing a deal is a symbolic moment of transaction, and it is a start of a new season of relationship cultivation. After closing a deal, we should continue to nurture the business relationship by finding out the clients' changing needs and wants, just like caring for a tree after the harvest. William Shakespeare (1623) says it best in the *Tempest*, "What's past is prologue." The next chapter elaborates on the preferences of different generations toward communication technologies and social media platforms.

CHAPTER 8

Digital Transformation in Relationship Building

Quotations to Ponder

We are in a digital transformation. An unsatisfied customer just went online to post an opinion. If you don't handle that incident correctly, it may start an epidemic of incidents, because a lot more people get to see that.

—Rick Cole, former Senior Vice President
Turner Broadcasting System

It's getting harder for companies to hide when they don't perform well, because it's all out there.

—Jessica Cork, Vice President
YKK Corporation of America

Regardless of the size of the company, you probably should have somebody checking those reviews on a regular basis so that it doesn't snowball into a major problem to impact the brand.

—Marcy Sperry, Founder
Vivid IP

Companies that do well have devoted people in those online forums, particularly if someone has a bad customer experience. Dedication to customer experience is paramount to any business.

—JR Wilson, Vice President for Tower Strategy & Roaming
AT&T

We monitor and engage with online reviews closely. That is your online reputation and if you don't watch it, it will get trashed, even if you are a great organization. Online reviews can dynamite or destroy a brand.

—Eddy Perez, Cofounder and CEO
Equity Prime Mortgage

We need to find the modern-day connection to get the information out to the young people who are thinking and developing the next generation of products in multiple time zones for us.

—David Kirk, President and CEO
Murata Electronics North America

Technology has empowered real estate professionals to evolve from the "gatekeeper of property information" to the "trusted guide for consumers" in making the right choice.

—DeAnn Golden, President and CEO
Berkshire Hathaway HomeServices Georgia Properties

Everything is on display now. If a large percentage of customers say good things or give a "thumbs up," that is your reputation. It's what others say about you, not what you say about yourself.

—Roger Neuenschwander, former President and CEO
tvsdesign

Chapter Summary

The ongoing digital transformation has a dramatic impact on corporate communication and business relationship building. This chapter encourages companies to engage with customers and clientele via online reviews and social media apps such as LinkedIn, Facebook, Twitter, YouTube, WhatsApp, Instagram, TikTok, WeChat, Pinterest, Reddit, and Tumblr. These are some of the social media apps that *virtually* facilitate people's relationships. This chapter spotlights virtual communication technologies to start, strengthen, and sustain relationships. This chapter unveils the communication preferences of five generations active in the workforce and marketplace at the time of this book's publication: The Silent Generation (born 1935–1950), Baby Boomers (born 1950–1965), Generation X (born 1965–1980), Millennials (Gen Y, born 1980–1995), and Generation Z (1996–2010). Challenges and opportunities of intergenerational communication are discussed.

CASE STUDY 8.1

Engaging with SAUPO Participants at Various Media Platforms

Inaugurated in 2011, the Symposium on ASIA-USA Partnership Opportunities (SAUPO) is a premier annual Asia business conference, alternating between Atlanta and Asia. During the COVID-19 pandemic, catching the trend of many conferences going virtual, we hosted a 100 percent online conference via Zoom webinar on April 2, 2021. In late February 2021, I tried to reconfirm with all speakers and sponsors, about one month before the virtual SAUPO. I realized that I had completely lost touch with Mr. Robert Striar, the president of M Style Marketing, based in New York City. He had agreed to speak in the panel on *pandemic, communication and organizations.* I called his cell, no answer. I texted him at the same number, no response. I went back to the LinkedIn message page, and followed up with a few messages, but no reply. I searched for his email address and discovered it expired. Where was Mr. Striar? How is he doing during the pandemic? Should we approach another speaker?

In the past decade, I learned to approach and engage with different SAUPO speakers, sponsors, participants, and volunteers on their preferred platforms of communication. After all these failed attempts to reach out to Mr. Striar, I explored new platforms. I downloaded WhatsApp and searched for Mr. Striar there. As his cell number was in my contact list, Mr. Striar appeared on the WhatsApp platform. I sent him a message of greetings. Almost immediately, he responded, apologizing for his lack of responses in the other platforms, explaining his overwhelming workload while conducting his entire business online during the pandemic. Empathizing with his challenges, I sent over a smiley face emoji, and asked if he could speak at the upcoming virtual conference via Zoom. Mr. Striar happily confirmed, a couple of minutes after we connected on WhatsApp!

Social media apps provide a multitude of platforms for communication, each with unique and beneficial features for certain communities and age groups. We unconsciously dedicate each app for connecting with people in different social arenas, business categories, cultural backgrounds, and relationship strength. For example, one may say text messages are used for family, LinkedIn message for clients, emails for colleagues, and Facebook Messenger for friends. As a professor, if I want to get messages to Millennials in the graduate programs and GenZers in the undergraduate programs, other than D2L virtual classrooms, *GroupMe* app is the best way to go. Some of my GenZ students say if they get messages on Instagram, they would respond quickly. If they are messaged via other platforms, such as email listserv, D2L, or texts, it might take them a few days to respond as they rarely check messages in those other platforms. One of my GenX graduate students has an account on *Snapchat*, so she can communicate as a "friend" with her GenZ son and Generation Alpha daughter. Snapchat map tracks the movement of her kids, providing a perfect peace of mind for her. *To build relationships with meaningful engagement, we must observe people's preferred communication platforms, trying to be "on the same page (app)" with them!*

CASE STUDY 8.2

YKK Responding to a Journalist
From the Associated Press

Around 10 a.m. on a Monday a few years ago, a Tennessee-based Associated Press (AP) reporter emailed Jessica Cork at YKK by Googling "YKK." Ms. Cork is the Vice President for Community Engagement and Corporation Communications at YKK Corporation of America, a Japanese multinational corporation with regional headquarters in Atlanta. Her email address was listed on the company website. The reporter's email indicated that one of YKK's competitors approached her, claiming that YKK took their business away. This email indicates that the AP reporter probably already made up her mind to write a negative news story about YKK.

Ms. Cork says that traditionally, Japanese companies tend to simply avoid reporters, dodging newspaper coverages, Twitter comments, and LinkedIn or Facebook posts. Their instinct is "no response, say nothing." Realizing that this AP reporter only had learned one side of the story from the competitor, Ms. Cork believed silence was absolutely the wrong way of responding to such media requests. On that Monday morning, YKK was hosting an important quarterly conference, with VIPs and executives from both Japan and the United States gathered in the room. Ms. Cork had learned from experience that AP reporters are on deadlines to publish news stories and that AP would publish this negative news story if YKK did not respond within a couple of hours.

Sensing the urgency, Ms. Cork pulled all YKK senior executives out of the meeting room, and gathered the legal counsel, and the company president. The YKK team sat together in a conference room, and within 30 minutes had drafted their response that basically disproved everything the competitor was saying. An official response email from YKK was submitted to the AP reporter within two hours. Consequently, the AP reporter did not run the negative story the next day as scheduled. The story did not run for another two months. After reviewing YKK's response, the AP reporter realized she did not know the whole story. She contacted some nonrelated third-party sources and gained more details.

The storyline shifted in the end. When the news story was published, it was favorable to YKK!

It is strategic to keep the lines of communication open for media requests. For crisis communication, *responsiveness* and *transparency* go hand in hand. A company should not be afraid of negative news, bad reviews, or problem reports, as they can be transformed into opportunities. Sometimes, the reviewers have the wrong information, and this is your chance to tell your side of the story. Other times, companies do mess up. Ms. Cork suggests this type of honest response: "Sorry about what happened. This is what we are doing to fix it. This is how we are going to improve. Thank you for sharing your information with us."

Discussion Questions for Readers

1. Why and how do we observe and discover a person's preferred platform of communication?
2. How should companies respond to mass media and social media regarding negative news and online reviews?
3. How can you effectively and efficiently engage with your employees, business partners, clients, and customers of different generations via mass media and social media?

Introduction

Based on a 15-year per generation division, I created Table 8.1 as an overview of generational differences in age, signature events, and their adoption of mass media and social media. There are unique opportunities and challenges in intergenerational communication. Kasasa (2021) suggests that generation labels are useful for understanding the combined experience of each generation. As each generation grows up in different cultural and technological environments, they develop generation-specific communication habits. Strategies for effective intergenerational communication can start from uncovering and mirroring each generation's preferences in communication platforms for mass media or social media. If an organization plans to cater to different generations of employees and customers, a multitude of communication methods and media platforms

Table 8.1 Generations and communication media preferences

Generation	Years of Birth	Signature Events Impacted Their Youth	Familiar Media	Notable Positions in 2022
The Lost Generation	1910–1935	WWI	Mass media	Elders
The Silent Generation	1936–1950	WWII, Cold War	Mass media: Print newspapers, magazines	Politicians, Leaders
Baby Boomers	1951–1965	Cold War, Korean War Vietnam War	Mass media (TV, Radio, newspapers)	Leaders
Generation X	1966–1980	Cold War, Globalization	Mass media and Social Media	Managers, Employees
Millennials (Gen Y)	1981–1995	Y2K, Internet	Social Media	Employees, Tech leaders
Generation Z	1996–2010	Smartphones, Social Media	Social Media	Employees, college students
Generation Alpha	2011–2025	Social Media, Pandemic	Social Media	K-12

This Table is created by Dr. May Gao based on a 15-year per generation metrics, to provide reference points for inter-generational communication. There are no definite cut off dates for any of the generations.

should be deployed. Intergenerational communication involves culture shock and misunderstandings, very similar to an intercultural communication experience. Effective communication cross generations can be achieved based on listening, respect, and mutual understanding. Regardless of age, everyone wants to be listened to, and no one likes being told what to do. Table 8.1 is created based on a 15-year per generation metrics, to provide reference points for intergenerational communication. There are no definite cutoff dates for any of the generations.

Mobile-First Approach and Netiquette

Made famous by Eric Schmidt, CEO of Google in 2010, the *mobile-first approach* refers to the practice of designing an online experience for mobile phone users before designing for users of desktop computers and other devices. Mr. Schmidt says that the current mobile ecosystem and its future incarnations are the result of three intertwining factors: *computing power, connectivity,* and *cloud computing.* As the high-volume end points of these trends, smartphones are the *defining products* in this ecosystem (Hamblen 2010). When engineers design platforms for desktop computers, there is a large "digital real estate area" to take advantage of as the screen of a desktop is much larger than the screen of a smartphone. When computer-friendly designs are repurposed to smaller smartphone screens, the user experience is often unsatisfactory. However, computer-friendly designs are no-longer compatible with our life in the digital age. *Smartphones have become the focal points in work and life. We are constantly "touching" smartphones during our time awake, while only "working" on desktops or laptops when we have to.* With the mobile-first approach, developers start with designing "the smaller real estate of the smartphone screen," with the flexibility to *scale up* for iPads, laptops, desktops, and other devices. Today, this mobile-first approach can go to the other extreme and this is why it is more convenient to update certain software on smartphones than on laptops.

Smartphones such as an iPhone, Samsung Galaxy, Google Pixel, Xiaomi, Huawei Mate, and Oppo are like a minicomputer. We can use a smartphone to browse the Internet and run software programs, almost anywhere with an Internet signal, for prolonged hours or fragmented segments. Touch screen smartphones allow people to interact virtually while socially distanced. Being present on the *smartphone real estate* is vital for a business to cultivate relationships with their customers. According to Statista, the number of smartphone users in February 2023 was 6.92 billion, accounting for 86.34 percent of global population. Global smartphone users increased by 49.89 percent from 2017 to 2022. World Advertising Research Center believes that by 2025, 72 percent of all internet users will solely use smartphones to access the web (Bankmycell website 2023). By 2027, smartphone subscriptions worldwide are estimated to reach 7.79 billion (Statista 2022a).

In October 2019, I served as the official translator for a delegation from the newly completed Beijing Daxing International Airport[1] at a global conference in Atlanta on airport communications. When discussing airport infrastructure, a leader from this delegation commented:

At Daxing Airport, other than facilitating all the flights, we care about two things: People need to be fed, and smartphones must be charged! There are a multitude of restaurants and numerous charging stations at Daxing, so that both humans and smartphones are satisfied.

I asked him how he would justify providing free electricity for millions of travelers to charge their smartphones. He said based on their study, the daily electricity provided to charging millions of smartphones is negligible in comparison with the electricity needed to operate the giant airport.

We spend so much time on smartphones, that our life partners sometimes get jealous of our smartphones. A survey with 11,000 respondents found that they spent an average of three hours and 15 minutes per day on smartphones (Zalani 2021). Data show that as of 2018, Americans aged 18+ spend more time on mobile devices than watching TV (Edison

---

[1] *Beijing Daxing International Airport (PKX)* is a large international airport in metro Beijing. PKX is Beijing's second international airport, after Beijing Capital International Airport (PEK). Looking like a golden phoenix, PKX began operations on September 26, 2019. PKX is a hub for SkyTeam alliance airlines and some Oneworld members.

Research 2021). This trend will continue. Consumers spending long hours surfing on smartphones provide a perfect entryway for companies to market their products and services on relevant social media platforms. Communication in the digital age requires special *netiquette*—digital etiquette, by which we expect people to act and communicate properly. Here are some tips:

- ***Treat others with respect***: In a Zoom meeting, mute your microphones when you are not speaking. Turn on your camera when the host wants to see everyone's faces.
- ***Be positive and supportive:*** On social media platforms or in other written messages, be positive on your messages. I tell my students to smile at their emails before they send those out. You may use emojis to add emotional tone to your messages when proper.
- ***Proofread and be careful with the auto-correction:*** Proofread your emails, texts, and posts; imagine how your readers might receive your messages and be sensitive with your word choice. The iPhone's auto-correction function uses your keyboard dictionary to spellcheck what you type, and automatically replaces the words considered *wrong*. You probably have been a victim of such auto-correction. It is better to take a deep breath, proofread the messages, before you touch the *send, post, or publish* buttons, although some apps provide *recall, edit, delete,* or *unsent* functions to unintended messages.
- ***Be sensitive to strong language usage:*** Using all caps and exclamation points may add emphasis, but they sometimes can offend readers for coming on too strong.
- ***Avoid improper content:*** Posts on all social media platforms are deemed as "published record." Employers and clients may check these records to do due diligence on you.
- ***Be professional:*** Even in a Zoom meeting, you can appear to be professional. Creating a professional background image, adding lamps around the laptop to luminate your face, and signing in early can leave good impressions for you in front of your team members, supervisors and clients.

Online Reviews

Do you read online reviews before you book a hotel room, purchase a laptop, visit a mechanic shop, approach a mortgage company, call a tree-cutting company, sign up for a doctor, or register for a class? This online decision-making moment is the important *zero moment of truth* (ZMOT) of the digital era. Comparing to the traditional way of consumers physically checking out a product/service in the *first moment of truth* (FMOT), ZMOT describes a revolution in the way consumers search for information and make decisions online. Recently I had an annual physical check, for which I had to fast. After the bloodwork and other tests, I Googled for *"McDonald's"* for breakfast with my smartphone. Beyond a few McDonalds with their locations, a nearby Wendy's was suggested by Google Ads. I ended up going to Wendy's as it was only 0.5-mile down the road. Wendy's benefited from my ZMOT via Google.

Online reviews can make or break a business nowadays. People see online reviews as an easy, honest, and unbiased view of the quality of a product and/or service. Online reviews are the digital word-of-mouth shared by numerous anonymous customers locally, nationally, and globally. From a researcher's perspective, most online reviews present both quantitative data (the five-point Likert scale score[2]) and qualitative data (the written comments). Many websites display online reviews of products and services, for example: Amazon, Google, Yelp, TripAdvisor, Hotels.com, Vrbo.com, Booking.com, Rotten Tomatoes, Yahoo, Yellow Pages, CitySearch, Airbnb, Trustpilot, ratemyprofessors.com, and so on.

Trust is the root of any relationship. Online reviews are testimonials by hundreds and thousands of trust intermediaries: customers who have personally used that product/service/brand. Online reviews are what nourish or inhibit the growth of a business these days. According to a survey conducted by Dimensional Research in 2013 with a sample of

---

[2] The *five-point Likert scale* is commonly used in survey research in social sciences for public opinion. It is a type of psychometric response scale in which responders specify their level of agreement to a statement typically in five points: (1) strongly disagree; (2) disagree; (3) neither agree nor disagree; (4) agree; and (5) strongly agree. The scale is named after its inventor psychologist Rensis Likert (Likert 1932).

1,046 customers in the United States, 90 percent of respondents claimed that online reviews influenced their buying decisions (Gesenhues 2013). *Phocuswright's U.S. Traveler Technology Survey* indicates that as many as 92 percent of travelers want to see reviews before booking hotels or short-term rental properties (Vrbo website 2022).

Each rating translates to money earned or not earned by the person or company being rated. A Harvard Business School study estimates that a one-star rating upgrade on Yelp measures up to an increase of 5 to 9 percent in revenues for a restaurant (Rushe 2013). Online reviews are helpful for any business to highlight services provided and to seek improvement. To a large extent, businesses live or die by online reviews in the digital age.

Effectively responding to online reviews helps to build business relationships, strengthen trust, engage with customers, and maintain brand equity. DeAnn Golden, president and CEO, Berkshire Hathaway HomeServices Georgia Properties says, "For negative online reviews, you need to immediately post your response in a way that is respectful but shows the other side." Jessica Cork, the vice president for Community Engagement and Corporate Communications at YKK Corporation of America, is a fan of online reviews. Seeing people's honest opinions is valuable to her. She claimed every address that YKK has in the Americas so that she would get alerted when someone posts anything about YKK in the Western hemisphere. If people post a question or a negative review, she responds. If people post five-star reviews, she thanks them. When consumers see brand ambassadors respond to negative and positive online reviews, it makes them even more interested in the brand and company. JR Wilson, vice president at AT&T, says that top companies have employees devoted to monitoring online forums, particularly if someone has a bad customer experience.

Some business owners have tried to manipulate their online review *scores* through the creation of fake reviews. However, fabricating online reviews is not only unethical, but also illegal. In 2013, New York Attorney General Eric Schneiderman cracked down on a fake online review case, with 19 firms fined a total of $350,000. Mr. Schneiderman cautioned some search engine optimization (SEO) companies offering fake reviews for profit. *Astroturfing*[3] is the 21st-century's version of false advertising, and prosecutors have many tools against it. Aaron Schur, Yelp's senior litigation counsel, says Yelp takes many steps to ensure the integrity of its reviews, including legal actions and sting operations (Rushe 2013).

Getting a bad review may be a shock at first, but responding to these bad reviews can be an opportunity for the business to achieve a better standing. It seems that no matter how hard you work at it, there is no guarantee of 100 percent customer satisfaction reflected in a 5.0-point full score. This does not mean a business should give up on trying to provide awesome customer service. Most of the problems displayed in the negative reviews are communication issues. When asked what made a customer service interaction bad, 72 percent of the respondents blamed having to explain a problem to multiple agents, while 51 percent blamed the problem not being resolved (Gesenhues 2013). In today's fast-paced society, people want instant answers in customer service. In the hospitality industry, being communicative matters as tourists move quickly with their travel plans. A proper response should be offered within 24 hours, ideally immediately or within one hour. Slow or no response may cause lower sales and poor online reviews.

Business Communication in Transformation

Digital transformation is a buzzword that often appears on boardroom agendas. Digital transformation derives from the application of digital capabilities to products, services, processes, and assets, for the purpose of improved efficiency, enhanced customer value, reduced risk, and new monetization opportunities. The ongoing digital transformation has a dramatic impact on corporate communication with both internal and external audiences. An organization's communication activities consist of

---

[3] *Astroturfing* is the practice of hiding the sponsors of a message to make it appear to be from grassroot participants, such as fake online reviews sponsored by business owners. The term astroturfing is derived from *Astro Turf,* a brand of synthetic carpeting designed to resemble natural grass.

written words (reports, advertisements, websites, promotional materials, emails, memos, press releases, responses to online reviews), *spoken words* (meetings, press conferences, interviews, videos, audios, podcasts), and *nonspoken communication* (photographs, illustrations, infographics, and branding). Corporate communication teams are supposed to manage branding, organizational identity, corporate social responsibility (CSR), corporate reputation, crisis communication, employee communication, investor relations, public relations, and media relations. A top priority in corporate communication is to create *favorable views* for the organization in front of stakeholders like employees, customers, clients, investors, communities, government agencies, and regulators. Organizations need to communicate consistent and credible messages to internal and external audiences.

Most executives understand the importance of maintaining their companies' reputations. Organizations strive to put their best feet forward, just like people do. Firms with positive reputations attract better employees and loyal customers. Deloitte's global executive survey revealed that a reputation risk that is not properly managed can escalate into a major strategic crisis (Deloitte 2015). Martin and Nakayama (2013) define *avowal* as the process by which individuals wish to portray themselves, whereas *ascription* is the process by which others attribute identities to them (p. 174). The concepts of avowal and ascription can be applied to corporate communication. Avowal is the ideal image an organization wants to present to the internal and external audiences, while ascription is the reputation the audiences assign to the organization. Unfortunately, many companies perform poorly in managing their reputations.

To bridge the avowal–ascription difference, a company must speak in one consistent and credible voice among all its units, as well as in both mass media and social media platforms. If one department creates expectations that another department fails to meet, or if the mass media and social media messages are not coordinated, the company's reputation suffers. For the sustainability of any organization, it is critical to study the communication preferences of the five generations active in the workforce and marketplace today: the Silent Generation, Baby Boomers, Generation X, Millennials (Gen Y), and Gen Z.

Intergenerational Business Communication

The communication traits and technological proficiencies of Millennials (Gen Y) and GenZers are highlighted here as they are the newer clients, customers, business partners, and employees. In the United States, there are over 72.2 million Millennials and about 90 million GenZers (Marketing Charts 2022). There are commonalities between these two generations. They are more technologically savvy then previous generations, having been born into a digital world. Social media is where Millennials and GenZers spend much of their time. They review contents on various apps by scrolling down their smartphones. This is their news feed.

Companies need to present products and services onto smartphones for Millennials and GenZers to access on Facebook, TikTok, Instagram, YouTube, LinkedIn, Twitter, WeChat, and so on. Selling through social media to these two groups is the logical strategy that will be a continuous movement as younger generations become a part of the business world. Both Millennials and GenZers respond to *influencer marketing*. Influencers give more interactive, creative, and authentic ways of selling than traditional commercials. Influencers serve as *trust intermediaries* for the business relationships between a company and these two generations.

David Kirk, president of Murata Electronics North America, expresses his viewpoint about intergenerational communication. Leading a company that produces parts for smartphones, Mr. Kirk says that his industry has many young employees, who are developing the next generation of products. He says there seems to be no time for traditional face-to-face communication with Millennials and GenZers. Some of his engineers are working virtually, in different time zones or at night. As the president of Murata, he strives to find new ways to connect with the younger generations of employees. He uses text messages, WhatsApp, and other apps to communicate with them while not intruding upon their privacy. Mr. Kirk asks, "How are you going to build that modern day connection with the younger people in the changing world?"

Engaging with customers via social media is the way to go for today's business. Brad Taylor, former brand strategist at The Coca-Cola Company, says his company is probably a leader in online consumer engagement space. For example, a consumer named *Jamal* just came inside a movie theater. Coca-Cola might send him a digital notification: "Your ice-cold Coca-Cola is right around the corner!" As a partner with movie theaters, Coke products are served in a special combo with popcorn, ready to win a share of the consumer's stomach.

Generational Preferences in Communication Media

Our families, communities, and corporations are made of people of all ages. Intergenerational communication creates challenges and opportunities. Reviewing profiles of employees, clients, and customers for your organizations, you may find that they can be categorized into seven generations: (1) The Lost Generation, (2) The Silent Generation, (3) Baby Boomers, (4) Generation X, (5) Millennials (Gen Y), (6) Generation Z (Gen Z), and (7) Generation Alpha. This chapter chooses to focus on the five generations from The Silent Generation to Gen Z, as they form the bulk of both the workforce and consumers. Each generation inevitably grew up with different communication technologies, and therefore has developed varied preferences for communication media and platforms. We will start with the tech-savvy Gen Z.

Generation Z and communication media: Generation Z (or GenZ, born between 1996 and 2010) were raised with smartphones and social media at their fingertips. When they were children or babies, they were given gadgets like iPhones, iPads, and video games to entertain and to bond. Being *self-taught tech geniuses*, GenZers grew up in a hyper-connected world. With the Internet in their pockets, smartphones and social media are their *norm* for communication. GenZers easily jump on new trends, and they are also creating or popularizing many new social media platforms. Instead of TV, GenZers entertain themselves with social media and streaming services such as YouTube. Aside from radio, they use music streaming apps such as Spotify (Edison Research 2021). GenZers communicate via images more than previous generations. They like photos and videos instead of paragraphs. Meeting GenZers through social media on their smartphones is the preferred strategy. GenZers prefer social media platforms like LinkedIn, Instagram, TikTok, YouTube, Reddit, Snapchat, and others. As GenZers spend so much time on smart phones and social media, they might lack interpersonal communication skills and experiences. Recently, one of my colleagues shared the story that his GenZ son just made a real phone call after two years of getting his new iPhone! Most of the time, he was just using the smartphone for text messages, social media, and Google. The COVID-19 pandemic from 2019 to 2022 left an *interpersonal communication vacuum* in many young people, as they endured social distancing, online learning, and isolation. Going forward, GenZers might enjoy having more face-to-face communication.

Millennials and communication media: Millennials (Gen Y, born between 1981 and 1995) are called *digital natives* as they are comfortable with all things digital: smartphones, computers, the Internet, and digital audio/visual (McMakin and Fletcher 2018). They are the generation who did not start with many digital technology innovations, but then during adolescence, they were surrounded by digital apparatuses. The abrupt transition from analog to digital technologies makes Millennials accustomed to adopting new digital gadgets and social media platforms. Digital technologies and social media play critical roles in the lives of Millennials. Typical Millennials love their cell phones, and the best way to communicate with them is through social media so that you appear on their radar screens. All millennial students in my graduate class confirm that communicating with and marketing to Millennials needs to be via mobile communication. Millennials make their purchasing decisions based on social media feedback, brand engagement, and online reviews. They have less brand loyalty and prefer shopping online (Kasasa 2021). Their purchasing habits are based on social media interactions and brand engagement. Social media platforms such as Facebook, Twitter, Instagram, and LinkedIn can be top channels for politicians and executives to communicate with Millennials.

Generation X and communication media: Born between 1966 and 1980, the GenX generation is the *middle child*. GenXers are in the middle of their careers, juggling jobs, children, and aging parents. They experienced economic recessions and technological changes from the dot.com boom to social media expansion. Xers are in their peak earning years, which enables them to save, boost their wealth, and achieve stability. For most GenXers, adapting to apps and online services is an integral part of their lives. Splitting time between mass media and social media, GenXers are reachable almost anywhere. Email works well for them as a communication tool. They prefer in-person meetings for important issues of finance and investment because it promotes trust and brand loyalty. While this generation is digitally curious, their social media usage tends to be narrower and less experimental than younger generations. Gen Xers usually do not like encountering ads on social media. According to a 2018 survey, 56 percent of Xers said there is too much advertising on social venues. One in three GenXers said they did not trust any social media channels or sharing personal information (Koch 2019). Gen Xers are willing to adopt new technologies with reservations.

Baby Boomers and communication media: Born between 1950 and 1965, right after the Second World War, Baby Boomers are a hardworking generation. The U.S. Baby Boomers experienced challenges during the Korean War, Cold War, and Vietnam War, as well as an extended recession, but they also enjoyed times of economic prosperity. They feel rewarded by money, recognition, and awards for their long hours at work. Baby Boomers enjoy traditional media outlets, such as television, radio, magazines, and newspapers. Baby Boomers grew up with face-to-face communication as the dominant method of workplace communication. During most of the boomers' careers, the telephone was an important tool in their offices. Email became available for people at work in the 1990s. Their drive for success gives rise to a *call me anytime* mentality, and they appreciate it when you seek their advice or use them as a sounding board. Boomers may prefer to use traditional forms of transactions such as checks or cash. They value handwritten thank you notes, birthday cards, and Christmas cards. Many Baby Boomers have transitioned toward social media to connect with family, friends, classmates, and colleagues, especially on Facebook and LinkedIn. About 90 percent of Baby Boomers in the United States have a Facebook account (Kasasa 2021). Baby Boomers adopt digital communication with reservations. For cost reduction, there has been a widespread push in organizations to transition from paper documents to online platforms. This transition can be challenging for leaders and employees in the Baby Boomer generation, as they are reluctant to move completely online without a hardcopy. Their reasoning may include cybersecurity, accessibility, and comfort. My millennial graduate students are appalled that some organizations they work for have cabinets filled with documents as far back as the 1950s!

The Silent Generation and communication media: Born between 1936 and 1950, *the Silent Generation* is also called *The Greatest Generation* or *Traditionalists*. Will they ever retire? The younger generations are fascinated with the work ethic of this generation. Although they are becoming scarce in the workforce, the Silent Generation is a *fountain of wisdom*. Some U.S. politicians and corporate executives belong to this generation. They grew up in a time when people communicated with face-to-face meetings, rotary dial telephones, manual typewriters, and Snail-mail. Members of the Silent Generation matured during political and economic uncertainties. They generally had a long tenure at a single job and pride themselves as being dedicated long-term employees (Galowich 2018). Like Baby Boomers, members of the Silent Generation appreciate traditional handwritten thank-you notes, birthday cards, and Christmas cards. A one-on-one communication approach works well with them. This generation believes in following rules and respects structure and authority. They expect you to present your information in a logical manner, using good grammar and manners, and formal titles of Mr., Ms., Dr., and so on. Comprehensive respect for this generation is critical, including respect for their age, experience, the chain of command, the histories and legacies of the organizations.

Conclusion

Effective intergenerational communication via proper media is essential for work and life. While each generation may have their preferred communication method, that does not mean effective cross-generation communication is impossible. Each generation grows up in its own political and economic environment, coupled with the availability of varied communication technologies and platforms. With respect for the other and humility for yourself, you may find out the preferred communication media of the other person, including your family members, supervisors, business partners, clients, and members of the community.

There is no more *one size fits all* in communication and marketing. We live in a digitalized and interconnected *global village* with the challenges of differed interests, conflicts, pandemics, and regulations. High-tech advancements create a paradox of digital connectivity. On the one hand, we can work, study, and entertain online. On the other hand, we miss the traditional social and community experiences. Each generation grows up with different popular cultures, signature events and technological innovations.

Mass media platforms are inherently one-way communication, while social media platforms are mostly relationship-based, facilitating two-way communication through likes, comments, and messenger texts. Each generation has their own preferences. With Millennials and GenZers entering the workforce and the markets, social media has become the mainstream, while traditional mass media is almost sidetracked. Forward-thinking companies are engaged in *social media marketing* or *SNS[4] marketing*, for which a dynamic and comprehensive strategy is adopted to promote products and services at social media platforms. Most social media platforms have built-in data analytics tools, enabling companies to track the engagement and effectiveness of ad campaigns.

Studying generational trends is important, but the generational labels do not tell the whole story. We want to avoid stereotypes, prejudice, and discrimination by simply categorizing people into groups. People of all ages can learn from each other and create harmony in our beautiful world. Effective intergenerational communication can be achieved with respect from both sides with the I-Thou perspective. While enhancing business strategies in social media for Millennials and GenZers, we need to not neglect other generations. Organizations need to become conversant and comfortable with both mass media and social media. Here are some additional tips on communication and media:

- Don't be left behind by technologies, including software updates and app downloads.
- Attend technological trainings in person and online.
- Learn tricks on apps to enhance your e-identities. For example, you may learn to set up a professional virtual background on Zoom.

---

[4] *Social networking services (SNS)* is an online vehicle with algorithms for creating connections with other people who share similar backgrounds or relationships. Companies that prosper from SNS profiles include Facebook, YouTube, Instagram, Twitter, LinkedIn, Reddit, Snapchat, Tumblr, and TikTok.

- Avoid text marketing. Text marketing can be seen as intruding into people's private territories, and it is considered annoying by most people. Receivers of text marketing usually immediately delete these messages, may further respond with *STOP*.
- Avoid robocalls, as these calls are the opposite of relationship building. Robo-callers usually address people with their legal names, which do not indicate any trust-based relationships. When vacation sellers or home buyers call our smartphones with unknown caller IDs, we almost never answer those calls.
- Do not overspend on hard copy colorful flyers. Upon arrival, they are usually thrown into trash cans, except those providing valuable coupons. Instead, you may transfer funding allocated for flyer advertisement to hiring employees for active engagement with customers on social media apps.

CHAPTER 9

Servant Leadership in the Digital Age

Quotations to Ponder

Listening is the most important skill for a leader, no matter the educational background. Listening leads to the greatest form of communication of a leader.

—Eddy Perez, Cofounder and CEO
Equity Prime Mortgage

If you want to see an organization getting enthusiastic, have a leader who wants to win and engrains in the culture that we are here to be the best in the marketplace.

—JR Wilson, Vice President for Tower Strategy & Roaming
AT&T

Good leaders have listening and influencing skills. They demonstrate empathy and authenticity.

—Brad Taylor, former Brand Strategist
The Coca-Cola Company

Leadership is vision, mission and passion.

—Robert Striar, President
M Style Marketing

We expect a leader providing a vision about what we should accomplish and how we get there.

—Masae Okura, Partner
Taylor English Duma LLP

You keep the language 8th grade simple as a leader. It's consistent and constant drumbeats. Tell them! Tell them what you told them! Tell them again!

—Roger Neuenschwander, former President and CEO

tvsdesign

You should never be jealous of your employees. You should be happy your employees are doing better than you, otherwise they can be out there starting a competing company.

—Li Wong, Publisher and CEO

Georgia Asian Times

Lead by example! Communicate with words, but always back it up with actions!

—Jessica Cork, Vice President

YKK Corporation of America

Chapter Summary

As inter-organizational relationships are cultivated through interpersonal encounters among leaders representing their organizations, it is imperative to examine the quality of leaders. *The Yellow Emperor's Classic of Internal Medicine* (黄帝内经) proclaims that the heart is "the commander in chief" for all inner organs of the human body. This chapter uses *heart* as the analogy for the leader(s) of an organization. The supreme value the heart provides to the human body mirrors the value of leader(s) to its people. Modern Western medicine teaches us that the heart is both the commander as well as the servant for the rest of the body. On the one hand, the heart is the "commander in chief" of a body's organs, all other organs (lung, stomach, liver, and kidney, etc.) obey the heart. On the other hand, the heart is the "servant in chief" for the body, as the heart never stops working during one's life, always pumping blood and energy to the rest of the body. Based on interview data, this chapter presents essential qualities of a leader in the digital age in these four areas of LEAD: *listing, empowering, adapting* and *decision making*. This chapter advocates *servant leadership* for the digital age, employees in the millennial and Z generations prefer leaders to be mentors who *coach* rather than *teach*.

CASE STUDY 9.1

Servant Leadership: Mr. Alex Gregory
Leads with Humility

When I teach the graduate course of Communication for Multinational Corporations, I often invite global business leaders as guest speakers. In spring 2021 during the COVID-19 pandemic, I taught an online version of this course via Zoom. For one of the evening classes, I invited Alex Gregory, the former president, CEO, and chairman of YKK Corporation of America. I also invited Jessica Cork, the vice president for Community Engagement and Corporate Communications at YKK. They shared their insights on and experiences with leadership, global business, organizational culture, and work/life balance. My graduate students learned that Mr. Gregory decided to retire in 2018 so that YKK could have a younger CEO, Jim Reed. They asked Ms. Cork what the employees at YKK missed about Alex Gregory the most. Jessica Cork mentioned a few aspects where people miss him, but then she said decisively, "What we really miss is that every morning, Alex used to take clean dishes out of the dishwasher before we got to the office." On my computer screen, I could see my students' faces shining with respect. They learned a new form of leadership: *servant leadership*. Alex Gregory was one of five CEOs featured in Hayes and Comer's (2010) book, *Start with Humility: Lessons from America's Quiet CEOs On How to Build Trust and Inspire Followers*.

Alex Gregory began his career with YKK Corporation of America (YCA) in 1973 with a BS in textile engineering from Georgia Institute of Technology (Georgia Tech). He was named the first non-Japanese president of YCA in 2001. From 2008 to 2010, he served on YKK Board in Japan. In 2011, he was named chairman of YCA, leading 3,000 employees at 12 locations in Canada, the United States, Mexico, Central America, and Colombia. During his 18-year tenure as YCA president, Mr. Gregory faced a series of challenges, including the shifting of apparel production from the United States to overseas, and the crippling global economic recessions in 2001 and 2008. Mr. Gregory launched a number of new initiatives, including the creation of the One Company concept, whereby YKK's companies offer customers a *One-company Solution*. Because of his lifetime leadership achievements, in 2015, Mr. Gregory was awarded the Foreign Minister of Japan's Commendation in Honor of the 70th Anniversary of the End of World War II. In 2017, he received the *Atlanta Business Chronicle*'s Most Admired CEO Award. In 2018, he was given the Leadership Character Award in the *CEO/President—Large Company* category from the Robert K. Greenleaf Center for Servant Leadership. I feel fortunate to have known Mr. Gregory as an extraordinary leader since 2010 when I invited him to speak at the 2011 SAUPO conference. Mr. Gregory has such a humble and encouraging demeanor that everyone feels comfortable around him.

Alex Gregory embodies some key qualities of a servant leader. *A servant leader leads by example, listens to and cares about the employees, and clearly communicates his/her vision. A servant leader sets a good example with a positive attitude, even during times of great challenges.* Mr. Gregory says he chose not to be angry at work. Sometimes he was dissatisfied and unhappy with certain situations, but he never felt the need to show anger. As a result, YKK employees often told Mr. Gregory that he had a calming effect on them. Second, a servant leader selects the right kind of people to join the organization while balancing diversity in their backgrounds, perspectives, and skills. This leader genuinely cares about the team, and seeks to understand their concerns, fears, and aspirations. Mr. Gregory says,

> As a leader, I ask myself: Why do people come to work every day? It is good to know the concerns of the employees from early on. You can lose talent to another company, and it might be over something very minor.

A servant leader clearly communicates his or her expectations for employees and insists upon those expectations being met to the point of terminating someone who does not comply with those guidelines. It is very important for a servant leader to practice active listening and two-way communication. A servant leader has strong desires to share information, be transparent, and build trust, even in tough times. In 2003, YKK experienced a massive decline in sales due to changes in the global supply chain. Most textile jobs were shifted from the United States to overseas, especially to East Asia and Southeast Asia. Mr. Gregory had to deliver some bad news to his employees about job cuts. From 3 a.m. to 10 p.m. on October 2, 2003, Alex Gregory met with 900 employees in groups of 50, spending one hour with each group, telling them why YKK was reducing their wages and changing their benefit packages. Out of 900 employees he met, only two spoke negatively. The message from the rest: "Alex, do what you have to do to save our jobs. We trust you to do the right thing." The next week, Mr. Gregory cut his own salary first, followed by a blanket salary cut for almost every employee so that YKK could stay competitive in the global market. During these challenging times, under Mr. Gregory's leadership, YKK Corporation of America ventured beyond zipper and textile productions. The company now provides products and services in the areas of architecture, automobiles, and health care.

CASE STUDY 9.2

Leaders Care: DeAnn Golden Treats
Others with the Platinum Rule

On July 1, 2022, DeAnn Golden became the new president and CEO of Berkshire Hathaway HomeServices Georgia Properties (BHHSGA), a full-service real estate brokerage with 29 locations in Georgia, over 1,500 sales associates, serving more than 12,000 clients. Ms. Golden most recently served as the senior vice president and regional manager at BHHSGA. The 26-year real estate veteran has been with BHHSGA since 2004. To learn more about her leadership style, I interviewed Ms. Golden in the first week of her becoming the *New Face of Real Estate* in Georgia.

DeAnn Golden, a *small town girl* from Athens, Georgia, participated in her first open house in 1978 as the young daughter of a real estate broker. She observed her mother acting as a de facto ambassador of the Athens community in assisting families buying homes, settling in, registering kids for schools, and joining community events. Early on, Ms. Golden learned that real estate is a relationship business, and she treasures her connections. Although she had worked as a pharmaceutical sales representative after college, it was a phone call in 1995 from her mother's client that made her realize that a real estate career was her calling. Ms. Golden is proud of helping homebuyers building wealth and investment, and gaining intangible benefits like the fulfillment of the *American dream*—home ownership. Over the years, Ms. Golden developed her unique leadership style rooted in optimism, care, and *the Platinum Rule*.

First, leaders are optimistic. Upon my arrival, DeAnn Golden greeted me with smile, warmth, and professionalism. I soon learned that her confidence came from hardship and perseverance. Her late husband, Mr. Golden, passed away in 2017, after 12 years of intense medical challenges that tested her physically, emotionally, and financially. She has been a single mom and a role model for their four children. She shares that when everything seemed lost, she surrounds herself with positive people and always believes in tomorrow. Ms. Golden says, "When people tell you that you can't do something, *don't stop believing*. It will lead you to places and moments you never thought possible."

Second, leaders care. Ms. Golden believes that our care for clients and colleagues gives us the ability to lift everyone up so we can all grow. Ms. Golden says: "When the clients succeed, we succeed; it's a simple equation." The foundational vision for BHHSGA is "The Right Choice," which not only places clients first but also focuses on the *relational* over the *transactional*. She says real estate relationships do not end when the deal is signed. Ms. Golden explains that when we choose an advisor for our finances or health, we expect to have an enduring relationship with that advisor, the same applies to real estate. Caring about the clients means cultivating a relationship before, during, and after a transaction, and throughout all their future home service needs. Ms. Golden asks all her employees and associates to be authentic, and to practice *active listening* to develop full understandings of the clients' real estate goals and homeownership dreams. Being a seasoned communicator, Ms. Golden empowers her employees and real estate associates with various resources of communication. She was responsible for launching the highly productive *smart office* concept. These *smart offices* are centrally located in communities, and they are stylishly designed spaces with state-of-the-art innovations in technology to enhance agent–client interactions. She advises us to seek out multiple mentors and ask them to coach us.

Finally, leaders are sensitive. To communicate with employees, associates, and clients, Ms. Golden practices *The Platinum Rule: Treating others as they want to be treated.* Various expressions of the *Golden Rule* can be found in the tenets of many religions, philosophies, and beliefs around the world. In *King James Bible*, Jesus says: "Do unto others as you would have them do unto you." Confucius said the negative form of this motto in *The Analects*: "Do not do unto others what you would not want others to do unto you." (己所不欲，勿施于人.) The Golden Rule implies that basic assumption that other people would like to be treated the way that you would like to be treated. Ms. Golden advocates *The Platinum Rule* for business: "Do unto others as what they want unto themselves." The Platinum Rule is popularized by Alessandra and O'Connor (2008) in their book of the same name. The Platinum Rule rejects reciprocity and asks us to practice empathy. In real estate business, every client has different needs and wants regarding sale, purchase, rental, and mortgage. A real estate agent should strive to do his/her best to communicate with the clients, in search of solutions to satisfy their needs and wants. Similarly, every client comes from different cultural, religious and ethnic backgrounds, we should respect their traditions and treat them as how they want to be treated.

I asked Ms. Golden how she gets everything done so well as a single mother of four children, and as a president and CEO of a large company. She smiled and said, "Mornings are magical. I get a lot done in the morning." She says she gets up around 4:30 am, has breakfast, coffee, then she will meditate, exercise, read, and work. She likes to take on the most difficult task first thing in the morning. She strives for efficiency at work and at home. At the end of the interview, she showed me a beautiful ring. After five years of facing the world alone, Ms. Golden is engaged. I am so happy for her.

Discussion Questions for Readers

1. In which ways do you think a leader should lead and communicate, considering different generations of employees and customers?
2. Why and how can a leader be a servant leader?
3. What are some good ways that a leader can listen to and care about his/her employees, customers, and business partners?
4. Is the Platinum Rule a good way to build relationships with customers and clients of different cultural backgrounds?
5. What does humility mean for a leader?
6. In your opinion, how should a leader lead by examples in good times and bad times?

Introduction

The term *leadership* may sound abstract and distant to many people. However, each of us fulfills certain leadership responsibilities. Everyone can be a leader. We are leaders of our own lives, our families, and our communities in various capacities. Interorganizational relationships are between two individuals, and two leaders. To build fruitful relationships, it is imperative to examine the quality of leaders. Taking advantage of interviewing 20 outstanding leaders from various industries, fields, and cultures, this chapter synthesizes the essential qualities of leaders and fundamental communication strategies used by effective leaders. This chapter advocates *servant leadership* as the leadership style in the digital age, especially for Gen Y and Gen Z followers. To better understand the concept of servant leadership, we start with two sets of inter-dependent terms: *leadership versus followership* and *direct versus indirect leadership.*

For someone to function as a leader, he/she must have followers. Followership is the action of people in subordinate roles that complement, support, and fulfill leadership goals. Followership as a role in a family, a team, or an organization is integral to the leadership process and success (Uhl-Bien et al. 2014). Followership is best defined as an intentional practice by the subordinate to enhance the synergetic interchange between the follower(s) and the leader(s). In a well-functioned organization, leaders and followers coexist. They are interdependent, collaborative, and supportive with each other. Without followers, there is no leader and vice versa. Followership makes leadership possible and successful. JR Wilson, a vice president at AT&T said,

> We speak up if we disagree, but once you have expressed your opinion, if the leader still disagrees, we follow through with whatever decision the leader has made. At the end of the day, our job is to make our leaders successful.

For decades, leadership scholars have been trying to answer this question: What is leadership? Does leadership mean authority, power, or prestige? Leadership author John Maxwell (2008) states, "Leadership is *influence*, nothing more, nothing less" (p. 20). When examining an organizational chart, we may see two types of leadership: direct leadership and indirect leadership. Direct leadership happens when someone has authority or supervising power over others. Indirect leadership is about influence, regardless of where an individual is positioned in the organizational chart.

In 1939, psychologists Lewin, Lippitt, and White (1939) identified three styles of leadership: *authoritarian, democratic, or laissez-faire.* The American Express company displays seven primary leadership styles as tools for its managers: autocratic, authoritative, pacesetting, democratic, coaching, affiliative, and laissez-faire (Martinuzzi 2021). A leadership style refers to a leader's character when directing, motivating, guiding, and managing groups of people. This book presents the *servant leadership style,* synthesized from interview research findings. To better explain the role of a leader, this chapter uses *heart* as the metaphor for the *leader.* The supreme value the heart gives to the human body mirrors the impact the leader gives to an organization. This chapter presents the essential skills of a servant leader: listening, empowering, proper attitude, and decision-making capacities (LEAD). This chapter highlights leadership communication strategies in the digital age, including vision statements, using simple language, and two-way communication via both mass media and social media.

Servant Leadership

The concept of servant leadership might appear to be an oxymoron. How can a leader be a servant? Robert Greenleaf, a former AT&T executive, proposed that service ought to be the distinguishing characteristic of a leader. Servant leaders serve the needs of others and find success and power in the growth of others. Greenleaf (2002) advocates that servant leadership would not only create better and stronger companies but also transform business leaders into happier individuals at work and at home. Spears (1998) synthesizes ten characteristics of servant leadership: *listening, empathy, healing, awareness, persuasion, conceptualization, foresight, stewardship, commitment,* and *community building.* As a growing field, servant leadership is shaped by the changing needs of our times.

The perspective of servant leadership enables the leader to be humble, sensitive, respectful, caring, and selfless. Servant leadership begins with the natural feeling that one wants to serve, support, and empower others. A servant leader shares power, places the needs of the employees first, and helps them to perform at their full potential. Instead of the people working to serve the leader, the leader exists to serve the people. When leaders shift their mindset to being servants for organizations, their employees are empowered, making it possible for the employees to gain stronger commitment to the organization. For a servant leader, while self-confidence is vital, too much emphasis on *ego* may deter the spirit of service. The cases of Alex Gregory and DeAnn Golden demonstrate that servant leaders care, coach, inspire, and support their followers. The servant leadership style promotes I-Thou dialogue between the leaders and followers, which in turn generates an innovative environment. Entrepreneur and billionaire Elon Musk, the leader, founder/cofounder of *Tesla, SpaceX, Boring, Neuralink* and *OpenAI*, reminds people that he is a "servant for his team." Elon Musk said,

> If you are a manager or leading at any level at SpaceX, we stress that your team is not there to serve you. You are there to serve your team and help them do the best possible job for the company. This applies to me most of all (Umoh, 2017, 1).

Leader = *Heart* Metaphor

To illustrate the function of a leader in an organization, I adopt the analogy of the heart. Both traditional Chinese medicine and modern Western medicine view the heart as possessing leadership qualities. *The Yellow Emperor's Classic of Internal Medicine*[1] is the earliest and cornerstone book of traditional Chinese medicine. It was compiled about 2,500 years ago during the Warring States Period (战国时代, 475–221 BC) and the Han Dynasty (汉代, 206 BCE–220 AD). *The Yellow Emperor's Classic of Internal Medicine* guides thinking in Chinese medicine, philosophical Taoism, and healthy

---

[1] *The Yellow Emperor's Classic of Internal Medicine* or *Yellow Emperor's Inner Canon* (Huang Di Nei Jing 《黄帝内经》) is composed of two sets of classic texts, each with 81 chapters, recording dialogues between the Yellow Emperor and his legendary teachers and physicians. In 2011, this book was accepted as a *Documentary Heritage* for inclusion in the Memory of the World Register by UN Educational, Scientific and Cultural Organization (UNESCO 2011).

lifestyle in China (Xu 2022). One major principle stated by this text is that "the heart is viewed as the commander in chief for all internal organs, the heart is where the soul dwells" (心者，君主之官，神明出焉). The heart is like the emperor, commanding over his officials who are the other major organs of the body: the lung, stomach, liver, and kidney. Modern science shows the human heart is made of a special tireless cardiac muscle. In one day, a heart transports all blood around one's body about 1,000 times (BBC Science Homepage 2020). Ever since a person is born, his/her heart has been working *nonstop*. If the heart stops beating, one's life comes to an end. The human heart is a tireless servant leader.

Most of the leaders and entrepreneurs interviewed like the heart metaphor to illustrate servant leaders. First, the heart pumps blood/nutrition to the rest of the body, just like a leader sends vital energy/information to the rest of the organization. Second, the heart beats non-stop, like a leader working tirelessly for the organization. Third, the heart hosts the soul, which parallels with the leader creating and influencing the organizational culture. Fourth, the heart coordinates with the brain, in a similar way to the leader consulting with the advisory board or thinking bodies of an organization. Fifth, the heart sets the heartbeat and other organs respond to this rhythm, just like the leader sets the agenda and his/her followers execute this agenda.

Further, the heart influences a person's body, personality, and emotions, just like a leader influences the health, culture, and reputation of an organization. We have heard cases when after someone has gone through a heart transplant, the new heart may be rejected by the body, or it may change the personality of the person. In a similar way, a new leader may be rejected by employees of an organization or may change the culture and style of an organization dramatically. Finally, the heart beats selflessly to serve the body, similar to an ideal servant leader working altruistically for his/her organization. Looking inward, we may realize that most of the time, we are not overly cognizant that the heart is beating. We take it for granted that our hearts are beating, keeping us alive. When one has to constantly think about one's heart, that is probably when one has some serious illness. Therefore, the healthiest state of leadership may be *a sense of nonexistence* for the leader to be felt or discussed by the followers. Taoism philosopher Laozi (471 BCE) wrote in *Tao Te Ching*, "A leader is

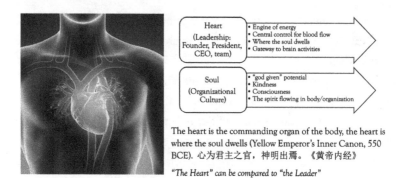

| Heart
(Leadership:
Founder, President,
CEO, team) | • Engine of energy
• Central control for blood flow
• Where the soul dwells
• Gateway to brain activities |
| Soul
(Organizational
Culture) | • "god given" potential
• Kindness
• Consciousness
• The spirit flowing in body/organization |

The heart is the commanding organ of the body, the heart is where the soul dwells (Yellow Emperor's Inner Canon, 550 BCE). 心为君主之官，神明出焉。《黄帝内经》

"The Heart" can be compared to "the Leader"

Figure 9.1 The metaphor comparing leader to heart

best when people barely know he/she exists, when the work is done and the aim is reached, the people say: We did it!"[2]

Similar to a heart, servant leaders are passionate, empathetic, and energetic. Marcy Sperry, the founder of Vivid IP says, "My team feeds on my passion and excitement." Alex Gregory, former president and CEO of YKK Corporation of America, said, "I had a job to do, and I had to take responsibility for my team's failures. I gave them credit for their successes." Rick Cole, former Senior Vice President of Turner Broadcasting System, talked about the scenario when an organization might reject a new leader, similar to a body rejecting a *transplanted heart*. Mr. Cole says, "Some new leaders are rejected because they did not give enough time to understand the environment, or the wants and needs of the organizations they are leading."

Four Leadership Skills: *LEAD*

After working with some of the greatest leaders across the globe, Hayes and Comer (2010) noticed patterns of difference between effective leaders and ineffective ones. Often, leaders who fail rule with arrogance, lack listening skills, and have poor communication practices. While interviewing the 20 global business leaders and entrepreneurs, I asked them: "What are some basic qualities of a leader? Decision-making power, listening skills, educational background, or other?" Most leaders downplayed the

---

[2] The original quotation in Chinese is "功成事遂，百姓皆谓我自然"(from *Tao Te Ching by Laozi*).

importance of educational background. Li Wong, the publisher and CEO of *Georgia Asian Times*, replied: "Not their title or education. You make the criteria based on their nobility, decision-making promise, civil contribution, and what they bring to the company." Rick Cole, former Senior Vice President of Turner Broadcasting System, says that he discounts *educational backgrounds* if someone obtains his/her knowledge purely from going to school. "Just because you went to Harvard means I should listen to you and that you have all the answers, trust me, you don't!" Mr. Cole says a leader can learn from both school education and life experiences. All leaders interviewed emphasize four key leadership skills: listening, empowering, proper attitude, and decision making (LEAD):

1. **Listening:** Finding out what people need and want in their contexts.
2. **Empowering:** Caring about others selflessly and letting them achieve their full potential.
3. **Attitude:** Proper *self and other* attitude, with humility for self and respect for others.
4. **Decision making:** Making decisions with calculated risk for organizations to move forward.

Leadership skill #1: Listening. We learn from reading, traveling, observation, meditation, and listening to others. Successful leaders listen to find out the needs and wants of their employees, customers, business partners, and competitors. Listening can be informative for leaders and therapeutic for followers. "People want to be heard," said Eddy Perez, cofounder and CEO of Equity Prime Mortgage. Mr. Perez believes that listening is the bedrock for the democratic way of leadership. Having more people at the table discussing issues might create longer meetings, but it will lead to stronger consensus and synergy. Roger Neuenschwander, former president of tvsdesign, shares,

> A good listener is the best leader. If you've got good listening skills, you don't talk over people, you don't come in and tell them what to do. You find a way to listen, let them talk and then guide them.

He says after you listen to your employees, *expectations* are put in motion, you need to show evidence that final decisions reflect their input.

Masae Okura, a Japanese lawyer in Atlanta, shared a story about how anyone can gain a leadership position through listening. After Ben Miller[3] graduated from college in 1995, he could not find a good job in New York City. One day, a friend told him that a Japanese company was hiring someone to move heavy boxes. He applied and got the job. While loading and unloading boxes to trucks, a Japanese manager noticed him. He would listen very carefully to the manager. Although Ben did not speak any Japanese, he listened for the meaning from the context. He observed relationships among people and paid special attention to the decision makers. Over time, Ben achieved a good understanding of the Japanese executives. Ben became a perfect liaison between these Japanese executives and their American employees. The Japanese manager liked him, made him a team leader, and promoted him to vice president of the company. He went up the ladder because of his dynamic listening skills.

Listening is critical for the success of joint venture relationships. Glad Cheng, the Chairman of China Window Group, says that sometimes an entrepreneur may face problems in an investment project. Some people may intuitively want to hide the problems or solve the problems alone. Mr. Cheng disagrees with this approach. He says the best strategy is to be transparent, display the problems at the table, and listen to the business partners for shared understanding. Even if the outcome may indicate financial loss, all partners would share responsibilities and commitment. Glad Cheng underscores the value of persistent listening, even for experienced leaders. It is easy for leaders to rest on past laurels. Some leaders tend to use frameworks generated from past success to guide current and future business, which might lead to failures as the context has changed. Elon Musk, the leader of SpaceX and Tesla, wants to listen to trusted individuals for their suggestions as these corrective feedback loops provide value for his corporations to move forward against *wishful thinking*[4] (Venture City 2020).

---

[3] This case about an American employee promoted to a top leadership position in a Japanese company is based on a real-life story. To protect the identity of the individual involved, the pseudo name of *Ben Miller* is being used.

[4] *Wishful thinking* is an attitude or belief that something you want to happen will happen, even though it is not likely or possible. Wishful thinking is based on what might be pleasing to imagine, rather than based on data, evidence, rationality, or reality.

Leadership skill #2: Empowering. Interviewing global business leaders made me realize one key difference between managers and leaders. Managers control time, money, and quality, while *leaders empower people.* I asked all leaders how they delegate responsibilities to others in their teams. Mr. Striar, president of M Style Marketing, says he is proud that he has hired phenomenal people. A couple of years ago, Mr. Striar hired Linda, an executive on his team. Mr. Striar asked Linda to think like him and be on the same wavelength with him. After some careful thinking, Linda responded politely:

> You did not hire me to be you, you hired me to be me. Just let me do my job. I will be your support structure, so you can do what you are good at. You are great at 40,000 feet, to look at the big picture and big strategy for client relationships. I can work on details on the ground, which you may not have the time, energy or skills for.

Mr. Striar said this was one of the most important conversations he has had in business. He learned to empower employees by letting them be successful in the skills they have. Empowering employees to achieve their full potential is an impactful leadership skill. JR Wilson, a vice president at AT&T, says, "As a leader, I have never found micro-management to be successful." He said you have to delegate tasks to people, empower people, and allow them to take risks. Leaders delegate responsibilities. Eddy Perez says a leader needs to know his/her limitations and be mindful of what is the best use of time. "If you can train people to replace you, that means you are a good leader," said Lucy Lu, founder of aiLegal Law Firm.[5] If you want the business to be successful, every team member needs to be energetic. For the longevity of an organization, a leader needs to develop the employees and look for people who can be the next generation of leaders.

Research shows that leaders need to provide special support to the *highly productive* employees, both for the happiness of these employees

---

[5] aiLegal, whose former entity was *Lucy Lu & Associates*, is a law firm based in Atlanta, Georgia, USA. aiLegal digitizes the entire document lifecycle to connect data, expertise, and processes for business growth.

and the success of the organization. Biederman and Bennis (1998, 45) state,

> Too many companies believe people are interchangeable. Truly gifted people never are. They have unique talents. Such people cannot be forced into roles they are not suited for, nor should they be. Effective leaders allow great people to do the work they were born to do.

Rick Cole, the former Senior Vice President of Turner Broadcasting System, shared his regrets:

> In my early career as a young manager, I put *way too much effort* into the mediocre employees, trying to develop them. What I was not doing was giving the outstanding employees the attention they deserved. If they can do so much with little attention, how much more could they do with great attention?

Alex Gregory stressed the urgency of identifying and developing *high-potential individuals* and moving them to different positions, if necessary. The original units often do not want to give up these good employees. Which is more important, the needs of the company or the needs of the individual? Mr. Gregory says both needs are important, but we ought to address the needs of individuals first; otherwise, they will become frustrated and unhappy. The company will lose talented employees. For these high-potential individuals, we can challenge them with new opportunities.

Empowering followers is a distinct skill of a servant leader. In today's workforce, Gen Y (Millennials, born 1980–1995) and Gen Z (born 1996–2010) employees especially need empathy and encouragement from their leaders, and this attitude was endorsed by my graduate and undergraduate students. Communication with Millennials should emphasize empathy and compassion, professional growth, frequent feedback, and respect.

Leadership skill #3: Proper attitude. Be yourself, be passionate, be real, be humble, and be approachable! A servant leader starts with a proper attitude: passionate about work, humble about self, and respectful to the other. Servant leaders are passionate. Servant leaders love what they do, and they are passionate about their work, their clients, their people, and their resources. Servant leaders are authentic. Roger Neuenschwander, former president and CEO for tvsdesign, shares, "As a leader, you can't be make-believe, you can't be play actor, you can't be scripted, because you are going to be seen in both good and bad conditions."

Being authentic asks for the courage of delivering bad news. Alex Gregory, former president and CEO of YKK Corporation of America, says, in business, you must be transparent and communicate both good and bad news in time. Mr. Gregory recalled,

> One time, we could not deliver our zippers on time because one of the suppliers had difficulty. We had some customer service people in the past who did not want to deliver bad news. What we understand now is that customers just want to have accurate information, good or bad. Customers might be disappointed, but they appreciate the ongoing updates for trust building.

Eddy Perez, cofounder and CEO of Equity Prime Mortgage, says he sometimes has to respond to his clients, "Unfortunately, I don't think I'll be able to help you, but I may know somebody else that can."

Servant leaders are humble. According to Taoism classic text *I Ching*, *being humble* is an ever-winning strategy among 64 scenarios in life (64卦). The symbol for *humility* (Qian, 谦卦) is depicted as *a mountain hidden underground*, illustrating that a person remains to be modest, despite standing on mountains of achievements. Alex Gregory always keeps a low profile, although he is decorated with outstanding abilities and laurels. Being humble does not mean lacking self-confidence or being less assertive. Glad Cheng, chairman of China Window Group, says the most important quality of a leader is self-confidence. A self-confident person does not need to flash the ego. A servant leader is not an egomaniac.

A humble leader respects the employees. Eddy Perez stated, "You'll let them down, you'll upset them. But if you lead with respect, you've given a human the highest level of dignity." A servant leader respects his/her employees, partners, and supervisors. A real leader will not be jealous of his/her own employees. Nagendra Roy, CEO of AanseaCore, says a leader who is insecure and disrespectful to the employees and coworkers will become unfit and a bottleneck for organizational growth, and potentially harmful for brand and company reputation. Roger Neuenschwander gives an example, "The insecurity may reflect on something small like getting mad about whose names were printed in the newspaper, or who are invited to the ribbon cutting ceremonies."

An ideal servant leader is selfless and altruistic. Jessica Cork, a vice president at YKK Corporation of America, suggests leaders to give without any strings attached: "It is important to help other people without the expectation of receiving anything back in return." This spirit of altruism reminds me of the virtue of water, as stated in *Tao Te Ching* by Laozi. As the river flows across the land, it nurtures all living things that it comes across. All the plants and animals benefit from the water in the river. Once it has done its work, water moves on without waiting for recognition or praise (The highest virtue is like water. 上善若水, Laozi 471BCE).

Leadership skill #4: Decision making. Decision making is the process of gathering information, assessing alternative options, and determining a choice. Leaders make high-quality decisions quickly with as much data as they can get. Depending on the position and power a leader holds, the decisions can be of different magnitudes. Leaders with decision-making skills can make quality and informed choices by having proper skillsets, being competent, and taking calculated risks.

Leaders often have to make tough decisions. Roger Neuenschwander says in his career, he has made two or three essential decisions, and thousands of small ones. Some of the small decisions can be very tough, including laying off people. Glad Cheng, the chairman of China Window Group, emphasizes that someone who cannot make firm decisions is not capable of being a leader. Marcy Sperry, the founder of Vivid IP, says, to be a leader, one needs to be decisive, and having the courage to take actions even in risky situations. Being decisive herself, Ms. Sperry relies on her team with complementary personality traits to balance her decisiveness. A strong leader makes decisions quickly and effectively with the facts available; otherwise, the organization will be *stuck* and not able to move forward.

JR Wilson, a vice president at AT&T, considers decision making a top leadership skill: "Not all leaders are good at making decisions. Some leaders only want to make decisions when they have 99 percent of the data to support their decision. A good leader will decide with 65 percent of the information." Mr. Wilson says that *not making a decision* will become a decision. This type of indecisiveness often hurts business. He said sometimes a leader decides on an issue, knowing that 45 percent of the people might not like that decision. A leader makes decisions by focusing on growing the business and creating opportunities for their people from a macro perspective.

Speed matters in business. Jeff Bezos, the founder of Amazon, recommends leaders making high-quality and high-velocity decisions. If a company desires to be a young and energetic *Day One Company*, the leadership needs to make quick and wise decisions, for which Bezos (2017) provided three suggestions. First, never use a one-size-fits-all decision-making process. Some decisions are reversible, and they can be made in a lightweight process. Second, try to decide with only about 70 percent of the information. If one waits for 90 percent of the information in order to make decisions, opportunities are lost. If a leader is agile at course correcting, being wrong in the beginning may be less costly as the initial decisions can be modified along the way, whereas being slow to react is expensive. Third, adopt the *disagree but commit* strategy to save time. If a leader has enough trust in his/her employees but disagrees with them on details of the project, the leader may say, "I disagree, but I commit and support you on this project." Bezos cites his disagreement with producers of Amazon Prime Videos but committed his support for their productions, which resulted in award-winning videos.

Leadership Communication Strategies

A servant leader communicates and unites the people through vision statements, actions, and simple language in mass media and social media. The interviews with the 20 global business leaders and entrepreneurs reveal universal strategies for effective leadership communication in the digital age. The best organizations have a talented leadership team, and they use vision statements and simple language to communicate with employees and customers.

1) Crafting a vision statement: Like a compass, an organization's vision statement guides the decision-making process and helps people stay focused to meet short- and long-term goals. Alex Gregory advises that everyone needs to hear the vision from their leaders. From the very beginning, a leader needs to communicate his or her vision to the people and then keep referring to this vision. A well-crafted vision statement keeps an organization on track, and unites the organization's teams of employees, investors, and stakeholders toward a shared purpose. Research shows that employees who do not find their company's vision meaningful have average engagement scores of only 16 percent (Folkman 2014). The first step to lead an organization is to create and interpret the vision statement. A good vision statement should be concise in language, encompassing in scope and reflective of the organization's values. Nagendra Roy, CEO of AanseaCore, says the vision statement should not be more than 8 to 10 words. Mr. Roy explains that vision and mission statements, underlying projects, and programs need to be aligned so that everyone in the organization knows what difference he/she is making to the organization. A good vision statement is written in an encompassing way that it allows the organization to be flexible in a changing marketplace. Many of the world's top companies have short and easy-to-understand vision statements (Brex 2021):

- BBC: "To be the most creative organization in the world"
- Ben & Jerry's: "Making the best ice cream in the nicest possible way"
- Disney: "To make people happy"
- Google: "To provide access to the world's information in one click"
- IKEA: "To create a better everyday life for the many people"
- Instagram: "Capture and share the world's moments"
- LinkedIn: "Create economic opportunity for every member of the global workforce"
- Microsoft: "To help people throughout the world realize their full potential"

- Nike: "To bring inspiration and innovation to every athlete in the world"
- Shopify: "To make commerce better for everyone"
- Sony: "To be a company that inspires and fulfills your curiosity"
- TED: "Spread ideas"
- Tesla: "To accelerate the world's transition to sustainable energy"
- Uber: "We ignite opportunity by setting the world in motion"

2) Using simple language: Servant leaders communicate in *simple* terms and sentences. In the Sunzi classic *The Art of War*, it is proclaimed that "an army will win if everyone from the generals to the soldiers has the same goal" (《孙子兵法》：上下同欲者胜). The best way to ensure everyone in a team has the same goal is to inform and motivate them with plain and simple language. Morkes and Nielsen (1997) studied how users read on the web and found that they do not actually read. Instead, they *scan* the content. A study of five different writing styles found that a website scored 58 percent higher in measured usability when it was written concisely, 47 percent higher when the text was scannable, and 27 percent higher when it was written in an objective style. A website that is concise, scannable, and objective at the same time resulted in 124 percent higher measured usability. The *Plain Writing Act of 2010*[6] (U.S. Congress 2010) requires federal agencies to communicate clearly in a way the public can understand. The Act defines *plain writing* as clear, concise, well-organized, and appropriate to the subject or field and intended audience. The U.S. Census Bureau (2021) allows only simple language to communicate with the general population in census forms and flyers. Plain language can save money, increase efficiency, and reduce the need for clarification.

An effective leader unites his people with simple words toward a clear goal. Leadership messages have to be presented in laymen's perspective

---

[6] The *Plain Writing Act of 2010*, signed into law by President Barack Obama, is a U.S. federal law that requires federal agencies use plain writing in every document issued or revised (U.S. Congress 2010).

with simple words so that all people understand what the organization is trying to do and how they can contribute. As employee experiences vary, the simple language catches most people's frames of references. A servant leader sends out consistent and constant messages in simple words. Roger Neuenschwander, former president of tvsdesign, advises: "It's 8th grade language and 8th grade vocabulary. Leadership communication is like a drumbeat." Mr. Neuenschwander shares one message that he gave at every meeting for 30 years at tvsdesign:

No matter how successful you are, or how many things we achieve, how much sunshine we get, just remember everything we do at this firm is through the hands of many. You can't do it alone, and you won't do it alone and we don't do it alone.

Communicating in simple terms enables everyone to know where to go, what to do, and how to behave. JR Wilson, a vice president at AT&T, appreciates leaders who communicate with their employees *directly* and *openly* in simple language. Jeff McElfresh, the Chief Operating Officer (COO) of AT&T, is humble, open, and transparent. He would share bad news and tell his employees where they have not done a good job and why it is important to change in certain ways. Mr. Wilson says Mr. McElfresh gains a tremendous amount of confidence from the employees. Mr. Wilson says Mr. McElfresh is well-educated, and he could show off with difficult vocabulary, but he prefers to speak in simple terms to let everyone understand.

3) Two-way communication via all media: A servant leader keeps up with two-way prompt communication on all media, including mass media and social media. Eddy Perez, the cofounder and CEO of Equity Prime Mortgage, says that overcommunication is better than under-communication. An effective leader communicates with people in a transparent and inclusive way. Leadership communication can travel via bulletins, magazines, list serves, group emails, individual texts, birthday and holiday cards, face-to-face and virtual meetings, phone calls, apps, and social media shares and tags. Wendy Lu, a partner at Aprio, reminds us that leaders should be technologically savvy so that they can use proper types of communication tools that fit with the situation. In some organizations, the vision statement and other key messages are not communicated enough to stay present and familiar to employees. It is not just the CEO's job. Every member in the leadership team can resonate and boost up the same drumbeats.

4) Leaders walk the talk: "Lead by example," said Jessica Cork of YKK Corporation of America. Actions speak louder than words. Roger Neuenschwander says leaders need to be present, available, and approachable, and they should be seen, heard, and felt by the employees in a positive way. Employees tend to follow their leaders who are passionate, strong, and walk the talk. Good leaders believe in what they say and follow through with actions that reflect conviction and determination. Communicating with a proper sense of humor can be the icing on the cake for a charismatic leader. People relate to an approachable leader, and the atmosphere at work becomes more rewarding and enjoyable. Mr. Taylor suggests, "Be real! Be who you are! The best leaders that I've ever known are comfortable in their own skin. They're not afraid to demonstrate some personality."

Conclusion

Unlike an authoritative boss or a dictator who rules with fear, a servant leader empowers employees to contribute for the organization. "When the heart is healthy, the whole body is in peace" (*The Yellow Emperor's Classic of Internal Medicine* (主明则下安). When a leader is wise and healthy, the organization stays vibrant. A servant leader creates a positive space and enables everyone to achieve their full potential. Laozi (571–471BCE) wrote about leadership in Chapter 49 of *Tao Te Ching* (道德经). I translated this verse from classic Chinese to modern English, based on a few translated versions at the Egreenway (2021) website. I changed the pronoun from third person singular to first person singular *I* for everyone to understand and internalize the meaning so that each of us can become a *wise leader*.

Laozi on Leadership, in Chapter 49[7] of Tao Te Ching

Translated by Dr. May Hongmei Gao on 09/20/2021

A wise leader has no ego
I adopt the hearts of the people as my own
I am kind to both good or bad persons
My virtue is kindness
I am trustworthy with both honest and dishonest persons
My virtue is trust
As a wise leader under heaven
I must be humble and low profile
All people are listening to me and watching me
I must purify my heart like a newborn baby

---

[7] Chapter 49 of *Tao Te Ching* (Laozi, 471 BCE) in classic Chinese: 《老子》第四十九章: 圣人常无心, 以百姓心为心。善者, 吾善之; 不善者, 吾亦善之, 德善。信者, 吾信之; 不信者, 吾亦信之, 德信。圣人在天下, 歙歙焉, 为天下浑其心。百姓皆注其耳目, 圣人皆孩之。

CHAPTER 10

Embracing Change in Business Relationships

Quotations to Ponder

In the United States, the pandemic forced what could have been a ten-year digital transformation into about a sixty-day window.
—DeAnn Golden, President and CEO
Berkshire Hathaway HomeServices Georgia Properties

We must consistently disrupt ourselves by doing things better, faster and cheaper.
—JR Wilson, Vice President for Tower Strategy & Roaming
AT&T

New is good. Change is good. If people become too complacent and prefer status quo, that organization is doomed to fail over time because the world is changing every day and we must adapt.
—Alex Gregory, former President and CEO
YKK Corporation of America

We must adapt to the cultures of the consumers. Always have a steady pulse on what consumers are thinking and doing, and what are important to them, so that you can reflect that in your products and marketing programs.
—Brad Taylor, former Brand Strategist
The Coca-Cola Company

If you cannot embrace technology and virtual networking tools to do business and develop clients, you are not going to be around very long. Adaptation is absolutely critical to success.

—Marcy Sperry, Founder
Vivid IP

The environment allows for big and bold moves. The environment will accelerate changes and it will take a lot of things out of the mix.

—Rick Cole, former Senior Vice President
Turner Broadcasting System

If you are not willing to make changes, you need to get out of business. The best leaders recognize that changes are coming.

—Robert Striar, President
M Style Marketing

Life is a series of natural and spontaneous changes. Don't resist them; that only creates sorrow. Let reality be reality. Let things flow naturally forward in whatever way they like.

—Laozi, Author
Tao Te Ching

Chapter Summary

Applying the perspectives of Taoism and Darwinism, this chapter illustrates why change is inevitable and coping with change is vital. Learning about megatrends in the next 30 years facilitates our strategies in dealing with change. Four megatrends are highlighted for the purpose of growing business relationships in a changing global environment: (1) the rise of a multilateral world; (2) the transformation of space and time of work; (3) technological advancements; and (4) changing global demographics. This chapter suggests three operational strategies to embrace change: adaptation, diversification, and innovation (ADI). The COVID-19 pandemic is discussed as an *agent for change* in ongoing digital transformations.

CASE STUDY 10.1

Virtual *Lunch-and-Learn* During the Pandemic: Vivid IP Style

Atlanta, with over six million people in its metro area, is the largest city in the Southeast region of the United States. In early March 2020, the COVID-19 pandemic started to hit home: panic shopping, grocery store shelves running empty, and nerves in a frenzy. On March 8, 2020, President Donald Trump declared a national emergency for the United States. On March 14, 2020, Georgia Governor Brian Kemp declared the state's first-ever *public health state of emergency.*[1] On March 23, 2020, a mandatory *shelter in place* order was issued for vulnerable populations. Quarantined. Alone. Nowhere to go. Streets empty. Overnight, the Atlanta airport (ATL), one of the world's busiest airports, became nearly empty. Businesses were closed. Schools were shut down. A *new normal* came to life: mask-wearing, social distancing, outdoor dining, and online learning. No more indoor business meetings, no more handshakes. For Vivid IP, it meant no more face-to-face lunch-and-learns.

Vivid IP is an Atlanta-based boutique law firm, specializing in branding and intellectual property (IP) protection. Vivid IP has attorneys representing clients in filing for new patent applications and oppositions to granted patents. As the founder of Vivid IP, Marcy Sperry is passionate about protecting the original works (creations, discoveries, and designs) of clients and inspiring them to create *bold and wise* brands (Vivid IP 2022). Before the pandemic, Sperry and her team enjoyed traveling around the nation to provide interactive lunch-and-learns to potential and existing clients. They provided delicious catered lunches to all participants at these informative presentations and training sessions. Providing seminars on legal topics of interest to clients with complimentary lunches has been a

---

[1] A *state of emergency* in the United States is a circumstance in which government officials determine that there is a threat to the safety of the citizens. During such a time, officials may implement procedures to protect or provide care for the affected population until the threat is deemed diminished. Military personnel may be called into action to set forth emergency plans (source: https://military-benefits.info/state-of-emergency).

successful business development tool. Sperry says, "After these lunch-and-learns, I usually walk away with either additional contracts from current clients or signed the prospects as new clients. It has been 100 percent successful." Other than lunch-and-learns, Ms. Sperry develops business through listening to clients at one-on-one lunches, breakfasts, dinners, happy hours, conferences, and events.

With COVID-19 shutdowns, businesses were forced to change their means of communication. *The pandemic drove innovations.* Ms. Sperry and her team started to host virtual seminars, meetings, and videoconferences frequently via Zoom. She still hosts lunch-and-learns, now virtual, with the help of food delivery companies such as Uber Eats, Grubhub, or DoorDash. Prior to these virtual lunch-and-learns, she would email a list of local restaurants with their menu links to clients and ask them to select the lunch boxes for delivery to their homes. When attendees of virtual lunch-and-learns are enjoying their custom-delivered lunches, Ms. Sperry presents her knowledge and insights on the legal topics of their choice. Although people are physically apart in different cities, they are virtually together in a Zoom room for her lunch-and-learn. Clients really appreciate Ms. Sperry's innovative and caring efforts. As a result, her business has grown steadily, even during the pandemic.

Discussion Questions for Readers

1. Why is adaptation essential for business survival and success? Give some examples of adaptive changes made by businesses.
2. How can a company diversify product and service offerings to satisfy customers' changing interests?
3. In what ways did the COVID-19 pandemic drive business innovation, such as the virtual *lunch-and-learns* by Vivid IP?

Introduction

Relationships are not static; they change and shift slightly or greatly over the years. "An intense relationship may become more distant; a superficial relationship may deepen" (Knapp and Vangelisti 2006, 132). Ancient Greek philosopher Heraclitus claimed, "No man ever steps in the same river twice, for it's not the same river and he is not the same man. The only constant in life is *change*." Leadership author Warren Bennis states that change is inevitable, and for business, change is vital (Biederman and Bennis 1998). In the past 10 years, a myriad of new job titles emerge, such as Chief Data Officer, Chief Sustainability Officer, TikToker, YouTuber, and Crypto Investor. New ways of work have emerged, changing from 9 a.m. to 5 p.m. traditional work routine to hybrid style, 100 percent online or remote working.

The COVID-19 pandemic accelerated the digital transformation of work and life around the world. Pressured by pandemic shutdowns in March 2020 in the United States, we were moved to online working, learning, shopping, and living almost overnight. DeAnn Golden, president and CEO of Berkshire Hathaway HomeServices Georgia Properties, gives specific example of the ongoing digital transformation. During the pandemic, real estate sales associates socially distanced themselves, utilized virtual showings, digital open houses, collaborative video conferences, and drive-through closings. After the pandemic, buyers will continue to request for homes with *Zoom rooms* or spaces for two sound-proof home offices. Exercise rooms and outdoor living spaces, fire pits, swimming pools, and outdoor kitchens are popular features for home-buyers as well. Moving forward, Berkshire Hathaway HomeServices Georgia Properties aims to combine *high-tech communication* with *high-touch relational service*, to create the most seamless and rewarding real estate experience for buyers and sellers.

Changes are in the workplace, in the way we use technologies, in the media platforms, and in work/life balance. When interviewing the entrepreneurs and global business leaders, I asked them to respond to these questions[2]: *(1) How does your organization deal with change? (2) How does*

---

[2] For the 14 entrepreneurs interviewed in 2019 and early 2020 before the pandemic shutdowns in the United States, they were not asked the second question about the impact of COVID-19 on work and life.

the COVID-19 pandemic impact communication and relationship build-ing? Based on interview data and megatrends, this chapter illustrates why change is inevitable and suggests three operational strategies: *adaptation, diversification,* and *innovation (ADI).*

Eastern and Western Perspectives on *Change*

Philosophical Taoism stresses the presence and vitality of change. *I Ching* (易经) is the foundational book of many classic schools of thought in China, including Taoism and Confucianism. The name *I Ching* can be translated into *The Book of Change.* The word *I,* (易, pronounces as Yi) traces its etymological root to chameleons. Ancient Chinese sages observed chameleons' abilities in changing their skin colors to camouflage with the environment for survival.

I Ching states that *change is the norm.* The word *I* (易) in *I Ching* stands for three layers of meaning: *flexibility* (变易), *simplicity* (简易), and *stability* (不易). First, we need to be flexible and adaptive to the changing world. Laozi (571–471 BCE), the author of *Tao Te Ching,* says that *being bendable* is the winning strategy to cope with the changing environment. *The flexible and the soft* always win over *the stiff and the hard* (柔弱胜刚强). Second, dealing with change should be as simple as following the indication in nature. Third, we can deal with change by

The pictograph word "YI" (易) came from the image and identity of "chameleons," who change their skin *colors* to fit with their environment.

Figure 10.1 The etymology of Chinese word change

Source: http://qiyuan.chaziwang.com/pic/ziyuanimg/E69893.png.

holding onto the "things that do not change for the time being." For example, the sun always rises from the East, and sets in the West. *Tao*, the core mechanism in the universe stays the same, while external phenomena change constantly. We can master the *core mechanism of the universe*, and adapt to the changing environment with mental readiness.

Darwinism denotes that the best way to deal with change is to adapt. Darwin (1859) introduced the notion that species struggle for existence by adapting to the environment through *natural selection* for the *survival of the fittest*. Adaptation is the biological mechanism by which organisms adjust to the changing environments. Giraffes in Africa have very long necks because only those giraffes feeding on tall trees can survive and reproduce. Responding to the turbulent environment, companies must interact with the environment as *living organisms* (Weick 1995). *Change is constant. Instead of wrestling against it, why not sail with it?*

Megatrends for the Next 30 Years

Leadership author Warren Bennis stresses that success in management requires learning as fast as the world is changing (Biederman and Bennis 1998). Critical issues challenging humans are globally connected: from climate change to public health, to food safety. No problem can be solved strictly within national boundaries. Recognizing major trends of the future helps us decide how to sail with changes. The COVID-19 pandemic, climate change, global trade, political conflicts, and the war in Ukraine[3] made headlines around the world in 2022. Despite these difficulties, the world economy is projected to grow in the next 30 years. Today's developing and emerging markets may become tomorrow's economic superpowers. This chapter synthesizes four megatrends defining the global skyline for the next 30 years: the rise of a multilateral world, transformation in the space and time of work, advancement in technologies, and changing global demographics.

---

[3] The *2022 war in Ukraine* was started on February 24, 2022, by Russia's invasion of Ukraine with ground troops. This was a major escalation of the Russo-Ukrainian War began in 2014. The United States and NATO countries provided military supplies to Ukraine while refrained from direct conflict with Russia, a nuclear power.

Trend #1: Rise of a multilateral world. On January 2, 2022, Kane Tanaka,[4] the world's oldest living person, turned 119 years old in Fukuoka, Japan. She was born in 1903 (Haq and Jozuka 2022). Five years before Ms. Tanaka was born in 1898, the United States of America became a superpower with overseas colonial dependencies, generated from the Spanish-American War. American people's support for the independence of Cuba enmeshed the United States in a war with Spain. The 1898 Treaty of Paris gave Cuba its independence, and ceded Spanish possessions of Puerto Rico, the Philippines, and Guam to the United States (U.S. State Department Website 2022). For everyone alive today, the United States has been the leading superpower for a long time. This geopolitical situation is gradually changing. For the next 30 years, we need to be prepared for a multilateral world. *Multilateralism* points to the process of organized partnerships between three or more nation-states. Multilateralism comprises connectivity among countries with shared interests in trade, security, and dispute resolution (Encyclopedia Britannica 2022).

The Regional Comprehensive Economic Partnership (RCEP) is a free-trade agreement between 10 Association of Southeast Asian Nations (ASEAN) members plus China, Japan, South Korea, Australia, and New Zealand. By 2030, RCEP will include nearly a third of the global population and about 50 percent of global gross domestic product (GDP). On January 1, 2022, tariffs on over 65 percent of trade among member states were reduced to zero, and more tariffs in the RCEP region will be eliminated in the next 20 to 30 years (Mullen 2022).

Emerging markets in Brazil, Russia, India, China, and South Africa (BRICS) countries extend from Asia to Africa and Latin America. The BRICS members are known for their significant influence on regional affairs. Since 2009, the governments of BRICS nations have met annually at formal and informal summits. The BRICS nations have a combined population of about 3.21 billion or about 26.7 percent of the world's landmass (Smith 2011). In 2022, Iran, Algeria, and Argentina applied to

---

[4] *Kane Tanaka* (田中カ子, 01/02/1903 – 04/19/2022) was a Japanese supercentenarian who passed away before her 120th birthday. She was the the oldest verified Japanese person and the second-oldest verified person after Jeanne Calment (Gerontology Research Group 2019).

join the BRICS five-nation bloc, and they may be admitted on the basis of *full consultation and consensus* (Business Standard Website 2022).

Finally, despite Brexit[5] and the 2022 war in Ukraine, the European Union (EU) balances the power of the United States with 27 member nations. The EU was formally established with the Maastricht Treaty[6] in 1993. EU creates a single market bloc with the euro as its main currency. Containing 5.8 percent of the global population in 2020, the EU generated approximately 18 percent of global nominal GDP (International Monetary Fund 2021). In 2022, after the invasion of Ukraine by Russia, Ukraine applies to become a full member of EU, and at the time of this book's publication, we have yet to see the results. RCEP, BRICS, and EU as nation partnership blocs have the potential to share the limelight with the United States on the world's stage. Awareness of these multilateral players enables new perspectives for international and intercultural business opportunities. In addition, the western calculation of GDP may not totally capture a country's capacity, resources, and resolve. Consideration of GDP per capita and purchasing power parity (PPT) balances a dynamic view.

Trend #2: Flexibility in work modality. The COVID-19 pandemic expedited the digital transformation in the operations of business and organizations. In the postpandemic era, companies have to be innovative in deploying flexible ways of work. In the United States, office vacancy rates increased to an average of 12.3 percent in the first quarter of 2022 (Statista 2022b). With a considerable part of the workforce working from home or following a hybrid working model, businesses are cautious when it comes to upscaling or renewing office leases. In June 2022, Jessica Cork, a vice president at YKK Corporation of America, says YKK

---

[5] Brexit is a portmanteau of *Britain Exit*, conceptualizing the withdrawal of the United Kingdom (UK) from the EU on January 31, 2020. The UK is the only sovereign country to have left EU since its inception. EU citizens can work in the UK after Brexit, but they need to apply under the Skilled Worker Visa or EU Settlement Scheme.

[6] The *Maastricht Treaty*, also known as the *Treaty on European Union*, is the foundation treaty of the EU. Concluded in 1992 between the then 12 member states of the European Communities, the treaty marked *a new stage* in the process of European integration (*Council of European Communities 1992*).

is downsizing its office space by moving to a smaller building, maintaining a hybrid work schedule.

Data show that millennials and GenZers tend to prioritize work–life harmony by viewing a flexible work schedule as a new *benefit perk*. To compete for the best talent, companies need to highlight flexible work arrangements preferred by millennials and GenZers. The increasing popularity of remote work has sparked demand for homes in the suburbs. Many Americans have decided to leave metropolitan and high tax areas and move to southern states with lower taxes, lower costs of living, milder weather, and a more relaxing lifestyle. Domestic immigration, coupled with record low interest rates, created a real estate boom in suburban and southern United States during the COVID-19 pandemic. Low inventory, low interest rates, and sky-high demand account for the surges in real estate prices during the pandemic.

Robert Striar, the president of M Style Marketing, says that his company is heavily involved in global business, with most of his employees speaking multiple languages. Prior to the pandemic, they used to travel a lot and frequently stayed in hotels. For postpandemic work, they plan to rent living spaces with kitchens in key cities such as London to accommodate face-to-face meetings, save costs, and to enable a more relaxed lifestyle for the employees. Wendy Lu, a partner at Aprio accounting firm, has been working at home since March 2020. She says her firm finds remote work more efficient and cost-effective. If Aprio partners need to meet with clients in person, they can simply *rent* offices by the hour.

Cloud technologies, the Internet, computers, and smartphones make it possible for teamwork when members are physically apart. Remote work saves time, effort, and costs for employees in driving and parking, while enhancing their emotional well-being and work–life harmony. Google, Apple, Amazon, Lyft, Uber, and others are allowing remote work permanently. On June 7, 2022, at the TIME 100 symposium in New York, Apple CEO Tim Cook called the shift to more remote work the *mother of all experiments*. Mr. Cook prefers the *serendipity* of in-person interaction but said a hybrid model will likely win out (McCluskey 2022). Andy Jassy, the CEO of Amazon, told *Amazonians* that Amazon will be experimenting, learning, and adjusting new ways of work to satisfy both employees and customers (Jassy 2021). Brian Chesky, cofounder and CEO of Airbnb, elaborates that prior to the pandemic, workers lived among three places: *home, work, and travel.* Nowadays for many people, there is only one place you need to be: *the Internet* (Patel 2021). Short-term rental businesses such as Vrbo[7] and Airbnb experienced a boom. Even the 91-year-old Marriott hotel chain (Marriott Website 2022) is offering *Marriott Executive Apartments* and *Homes and Villas.*

Technology changes how we communicate. Robert Striar, the president of M Style Marketing, points out that online meetings are *equalizers* of corporate hierarchy. In a 20-person Zoom room, there is no traditional hierarchy with a presiding chair at the end of a rectangular table. The CEO has almost the same ability to talk as someone who is a mid-level account executive. The postpandemic new normal entails increased online communication, remote working, and creative ways to promote products. However, we do need to remember that it is a *privilege* to be able to work remotely. Health care workers, cleaning crews, grocery store managers, and truck drivers keep our communities running by being physically present on the frontlines.

Some employers have expressed concerns regarding methods in mea-suring productivity in the remote or hybrid work formats. For example, in a law firm, the attorneys can work at home, or meet with clients at coffee shops, saving time and energy on the commute between home and office. The attorneys are measured by the profit they bring in and billable hours they document. How about the paralegals in a firm? How do we know that the paralegals are working at home, or are they just doing laun-dry, watching movies, or having a house party? Some have suggested to use certain software to record the paralegal's headshot in front of his/her computers, others have asked these paralegals to document their hourly activities every day. These measures indicate distrust from the employer to the paralegal, and they are probably not effective. For example, a para-legal may be on phone with a client or texting with an attorney on his/her smartphones, thus not being recorded in the *automated computer headshot.* The best measurement is *consumer satisfaction!* In this situation,

---

[7] *Vrbo* (originally VRBO, acronym of Vacation Rentals By Owner) is a global short-term rental online platform. In 2006, VRBO was acquired by HomeAway, which was further acquired by Expedia Group in 2015. On March 27, 2019, VRBO was rebranded as Vrbo, including a new logo and pronunciation (Vrbo website 2022).

the *consumers* of a paralegal may include the attorneys and their clients. Perhaps you can have a bi-weekly consumer satisfaction online review for each of the paralegals? Perhaps you don't have to hire full-time paralegals, you can just rent those five-star paralegals whom you trust.

Trend #3: Technological advancements. In 2009, U.S. President Barack Obama made headlines when he was able to retain his *beloved* Blackberry mobile phone after modifications were made to strengthen its security. In 2022, Blackberry officially decommissioned the use of this iconic keypad phone. Newer Blackberry phones have touch screens, like an iPhone. CEO John Chen announced that the company was transitioning to become a software company, focusing on cybersecurity. At its peak in 2009, Blackberry owned 20 percent of the global smartphone market, but it was soon overtaken in 2010s by touchscreen devices like the iPhone and Samsung Android phones (Teh 2022). Facing the advancement in technologies, companies cannot afford to be left behind. Accurately recognizing and following technological trends and consumer preferences can make or break a business.

In the next 30 years, we will witness the rise of new technology unicorns. These companies eventually could be more powerful than today's companies such as Apple and Amazon. We will witness tremendous advances in 3D printing, autonomous vehicles, electric cars, drones, androids, virtual reality and gaming industries, voice technologies, artificial intelligence (AI), automation technologies, blockchain, space exploration, asteroid mining, and renewable energy (Sivathas and Lanfranconi 2022). While rapid technological advances and the increasing integration of technology into our lives have the potential to benefit society, there will be a gap between those with access to this transformation and those left behind. Similar to the concept of *haves versus have-nots*, the digital divide can widen the economic hierarchy.

Jeff Bezos, the founder of Amazon, advocates embracing external trends as they represent the future. Bezos said, "Embrace them and you have a tailwind." Bezos (2017) highlights Amazon's adoption of *machine learning and AI*, with applications in autonomous Prime Air delivery drones, the Amazon Go convenience store, Alexa, and cloud-based AI assistant. Machine learning drives Amazon's algorithms for demand forecasting, product search ranking, product and deal recommendations, merchandising placements, fraud detection, and translations. Machine learning improves core operations for customer service.

Trend #4: Changing global demographics. In the next 30 years, all around the world, much of the workforce and consumer market are made up of millennials (Gen Y) and GenZers, who are tech-savvy. They are usually inseparable with their smartphones and are very active on various platforms of social media. Generation Alpha, born between 2011 and 2025 will be entering the labor force soon, and this is a generation that plays, connects, and studies online, due to the impact of the COVID-19 pandemic. Looking to the near future, life and business will be different due to changing demographics. To manage the incoming members in the workforce and to satisfy future consumers, we must change our business offerings.

- The world population is expected to reach 8.5 billion people by 2030.
- We are entering an aging society. The fastest-growing demographic in the world will be the elderly: the number of 60+ people will be over one billion. In any given community, there may be more grandparents than grandchildren.
- In 2023, India overtakes China as the most populated country in the world.
- Nigeria will overtake the United States as the third most populous country.
- The middle-class and millionaires in Asia and Africa will outnumber those in North America and Europe.
- The global economy will be driven by non-Western consumers.
- More global wealth will be owned by women than men. More and more women will be promoted to executive leadership positions.

ADI: Operational Strategies for Changes

Albert Einstein once said, "In the midst of difficulty lies opportunity." The Chinese word for *crisis* (危机) implies that "in every crisis lies opportunity." Facing inevitable changes, adaptation brings opportunities in business for new products and services. Laozi, a founding philosopher in Taoism, taught us that being adaptive and flexible is being on the side of life, because only living things are bendable. Interviews with global business leaders reveal the ADI strategy to deal with change: adaptation, diversification, and innovation.

Operational strategy #1: Adaptation. Organizational communication scholar Karl Weick (1995) applies Darwinism to business, stating it is natural for organizations to adapt to their environments. Organizations that plan and alter strategies in accordance with the changing needs and wants of customers will survive and be successful. The entrepreneurs I interviewed stressed the importance of constant adaptation, from creating soft drinks to producing movies. Rick Cole, former Senior Vice President at Turner Broadcasting System, says that in the media and entertainment industry, they have known for years that online streaming was going to kill traditional business, and that they would have to make changes to collapse the windows of viewing. Prior to the pandemic, a new movie would go to theatrical release, and after six to eight months, the movie would be available in DVD format. Then the movie would go to its first commercial premier and cable window. The pandemic changed it all. New movies are now directly released to consumers. The movie producers realize that they do not have another avenue. Mr. Cole says that before the pandemic, movie theater partners would not have allowed such direct releases. They would have shown up with a contract and a lawsuit!

Brad Taylor, former brand strategist of The Coca-Cola Company, recommends businesspeople go where consumers are and deliver products and services to satisfy consumer wants and needs. The 130-year-old Coca-Cola Company strives to stay relevant to consumers and give them what they want. Mr. Taylor elaborates that beyond the one brand *Coca-Cola* with heavy sugar content, the company offers over 500 brands, and about 50 percent of them do not contain sugar, as many consumers are health conscious. On June 13, 2022, the company announced a new portfolio of alcohol beverages, created with consumers in mind. The ready-to-drink *Jack Daniel's & Coca-Cola*, inspired by the iconic bar cocktail was offered in Mexico in late 2022 (The Coca-Cola Company Website 2022).

The communication method of *strategic ambiguity* allows a company/organization the freedom to interpret meaning based on changes in the business environment. Eisenberg (1984) argues that while most organizational communication scholars encourage *clarity*, clarity is both a non-normative and ineffective way to gauge individual or organizational productivity. When surfing in the turbulent changing environment, *strategic ambiguity* can be a visionary communication strategy to: *(1) promote unified diversity; (2) facilitate organizational change; and (3) amplify existing source attributions and preserve privileged positions.* Government leaders in various countries also practice strategic ambiguity by being intentionally ambiguous on certain aspects of their foreign policies. Being ambiguous in certain terms and policies provides the flexibility and room for change.

Operational strategy #2: Diversification. "Don't put all your eggs in one basket." This popular saying advises people to diversify investment and business against unforeseeable risks. Diversification in the offering of products, services, and business relationships helps companies to minimize risks and maximize profits. Alex Gregory, the former president and CEO of YKK Corporation of America said, "We've gone through a lot of restructuring over the years. It takes ten seconds to say that, but it took years to accomplish." YKK came to the United States in the 1970s to produce zippers. In the 1990s, YKK's biggest customers were 59 brand-name jeans manufacturers in the United States such as Levi's, Gap, and Madewell. By the mid-2000s, the clothing companies mostly went overseas and therefore no longer needed to buy from YKK Corporation of America. Diversification was needed for YKK's survival.

First, YKK diversified zipper offerings by finding out what the American market needs and wants, beyond the textile industries. Some of these diversification strategies include making zippers with heat protection for firefighters, flexible zippers for car seats, and ultra-strong zippers for astronauts. YKK sells its fasteners in new markets such as automotive, safety, medical, hygiene, military, and space applications. Second, in 1992, YKK built a $45 million aluminum plant on 202 acres in Dublin, Georgia, USA. YKK began production of architectural products (AP) for the residential market on its Macon campus in 2007. In 2015, YKK AP doubled its production capacity at the Macon plant. YKK AP's strong anti-hurricane aluminum doors and windows are very attractive in the U.S. market. Finally, to better serve its industry customers, the company expanded into machine production and engineering services. "We provide machines that help our customers attach or dispense our products into theirs," Jim Reed, the President of YKK explained. YKK sends its engineers to meet with customers to solve problems and this focus pays off. "It's really good to work with YKK," said a manager at AccuMED. "They help us with the engineering and technical aspects of our products. They customize products for us if needed." Truck Hero, a producer of truck accessories, agrees: "They provide hook and loop closures for our soft roll-up covers. They've been very receptive to doing further R&D work for us" (Vinoski 2021). YKK's business in the United States not only survived, but prospered, through diversification and listening to customers.

Operational strategy #3: Innovation. During the 2019–2022 global pandemic, many people worked remotely at home, transforming from *office executives* to *couch potatoes.* As Americans seek comfort food amid the coronavirus pandemic, the snacking business experienced a boom. Frito-Lay quickly sensed the pulse of customers and launched new direct-to-consumer sites (Troitino 2020). In 2020, the snacking giant that already had a presence in 94 percent of pantries across the United States when it launched *Snacks.com,* focusing on delivering brands like Tostitos and Ruffles straight to consumer homes. In the meantime, another Frito-Lay website, *PantryShop.com,* was launched, offering pantry kits containing bundles of related products across the Frito-Lay portfolio. "We started thinking about this even before COVID hit," explained Frito-Lay Chief Transformation and Strategy Officer Michael Lindsey. Facing unpredictable offerings at grocery stores, consumers turned to online ordering of snack food from home (Troitino 2020). The pandemic drove rapid changes, and many companies profited by being innovative. If it benefits customers, why not do your business in a new way?

Conclusion

When viewing organizations as living organisms in an ever-changing environment, adaptability is crucial to the survival and health of a company. Waves of globalization in the past few decades have created deep interconnections among countries of different geographical regions. Multilateral production centers, markets, and economic zones attract opportunities beyond the borders of the United States. To be a winner in business, you must be open-minded and flexible. When letting employees work remotely, it is strategic to balance employee need for schedule flexibility with company need for business growth. On the one hand, I have heard employees who work at home complain about lacking a sense of organizational belonging. Consequently, the turnover rate can be high as these employees usually may not strongly identify with such "remote" companies. On the other hand, although some projects can be done remotely, interpersonal relationships are usually nourished during face to face conversations, at meeting rooms, company hallways, coffee shops or restaurants.

The pandemic, as a de facto *agent for change*, pushed organizations to develop more presence in the digital world. It is important for businesses to be always aware of the needs and wants of their consumers and employees. It is essential that we make the technology both an enabler and accelerator of needed changes for our work and life. There are the old normal, the new normal and the next normal. Change happens. We must adapt to these changes. The next chapter discusses ways to achieve work–life harmony amid stressful changes in work and life. Let me end this chapter on change with a quotation from *Tao Te Ching* (Laozi 471 BCE).

Laozi on "The Soft Overcoming the Hard", in Chapter 76[8] of Tao Te Ching

Translated by Dr. May Hongmei Gao on 04/18/2023

Humans are born soft and supple
When dead, they are stiff and hard
Plants and animals are born tender and pliant
When dead, they are brittle and dry
Thus, whoever is stiff and inflexible is a disciple of death
Whoever is soft and yielding is a disciple of life
Therefore a bully might not win
Tall and big trees will be cut
The hard and stiff will be broken
The soft and supple will prevail

---

[8] Chapter 76 of *Tao Te Ching* (Laozi, 471 BCE) in classic Chinese: 《老子》第七十六章：人之生也柔弱，其死也坚强。万物草木之生也柔弱，其死也枯槁。故坚强者死之徒，柔弱者生之徒。是以兵强则不胜，木强则共。强大处下，柔弱处上。

CHAPTER 11

Aspiring for Work–Life Harmony

Quotations to Ponder

Work/Life balance is a myth. We should not dichotomize these two things because work is a part of life. Try to take the time to notice the joy in both work and life.

—Jessica Cork, Vice President
YKK Corporation of America

So many people don't forgive themselves and they carry that around and never get past it. Life is meant to be lived through the windshield, not the rearview mirror. Shift your lens to forward.

—DeAnn Golden, President and CEO
Berkshire Hathaway HomeServices Georgia Properties

I told Japanese company executives that working all the time is the easy way out. What's hard is to make daily decisions such as "I am going to leave at 5 p.m. today to go to my son's baseball game." That's tough.

—Alex Gregory, former President and CEO
YKK Corporation of America

To achieve work-life harmony, I try not to work more than I want to. It is about establishing boundaries and then staying in those boundaries.

—Brad Taylor, former Brand Strategist
The Coca-Cola Company

Not everyone can be a business owner. Being an entrepreneur means you have to do a lot of sacrifice to your family and yourself. Be ready to cope with that.

—Lucy Lu, CEO/Founder
aiLegal

Health is the wealth. If you don't take care of your physical and emotional health, respective plans will not produce that degree of success with the desired outcomes and impacts.

—Nagendra Roy, CEO
AanseaCore

As women, we put much pressure on ourselves to achieve the mythical work-life balance. Make sure you are fulfilling yourself emotionally, professionally, physically, and spiritually.

—Marcy Sperry, Founder
Vivid IP

Chapter Summary

The traditional concept of *work/life balance* is a myth. We shall not dichotomize work and life because work is a part of life. Instead, we may experience joy in both work and life, achieving *work–life harmony*. Progressing from the concept of conventional *work/life balance*, this chapter recommends *work–life harmony* in the digital age when work and life are intertwined in the same smartphone. Synthesizing interview data from entrepreneurs and ongoing trends, this chapter proposes strategies to achieve *work–life harmony*, including task prioritization, choosing flexible work schedules, reducing desires, seeking inner peace, and living in the moment.

CASE STUDY 11.1

Respecting Cultural Subtleties: Mr. Jackson in Hong Kong[1]

Located at the heart of Asia, Hong Kong is known as the *Gateway to China and Asia*. With a hybrid Chinese and British cultural, linguistic, and legal heritage, Hong Kong has been a global business and financial hub for almost a century. Hong Kong is one of the world's most dynamic and cosmopolitan cities with opportunities for people from around the globe to work and live (Hong Kong Economic and Trade Office in NYC 2022). To conduct a smooth global business, most multinational corporations have regional headquarters in Hong Kong.

Mr. Jackson was a vice president at an American entertainment firm. In 2018, he was sent to work in the firm's Hong Kong office for three months as the interim division head. Mr. Jackson was a hardworking and hands-on leader. Mr. Jackson did not mind climbing under a table to fix computer wires, carrying heavy file folders to a meeting, or making coffee for himself at the office. He considers these tasks as *mundane* work that he can do himself, without involving his Chinese staff members. Two weeks into his time in Hong Kong, he experienced a dramatic episode. Irene Zhang was the executive assistant assigned to Mr. Jackson's post. Every morning, Irene would come to his office with freshly brewed coffee and help arrange Mr. Jackson's daily schedule. One morning, Irene walked to his office with a cup of office and a smile as usual. Mr. Jackson looked up from his desk and said to Irene: "From tomorrow on, you don't need to make the coffee for me. I will make the coffee myself. Thank you for your efforts, though." Irene apologized and walked out. She burst into tears with her colleagues. Staff members in Hong Kong did not know what to think of this new boss from the American headquarters. Born and raised in Hong Kong, these young employees were taught to respect their leaders and practice cultural hierarchy. They considered it their duties to make coffee, carry file folders, or fix computers for their bosses.

---

[1] Mr. Jackson is a pseudo character created by summarizing a few American entrepreneurs' experience in Hong Kong, based on the interview data.

The next morning, Mr. Jackson was waiting for Irene to come in and arrange his daily schedule. He called her office, no response. Then he walked to the front desk to look for her. The receptionist said, "Oh, Mr. Jackson, Irene quit her job yesterday." "What?! Why did she quit her job? She was a good assistant." The receptionist responded cautiously, "Irene said you asked her to stop making coffee for you. Usually, that is a sign around here for someone to be fired."

Mr. Jackson quickly learned his lesson on cultural subtleties and apologized. Mr. Jackson's hands-on approach did not help to build trust with his new team of Chinese employees. They felt Mr. Jackson did not trust them to do their work, and they were *horrified* to see their boss climbing under the conference table to fix computer wiring himself. In a cultural hierarchy, everyone has a *place* based on his/her social and organizational status. Mr. Jackson said to his new team, "I trust your work. Never did I try to disrespect your culture. You were working so hard, and I felt like I needed to pitch in. I am sorry about any misunderstandings that I have created." They understood, and each person followed the unwritten protocol from then on. Mr. Jackson says he observed similar hierarchical scenarios in Asia, including Mainland China, Vietnam, Korea, Japan, Malaysia, Singapore, Thailand, and India while on duty there. Since then, Mr. Jackson makes extra efforts to understand the various cultures when he meets with CEOs of Asian companies. *A small intercultural misunderstanding can grow into a complex business problem. Culture determines communication styles and business models* (Gao 2013).

Whether for an American entrepreneur in Hong Kong, a Chinese businessman in Germany, or a Japanese executive in Thailand, I recommend *a localization process* for their cultural understanding. Through learning and experience, one can achieve the competency level of *cultural multiphrenia*, when one can function in a foreign culture with local knowledge. With cultural multiphrenia, American entrepreneur can behave as a local in Hong Kong, a Chinese businessperson can communicate in German, and a Japanese executive can be as culturally fluent as a Thai.

Culture is the *software of the mind (Hofstede 1991)*. Just like computers, tablets, and smartphones need to be installed with multiple software to function, a human brain can learn multiple cultures to interpret the meaning of life in various cultural contexts. The concept of "*multiphrenia*" was coined by Kenneth Gergen (1991) who conceptualizes that globalization and technological developments enable us multiple identities. Through this book, I advocate *"cultural multiphrenia,"* which means adopting and maintaining multiple cultural identities. Entrepreneurs can learn multiple languages and cultures, and act as locals wherever they travel, work, and live. *Through cultural multiphrenia, one can achieve multicultural competencies. An entrepreneur equipped with cultural multiphrenia can function as a local wherever he/she works and lives. Practicing intercultural sensitivity and achieving cultural multiphrenia bring happiness to anyone living in a multicultural world.*

Discussion Questions for Readers

1. How do you obtain cultural knowledge about your target market?
2. Have you ever offended a group of people because of cultural differences? If so, how did you resolve intercultural misunderstandings?
3. How can we achieve *cultural multiphrenia?*

Introduction

You might have seen people working long and hard hours for jobs they hate, purchasing things they don't need, or impressing people on social media they don't like. Many of us are less than healthy and mentally stressed out. We may have neglected our families and relationships due to our busy work schedules. It seems that certain job choices are fundamentally incompatible with meaningful self-fulfillment and family engagement. As a result, some people with less-than-optimal job choices may eventually change jobs to maintain physical and mental health.

The widespread usage of smartphones and the impact of the COVID-19 pandemic have transformed the way we work and live. Hybrid working and teleworking have become common practices. Consequently, we lose traditional physical boundaries between work and life. We can no longer *leave work* and *go back to life*. We need to realize that taking a vacation is not only about getting away from work, but also about an attitude of protecting yourself from the hassle of work. Otherwise, you are just teleworking from the beach. Entrepreneurs interviewed for this book suggest that work and life shall not be viewed as two opposing forces. The traditional *work/life balance* seems to be an unrealistic goal in the digital age. We are the same person at work and in life, tapping the same smartphones. To thrive in the digital age, we must try to embrace both work and life and maintain a dynamic work–life harmony. In this concluding chapter, practical strategies are suggested for work–life harmony.

Entrepreneurs Overwork Themselves

At the end of my interviews with the 20 global business leaders and entrepreneurs from various cultures, I asked them to share their strategies for searching for happiness while coping with demands from both work and life amid busy schedules. Most of the leaders and entrepreneurs interviewed said they could not maintain work/life balance because they spent too much time, effort, and energy on work, often at the sacrifice of their health, families, and quality of life. Data indicate that entrepreneurs of all cultures take passionate ownership of their business, and they work extremely hard to stay afloat in the competitive and turbulent global business environment.

Thomas Edison once said that innovation is 1 percent inspiration and 99 percent perspiration. It is clear that hard work paves the way to success. Here are some personal stories shared by the entrepreneurs and leaders interviewed, whose names are hidden for privacy.

Entrepreneur #1:

Over the course of my life, I could have done much better. There was a period in my life when I was just all into work, building my company. When I did that, I sacrificed family and I cannot ever get that time back. I have to ask for forgiveness of my family, and also to forgive myself.

Entrepreneur #2:

I have struggled with work/life balance. I gave a lot to work and sometimes to the detriment of my personal relationships. That is very unhealthy. I did not have a college degree until I was 20 years into my corporate life. I overcame that by working harder than others. I put in 60 or 70 hours per week. Working in a global business, I don't get a real day off. The business is going 24/7. My Sunday is already Monday in Asia.

Entrepreneur #3:

As the owner and founder of my company, I do not have a work/life balance. I often joke that I am open 36 hours a day, nine days a week. That is not right for everybody. It depends on who you are within your organization and what fuels your passion. I am excited every day at work because I like what I do. I answered emails at 3:30 a.m. because I could not sleep on something last night. I used to be offended that I got a ton of emails on the weekend when I was working for a company. But now I say: "By all means, text me at 2 a.m."

Entrepreneur #4:

Work/life balance is a question without a solution. I never think of my life to be balanced. Here is my approach. When I am with family, I focus on my family. When I am at work, I fully focus on business.

Entrepreneur #5:

I think work-life balance is a fallacy in the world we live in today. There is always a scenario when I am on vacation with my family, and I have to take an important business call. I have to sacrifice, and my family has to sacrifice. Technology is a double-edged sword. My office is in my pocket.

Entrepreneur #6:

Sometimes I have stressful clients or pressing projects. I was taking a lot of headache pills and that further triggered my health issues. I am scared of going into my home office. Once I'm in my home office, I'm in there for the whole week. I sleep on the couch so that I can wake up and go back to work.

The Impossible *Work/Life Balance*

Cambridge Dictionary (2022) defines *work/life balance* as "the amount of time you spend doing your job compared with the amount of time you spend with your family and doing things you enjoy." The Cambridge definition juxtaposes *work* as something one inherently does not enjoy. Based on these *official* and perhaps *outdated* definitions, it is nearly impossible to achieve work/life balance by distributing an equal amount of time and energy toward work and life. When discussing work/life balance in class, a graduate student responded: "I am always told that work and life are meant to be separate. Work and life seem to be two enemies fighting in our schedule." Another student asked, "Some people have tons of money and do not need to go to work. How come they seem to be unhappy with their lives?"

In the digital age, work/life balance is often disrupted by smartphones. In 2007, Steve Jobs, the cofounder and chairman of Apple debuted *iPhone 1*, the original iPhone, to be an all-in-one device for a music player (iPod), a mobile phone, and an Internet communicator. The iPhone 1 featured a revolutionary 3.5-inch touchscreen with multiple app capabilities. The *Wall Street Journal* touted the phone as "a beautiful and breakthrough handheld computer." *Time* magazine hailed it as the "Invention of the Year."[2] The iPhone has been the flagship of

---

[2] This story about *iPhone 1* was summarized by Dr. Gao from Verizon website data, Accessed in 2022.

smartphones of various brands over the years. Since then, technology companies like Samsung, Xiaomi, OPPO, Vivo, and Google have developed their version of Android-based smartphones. The invention of smartphones and the subsequent adoption of various apps transformed our work and life. On the one hand, smartphones and apps provide convenience for work and life. On the other hand, the usage of smartphones disrupts the traditional concept of work/life balance. A smartphone is like an all-in-one *miniature office*, complete with some or all functions of a computer, phone, text message, pager, beeper, music/video/game player, online meeting platforms, and e-wallets. With such a miniature office fastened to one's body, sometimes even as *wearables* like an Apple Watch, one cannot truly escape from work.

In most industries, competition is constant, challenges are abundant, and workloads pile high. Engineers working in high-tech companies feel the burn. In China, among some technology companies, there are *996* or *007* work cultures. *996* means engineers work from 9 a.m. to 9 p.m. for six days a week, while *007* means engineers work from midnight to the next midnight nonstop 24 hours a day, for seven days a week. Although intense working hours are against labor laws in China, they are sometimes practiced. Some employees from these companies complain: "When we are young, we sacrifice our health for jobs. When we grow older, we spend the money earned going to hospitals."

Overwork creates high stress and mental health issues. Depression is a real thing for many of us. In the United States, where people believe in the *solution of a pill* in most health matters, many people take daily antidepressants. When depression deepens, some quit their jobs. Over 4.5 million Americans quit their jobs in November 2021 (Reuters 2022). The reasons driving this great resignation transcend a desire to work less, ranging from avoiding pandemic frontlines, to securing accessible child care, to searching for a higher meaning in life. A growing number of people *chose to be happy* rather than maintaining an office job. CEOs also joined the *great resignation*, trading fatigue at work for relaxation with family. The number of departing CEOs in the final quarter of 2021 was up 16 percent on a year-over-year basis (White 2022). Work was *pointless* at best and "degrading, humiliating, and exploitative" at worst, says *Reddit* moderator behind the *antiwork* thread with over 1.6 million members (Jones 2022a).

Introducing *Work–Life Harmony*

With the widespread adoption of smartphones, the traditional concept of *work/life balance* is obsolete as we can no longer *leave work for life*. Instead of struggling with the work and life dichotomy, this chapter advocates *work–life harmony*. We all have the potential for enjoying both work and life while allowing work and life to energize each other. Data show that maintaining work–life harmony reduces stress, prevents workplace burnout, and enhances health and happiness. The cornerstone book in traditional Chinese herbal medicine, *The Yellow Emperor's Classic of Internal Medicine* (黄帝内经, pronounced as "Huang Di Nei Jing"), points out that each human being has the potential to live for 120 years (two of 60 years, 两个甲子), the longevity bestowed to us by the Heaven. However, most people do not live to be 120 years old, because of various reasons, including poor choices in profession, attitude, lifestyle, and diet. Chinese medical doctor Dr. Xu Wenbing explains that a good job brings health and happiness to one's life. Dr. Xu (2022) interprets that a good job should properly follows laws in nature. For example, night shift jobs can be harmful to one's physical and mental health as they prevent good sleep and proper immune functions. A night shift job may reduce one's prospect for longevity and increase one's medical bills.

On any given workday, many of us spend more time with co-workers than with our family. Steve Crabtree (2011) from *Gallup Poll* states that the leading determinant of happiness is *having a good job*, a meaningful job that employees feel engaged with. Among the 47,361 employees surveyed in 120 countries, 45 percent of those reported as "engaged with the company cultures" describing themselves as having a "thriving life." Among those who are disengaged with the company culture, just 13 percent reported having a thriving life. Happy workers are more productive, more likely to help coworkers, less likely to quit, and are friendlier to customers. Engaged and happy workers are a great resource for a business, and their health care costs tend to be lower as well. Li Wong, the publisher of the *Georgia Asian Times,* advocates a four-day work week. Consequently, a three-day weekend would give the employees proper time for themselves and their families. As an experiment in 2018, employees at Microsoft Japan worked four days per week and received five-day per week paychecks. The result was a productivity boost of 40 percent, with

23 percent less spent on electricity, 60 percent less documents printed, and shorter meetings (Kohll 2018). At different stages of their lives, people change their allocation of resources to work and life, not at a constant 50/50 ratio. Roger Neuenschwander, former president of tvsdesign said,

> I need more work than life. My family knows that, and everybody who works with me knows that. This ratio changed over the years. When I was 35, it was 90 percent work and 10 percent life because I was building my career. As I aged and matured, I found joy in international work by exploring new cultures, making new friends, and working on projects on the other side of the world.

People of various generations perceive the meaning of work and life differently. For the Millennials and GenZers, the traditional concept of a 9 a.m. to 5 p.m. workday seems less attractive. Some companies try to compensate by adding free coffee, game rooms, and beanbags to spice up the work environment. An entire industry has popped up surrounding making workspaces more *Millennial and Gen-Z-friendly.*

Cultivating a Relationship with Your Inner Self

Relationships with business partners, clients, and customers is only one of many relationships that we need to cultivate in our lifetime. Other than business relationships, we need to care for our relationships with family members, the nature and/or God, and the inner self. Giving each of these relationships proper attention sustains career success, family happiness, physical and mental well-being, and overall work–life harmony. One foundational relationship to care about is between you and your inner self.

In the Taoism paradigm, inside the physical body of each human being, lives a *soul*, which is one's *inner self.* The inner self accompanies us from birth; thus, we are never lonely. Taoists believe that the *soul* gives life to the physical body, and therefore, it is essential to keep the soul happy by cultivating a good relationship with our *inner self.* This *I–inner self* relationship can be cultivated through meditation, self-talk, and doing things that satisfy the spirit and body. Hobbies such as music, gardening, yoga, traveling, jogging, painting, and writing poems can delight the soul for your happiness. Yellow Emperor and his advisors say, "When you keep your soul happy inside your body, how can you become unhealthy?" (精神内守，病安从来？" Xu 2022).

Ways to Achieve Work–Life Harmony

Achieving work–life harmony depends on the proper cultivation of the four essential relationships. Work–life harmony is possible from finding your passion, harnessing energy from your passion, and prioritizing your major goals. We need to pay attention to all categories of relationships, including the four essential relationships: "I + Inner self," "I + God/ nature," "I + Family," and "I + Communities (business partners, coworkers, classmates, clients, friends)." Spending time with your inner self through meditation and reflection helps you to know more about yourself. Spending time with God/nature, family and communities help you to enjoy your life to the fullest.

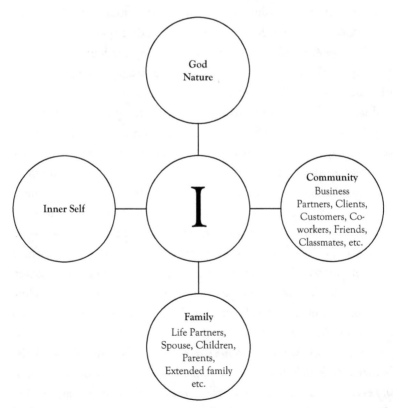

Figure 11.1 Cultivating Four Essential Relationships for Work–Life Harmony

Strategy #1: Finding your passion. Your relationship with your inner self makes up your identity and forms the foundation of all your relationships. It is critical that you observe your inner self in search of your passion. Your passion is usually revealed in hobbies and qualities that make you who you are. You can cultivate a relationship with your inner self through meditation, fulfilling your passion, and acting on your hobbies. Finding your passion, then harnessing the energy from your passion can enrich your relationships with your family, God/nature and communities. *Learning about yourself and finding your passion is the first step toward a work-life harmony.* Mr. Neuenschwander, former president of tvsdesign asked this question: "Are you working toward your passion? Is your work generating energy or depriving you of energy?" Finding your passion demands *quality me time.* Block some time per week or per day for yourself, examine your physical and mental health, meditate, and figure out what you really want in work and life. Physical activity and sufficient rest can help your mood, creativity, and productivity. Make time for exercise, walking the dog, hiking with your kids, or practicing yoga.

Strategy #2: Calculating priorities. Among the four essential relationships, each may need different amounts of attention at various stages of your life. Establish realistic goals and priorities for work, school, and family. This will help you focus on tasks that give you satisfaction, happiness, and a sense of accomplishment. Concentrate your resources on the important projects, and avoid procrastination on menial tasks. Try to delegate work that others are capable to handle, and eliminate those that do not contribute toward your passion. If you feel overwhelmed when evaluating your time, you may be overcommitted. Try to delegate some tasks to others. Career women face unique challenges in managing work and life. Marcy Sperry, the founder of Vivid IP, spends quality time on weekends with her sons when they go on nature walks or play soccer. She feels she develops a stronger connection with her boys by spending time together outside. Ms. Sperry said, "The pandemic forced us to stop and slow down, and take stock in what really matters."

Strategy #3: Setting up boundaries. When the physical boundaries between work and life disappear, we need to adopt a *psychological boundary* between work and life and learn to say *no* more often. Saying *no* to things that might distract us from our passion helps us to focus. Brad

Taylor, former brand strategist for The Coca-Cola Company, highlights the value of setting boundaries: "I make decisions. I create boundaries. I'm not going to get myself in a situation where I would be working more than I want to. It's about establishing boundaries and then staying in those boundaries." Marcy Sperry, the founder of Vivid IP, advocates taking off completely on Saturdays and Sundays to be more productive on weekdays. JR Wilson, vice president at AT&T said, "There are times when people call me, and I let them leave a message. Based on that, I determine whether I'm going to call them back on a Friday night or Monday morning."

Setting up boundaries can be a difficult practice. In the United States, there is an unwritten rule. After 5 p.m., many people do not respond to emails or answer phone calls. Nagendra Roy, the CEO of AanseaCore, clarifies that if I call him after 5 p.m., he would probably answer because "when it comes to relationship, it gets beyond that time frame." Glad Cheng, chairman of China Window Group says, "In China, it is impossible to separate work and life. The two are always mixed together." As a *sophisticated relationship manager*, we need to be sensitive to people's private resting time, and refrain from sending them emails at night, on weekends, or during holiday times. Here are some more tips for managing time:

- **Learn to say no:** If you feel overwhelmed with work and are asked to take on a new project, discuss your concerns with your supervisor. If you feel overburdened with obligations in your life, it's OK to cancel plans or decline invitations to events.
- **Accept your limits:** Do you feel as if you need to accomplish everything by yourself? It's OK to delegate and seek help from others who might feel pleased and honored to help.
- **Shorten meeting times:** Meetings can be shorter. The systems of iPhone or Zoom tend to set meetings automatically at one hour, but most issues can be resolved with 10-, 15- or 30-minute shorter meetings.

Strategy #4: Flexible work schedule. Work smart instead of work hard. Due to advancements in communication technologies, pandemic impacts, and employee demands, more and more organizations have adopted flexible work schedules, including in-person, hybrid, and remote formats. The hybrid work format spans from half a day in the office to one to four days per week in the office. A 2021 survey by American Express concerning work format preferences indicated that about 20 percent of employees wanted to remain virtual, 75 percent voted for hybrid working, and only 5 percent wanted to be in the office full-time. Working *in person* in offices should be purposeful and beneficial for relationship building among team members. Stephen Squeri, CEO of American Express said, "It makes no sense for people to trek into the office just to sit on Zoom" (Jones 2022b). Airbnb CEO Brian Chesky believes the office is *an anachronistic form* from a predigital age. Based on the productivity data of remote working, in order to secure the best talents, Airbnb decided that starting May 1, 2022, employees can work remotely forever with no pay cuts (Jackson 2022).

Working from home does not guarantee work–life harmony. First, when people work where they live, work blends into their lives. Some people do not like working at home, as their spouses keep giving them *honey-do-lists,*[3] and their children and pets keep asking for attention. Robert Striar, president of M Style Marketing, shared, "I find working at home during the pandemic very challenging. My kids are around me more, which I love, but I often tell them to wait. They want to go out and play, but Dad has important phone calls." Second, hybrid and remote work leaves employees feeling *Zoom fatigue* and disconnected from one another. DeAnn Golden, president and CEO of Berkshire Hathaway HomeServices Georgia Properties, says that online meetings can work for certain tasks, but interacting *outside of the screen* in the real world brings the human element to communication, which is critical for relationship building. When discussing collaboration, *off-line* face-to-face communication has the potential to create limitless opportunities. While

---

[3] *Honey-do-lists* are lists of chores, tasks, requests, or household repairs that one spouse makes for another. Very commonly, it is the female who makes up this list for her husband or partner. The list can be a helpful reminder of things that need to be done, or a drain on a person's free time.

modern technology is wonderful, it is not the same as connecting in person. Efforts need to be made to achieve a balance between *human needs for bonding* and *computer-aided communication*.

This ongoing global movement that rejects the traditional idea of a *nine-to-five job* are led by Millennials (GenY) and GenZers, who seek for careers with greater flexibility. Data show that Gen Y and Gen Z workers in the United States choose work flexibility over health care coverage when comparing jobs (Chappell 2019). Employers of today and tomorrow must determine ways to appeal to millennial and Gen Z workers, who are projected to be more than 75 percent of the workforce by 2025 (Kohll 2018).

Many organizations have adopted monthly or quarterly face-to-face team building routines for those remote workers to meet with their peers and be refreshed with organizational cultures. Face-to-face activities often create unforgettable shared memories for trust-building among team members, which strengthen their future online communication. What's more, online meetings and face-to-face meetings carry different weights on one's *visibility* in front of supervisors and peers. Although some organizations say certain meetings are hybrid that you can attend either in person or online, leaders would most likely judge those attending online as less visible than those attending in person. For those who want to excel in your organizations, it is strategic to attend meetings in person once in a while to increase your visibility, and connect with your supervisors and your peers off the screen.

Strategy #5: Achieving inner peace and living in the moment. Inner peace refers to a deliberate state of psychological or spiritual calmness despite the potential presence of stressors. In our lifetime, we accumulate material processions, real estate, bank savings, and experiences because we believe they make us happy. By continuing to search outside of ourselves for pleasure without a strong inner peace, we may be always feeling hungry for something else. *Keeping up with the Joneses* can distract us from who we are. "All of humanity's problems stem from our inability to sit quietly in a room alone," wrote The French philosopher Blaise Pascal. Medication, prayers, listening to yourself, and other inward thinking methods help to build inner peace. As I was discussing work–life harmony with my Gen Z undergraduate students, one of them said, "I was told by my parents and grandparents to always strive for better and to *never settle.*" This mantra seems to be in contrast to our mental need for inner peace. How much money is enough? A common Chinese idiom says, "Those who know when is enough find happiness" (知足常乐). "Letting Go" may be the best strategy for achieving inner peace. We can let go certain things, projects, relationships, status, and desires.

When we watch the moon, we can notice the shape of the moon changes slightly every night. The span between one new moon and the next is called a lunar cycle, lunation, or lunar month, which lasts for about 29 days (Almanac 2022). The full moon night is usually the 15th day in this lunar cycle. While the new moon is totally dark, the full moon is bright and round. People often get excited on full moon nights. Poets in ancient China often would host *poetry parties* during full moon nights, complete with music, dances, and drinks. However, the ideal *full moon night* that people want only exists once per lunar month. In the eyes of people on earth, the moon shrinks after the full moon night, advancing to the next lunar cycle. If we compare our lives to the stages of the moon, perhaps the best stage is the night before the full moon, before the decline? Reflecting the same spirit, in the *Qian Gua* 乾卦, the first Gua of I Ching (易经), there are six strokes from the bottom to the top. The fifth stroke, which is slightly lower than the sixth stroke, is considered the luckiest stroke in the Qian scenario (九五至尊). It takes wisdom and careful thinking for us to identify the *pause points* in our pursuit of material processions and ambitions so that we stay at the territory of fortune (almost full moon), before the situation declines.

Achieving inner peace allows us to *live in the moment.* Some people live in the past, blaming themselves for what "would have, could have, or should have been." Some people live in the future, and they dream about retirement life. Alex Gregory, former President and CEO of YKK Corporation of America, told my class, "Try to enjoy your life now as graduate students. Enjoy the moments that you are learning and growing. Don't always dream about retirement. Look at me, I am retired and there is nothing to be envied about here!" *Life is more about the journey than the destination!* Here are a few tips for you to enjoy the moment, whether you are working or taking a break.

- **Enjoy what you do:** If you are not passionate about your work, find purpose in what you do and embrace it. If you cannot find any purpose in your work, it may be time to explore an alternate career or a different job.
- **Be present:** When you are working, make sure you are fully engaged with your tasks and activities. Then, put your work responsibilities out of mind when you are off work.
- **Reduce ruminating:** When you are resting or spending time with family and friends, try not to think about work or business.
- **Go with the flow:** Things have ways to naturally settle themselves. By adapting to the environment and through effortless action (wu wei无为), we can go with the flow and achieve goals with higher efficiency.
- **Be kind to yourself:** Set manageable goals, take breaks, stay physically active and mentally positive. Take care of yourself, as your health and mind form the foundation for your dreams, work and relationships with others.

Conclusion

Consider life as your full-time job and view work as your part-time job. During your lifetime, you never lose your job of living your life. You just change your projects, jobs, and careers from time to time. According to Yellow's Emperor's Inner Canon, each of us has the potential to enjoy 120 years of healthy and happy life. While striving to win business with relationships, we should be aware that business relationships are only one kind of the four essential relationships we cultivate in our lifetime. The four essential relationships that we need to cultivate include our relationships with the inner self, God/nature, family, and communities (business partners, clients, customers, classmates, co-workers, and friends). Proper attitude for the relationships between the self and the other can be the *best pill of solution* for life's many challenges.

Mark Twain once said, "The secret of success is making your *vocation* into your *vacation*." For some people, *work* means bringing home the check while enduring hardships. It does not have to be this way. From a holistic perspective, work–life harmony involves incorporating work into life in a way that promotes happiness both at home and work. Attitudes toward work–life harmony will continue to evolve with cultural, generational, and economic changes. Flexible leaders adapt to the environment and reinvent their workplace cultures to promote happiness and productivity among employees. Smart employees look for jobs that sustain their mental and physical health. Work–life harmony can be achieved if we consciously seek for it.

Epilogue

From a relational perspective, customer service means providing other human beings with products/services they want and need at the right time in a convenient way. No matter where you are from or what culture you grow up with, we have a lot more in common than in difference. The Tao of the universe transcends. Perhaps we are in different businesses or industries, but we are all doing *customer service* through communication with other human beings. We are providing customer service for people in our communities: consumers, clients, business partners, students, patients, and pet owners. Mistakes have been made by companies in giving customers wrong products, lousy services, and/or via inconvenient formats at improper times. In the past 30 years, for cost saving, a large portion of customer service jobs have been outsourced overseas, especially to India. Outsourced customer service means that a company is utilizing a third-party provider overseas or *AI-powered chatbots* to handle communication with customers. While employees in India read scripts with an accent to respond to customer inquiries, many of them have no idea of the American way of life and American consumers' struggles with these products and services. Without the proper frames of reference, can Indian employees sitting in call centers in Bangalore solve problems for an American family traveling in Montana?

Respect every customer as a potential "repeat customer." If you have successfully persuaded a customer to buy your product, you have earned his/her trust for more potential business. For real estate, each household usually only buys one home from an agent at a given time. However, this household can be a *golden goose* for the agent. First, the household can provide word-of-mouth referrals and online reviews for this agent to their neighbors, employees, families, friends, and online communities. Second, this household may be moving to another state in a few years, which means selling a home in one state, and buying a home in another state. Keeping in touch with these customers and finding out their wants/needs at different times are the *key* in all businesses. With proper care, a relationship may yield fruits every harvesting season. I have heard that only 6 percent of real estate agents keep in touch with their customers to enjoy these encore and bonus business deals.

Be a loyal long-term consumer of your own products and services. That way, you find out what the consumers want and need firsthand, and you will experience their happiness and difficulties while using your products and services. You will then get closer to consumer hardship in user experience: a gardener cannot open insect-killer containers, a patient with arthritis struggles with medicine bottles, and a car accident victim wrestles with insurance claims. Ask your employees and family members to become consumers of your products and services. You will be able to discover people's experiences from different backgrounds. Strive to be user-friendly in every product and service for win–win–win results.

Increase the diversity of your employee and leadership team so that their backgrounds in age, gender, culture, and lifestyle *reflect and match* those of your target customers. To keep a steady pulse on your customers, it is essential that you practice the principle of *requisite variety* in your hiring. Diversity in viewpoints is required for companies to address complex issues. Explaining "the cybernetic principle of requisite variety," Ashby (1957) suggests that the internal diversity of any self-regulating system, such as a company, must match the variety and complexity of its environment for sustainability. Hiring more diverse, women, and younger employees can increase the strength of a company by reflecting and relating to the changing consumer demographics.

To conclude my interviews, I asked the leaders and entrepreneurs for some key words in building relationships for business success. Masae Okura, a partner at Taylor English Duma LLP says, "Anything could be networking: volunteering, lunch, and golf." Eddy Perez, the Cofounder and CEO of Equity Prime Mortgage gives a *show up + follow up + luck up* equation. Mr. Perez says,

> 90 percent of the game is just showing up in relationship platforms. Showing up means you care to give good content to others. By being on their radar screen, you've already done more than most people. Then 5 percent is following up. Many people lack

the tenacity to follow up. The last 5 percent is just circumstances, such as timing, trends, and luck.

Embrace changes. Instead of fighting with mega-changes, flow with these changing trends, such as flexible work schedules, smartphone-aided communication, and a younger workforce. In June 2022, a CEO of a headhunting company told me the first question most jobseekers ask is, "Does this job allow remote work?" In real estate, iBuyers[1] have entered the market, and a real estate agent may want to embrace them for new business. Social media is replacing mass media as the main source of information. Social media is inherently relationship-based, while mass media usually provides one-way communication.

Be a giver instead of a taker. By giving others your time, efforts, money, attention, and other resources, you are appreciated. Giving makes you visible! You will be highlighted on their radar screens. Usually the more value in products and services you give to your business partners, clients, and customers, the more they will reward you with business deals and cash flow. The universe has a remarkable way of karma. When you provide extra value to your customers, opportunities and money will follow. In Shakespeare's (1597) play *Romeo and Juliet*, Juliet said to Romeo:

My bounty is as boundless as the sea
My love as deep
The more I give to thee, the more I have
for both are infinite

---

[1] "iBuyers" are real estate buyers that use online home value assessment tools, incorporating machine learning and AI to make instant offers. Top iBuyers in 2022 in the United States were Opendoor, Offerpad, Zillow Offers, and RedfinNow. These iBuyers purchase residential properties directly from private sellers to eventually resell them.

The 20 Entrepreneurs and Leaders Interviewed

These semistructured in-depth interviews were conducted between April 3, 2019 and July 6, 2022, to collect data for this book. The entrepreneurs are listed with the job positions they held at the time of the interview, in chorological order of interviews. The length of each interview duration is shown in minutes (') and seconds (").

#	Entrepreneurs interviewed	Job title and organization/company (At the time of interview)	Business area	Day of interview	Interview duration
1	Nagendra Roy	CEO, AanseaCore	IT	04/03/2019	64' 45"
2	Glad Cheng	Chairman, China Window Group	General	06/23/2019	40' 35"
3	Roger Neuenschwander	former President and CEO, tvsdesign	Architectural design	09/05/2019	83' 49"
4	Alex Gregory	former President, CEO and Chairman, YKK Corporation of America	Manufacturing	09/09/2019	90' 18"
5	Jessica Cork	Vice President, YKK Corporation of America	Manufacturing	09/11/2019	115' 08"
6	Lucy Lu	CEO/Founder, aiLegal	Law	11/05/2019	54' 06"
7	Masae Okura	Partner, Taylor English Duma LLP	Law	11/10/2019	109' 03"
8	Li Wong	Publisher and CEO, Georgia Asian Times	Media	11/13/2019	24' 09"
9	Brad Taylor	former Brand Strategist, The Cola-Cola Company	Marketing	11/18/2019	71' 39"
10	Cathy Garces	former Sales Executive Emirates Airlines, Japan Airlines	Sales	11/22/2019	59' 11"
11	Stan Wang	President, Tenfunder Investment Group	Investment	12/07/2019	70' 47"
12	JR Wilson	Vice President, AT&T	IT	01/23/2020	73' 08"
13	David Kirk	President and CEO, Murata Electronics	Tech	02/10/2020	105' 12"
14	Eddy Perez	Cofounder and CEO, Equity Prime Mortgage	Finance	02/14/2020	60' 20"
15	Robert Striar	President, M Style Marketing	Marketing	04/16/2020	77' 02"
16	Wade Edwards	former Fundraising Director, Habitat for Humanity International	Nonprofit	04/17/2020	70' 13"
17	Rick Cole	former Senior Vice President, Turner Broadcasting System, Inc.	Media	04/21/2020	119' 28"
18	Wendy Lu	Partner, Director of China Practice, Aprio	Accounting	04/23/2020	75' 05"
19	Marcy Sperry	Founder, Vivid IP	Law	04/30/2020	76' 55"
20	DeAnn Golden	President and CEO, Berkshire Hathaway HomeServices Georgia Properties	Real estate	07/06/2022	53' 47"

References

Alessandra, T. and O'Connor M. J. 2008. *The Platinum Rule: Discover the Four Basic Business Personalities and How They Can Lead You to Success.* New York, NY: Grand Central Publishing.

Almanac. 2022. "Moon Phase Calendar for 2022." www.almanac.com/astronomy/moon/calendar#:~:text=As%20mentioned%20above%2C%20the%20span,44%20minutes%2C%20and%203%20seconds (accessed May 10, 2022).

Altman, I. and D.A. Taylor. 1973. *Social Penetration: The Development of Interpersonal Relationships.* Canada: Holt, Rinehart & Winston of Canada Ltd.

American Express Website. 2020. "Business Development and its Importance." www.americanexpress.com/en-ca/business/trends-and-insights/articles/business-development-and-its-importance/ (accessed December 29, 2020).

Architect Magazine. 2021. "TVSDESIGN." *Architect Magazine.* www.architectmagazine.com/firms/tvsdesign (accessed May 24, 2021).

Arteca, R. 2015. *Introduction to Horticultural Science*, 2nd ed. USA, Stamford: Gengage Learning.

Ashby, W.R. 1957. *An Introduction to Cybernetics*, 2nd ed., p. 294. London: Chapman and Hall.

Aten, J. 2020. "Jeff Bezos Says People Trust Amazon More Than Congress. Why That Matters." *Inc.com.* www.inc.com/jason-aten/jeff-bezos-says-amazon-is-more-trusted-than-congress-why-that-matters.html (accessed May 19, 2021).

Auyang, S.Y. 1999. *Foundations of Complex-system Theories in Economics, Evolutionary Biology, and Statistical Physics.* Cambridge University Press.

Bakhtin, M. 1984. *Problems of Dostoevsky's Poetics.* Minneapolis, MN: University of Minnesota Press.

Bakhtin, M.M. 1981. *The Dialogic Imagination: Four Essays by M.M.* Translated by C. Emerson and M. Holquist. Austin, TX: University of Texas Press.

Bankmycell Website. 2023. "How Many People Have Smartphones in the World?" https://www.bankmycell.com/blog/how-many-phones-are-in-the-world (accessed February16, 2023).

BBC Science Homepage. 2020. "Organs—Heart. Science: Human, Body & Mind." www.bbc.co.uk/science/humanbody/body/factfiles/heart/heart.shtml (accessed March 29, 2020).

Beinart, P. 2010. *The Icarus Syndrome: A History of American Hubris.* New York, NY: HarperCollins.

Bertalanffy, L.V. 1972. "The History and Status of General Systems Theory." *The Academy of Management Journal* 15, no. 4. pp. 407–426.

Bezos, J. 2017. "What Is 'Day One' Philosophy: Interview Transcript With Jeff Bezos." *Forbes.* www.forbes.com/sites/quora/2017/04/21/what-is-jeff-bezos-day-1-philosophy/#7fa05bca1052 (accessed February 8, 2022).

Biederman, P.W. and W. Bennis.1998. *Organizing Genius: The Secrets of Creative Collaboration.* New York, NY: Basic Books.

Billings, S.A. 2013. *Nonlinear System Identification: NARMAX Methods in the Time, Frequency, and Spatio-Temporal Domains.* New York, NY: Wiley

Blau, P. 1964. *Exchange and Power in Social Life.* New York, NY: Wiley.

Bohm, D. 1996. *On Dialogue.* London and New York: Routledge.

Branson, M. 2019. "5 Memorable Reverse Mortgage Spokesmen." *All Reverse Mortgage Inc.* https://reverse.mortgage/5-memorable-spokesmen (accessed May 9, 2021).

Brex. 2021. "22 Vision Statement Examples to Help You Write Your Own." *Brex Company Website.* www.brex.com/blog/vision-statement-examples.nt (accessed November 19, 2021).

Bryant, S. 2020. "How Many Startups Fail and Why?" *Investopia.* www.investopedia.com/articles/personal-finance/040915/how-many-startups-fail-and-why.asp#:~:text=Key%20Takeaways,70%25%20in%20their%2010th%20year (accessed December 29, 2020).

Buber, M. 1970. *I and Thou.* New York, NY: Charles Scribner's Sons.

Burt, R.S. 1995. *Structural Holes: The Social Structure of Competition.* Cambridge, MA: Harvard University Press.

Business Standard Website. 2022. "Iran and Argentina Apply to Join BRICS Bloc After Recent Summit." www.business-standard.com/article/international/iran-argentina-apply-to-join-brics-bloc-after-recent-summit-report-12206 2800935_1.html (accessed July 20, 2022).

Cambridge Dictionary. 2022. "Work/Life Balance." https://dictionary.cambridge.org/us/dictionary/english/work-life-balance (accessed February 21, 2022).

Chadwick, S. 2021. "A Deficit of Trust." *Research World.* www.researchworld.com/a-deficit-of-trust/ (accessed May 20, 2021).

Chappell, B. 2019. "4-Day Workweek Boosted Workers' Productivity By 40%, Microsoft Japan Says." *NPR.* www.npr.org/2019/11/04/776163853/microsoft-japan-says-4-day-workweek-boosted-workers-productivity-by-40 (accessed February 22, 2022).

Cisco. 2021. "What is a VPN?" www.cisco.com/c/en/us/products/security/vpn-endpoint-security-clients/what-is-vpn.html (accessed February 13, 2022).

Cissna, K. and R. Anderson. 1994. "Communication and the Ground of Dialogue." In *The Reach of Dialogue: Confirmation, Voice, and Community,* eds. R. Anderson, K. Cissna, and R.C. Arnett. New York, NY: Hampton Press.

Cohn, Scott. 2022. "One Year After the 737 Max's Return, Boeing is Still Trying to Get Back on Course." *CNBC*. www.cnbc.com/2022/01/24/the-737-max-may-be-back-but-boeing-is-still-trying-to-get-back-on-course.html (accessed June 14, 2022).

Corporate Finance Institute. 2021. "What is Return on Investment (ROI)?" *Corporate Finance Institute*. https://corporatefinanceinstitute.com/resources/knowledge/finance/return-on-investment-roi-formula/ (accessed June 2, 2021).

Council of European Communities. 1992. *Treaty on European Union*. Luxembourg: Office for Official Publications of the European Communities.

Covey, S.M.R. and R.R. Merrill. 2006. *The Speed of Trust: The One Thing That Changes Everything*. New York, NY: Free Press.

Covey, S.R. 2015. *The 7 Habits of Highly Effective People*. Infographic Edition. FranklinCovey. Coral Gables: Mango Publishing.

Crabtree, S. 2011. "A Good Job Means a Good Life: Employee Engagement Enhances Personal Well-being." *Gallup*. https://news.gallup.com/business journal/147443/good-job-means-good-life.aspx (accessed December 30, 2021).

Creswell, J.W. 2009. *Research Design: Qualitative, Quantitative, and Mixed Methods Approaches*. Thousand Oaks: Sage.

Darwin, C.R. 1859. *On the Origin of Species*. London, UK: John Murray.

Dawson, S. 2019. "What Boeing's 737 MAX Has to Do with Cars: Software." *Wired Magazine*. www.wired.com/story/boeings-737-max-cars-software/ (accessed May 20, 2021).

Deloitte. 2015. "Global Survey on Reputation Risk." *Deloitte Website*. www2.deloitte.com/content/dam/Deloitte/za/Documents/risk/NEWReputation RiskSurveyReport_25FEB.pdf (accessed August 16, 2021).

Dolan, S. 2021. "The Challenges of Last Mile Delivery Logistics and the Tech Solutions Cutting Costs in the Final Mile." *Insider*. www.businessinsider.com/last-mile-delivery-shipping-explained?IR=T (accessed August 5, 2021).

Dorton, D. 2019. "tvsdesign Reaches Sky-scraping Heights With a Sage Intacct Implementation." *Dean Dorton*. https://deandorton.com/case-study-tvsdesign-sage-intacct-implementation/ (accessed June 2, 2021).

Edison Research. 2021. "Radio's Roadmap to Gen Z Listenership." www.edisonresearch.com/radios-roadmap-to-gen-z-listenership/#:~:text=Gen%20 Z%20listeners%20spend%2050,they%20are%20in%20the%20care (accessed August 1, 2021).

Egreenway Website. 2021. "Translation for Chapter 49 of *Tao Te Ching*, Compiled and Indexed by M.P. Garofalo." www.egreenway.com/taoism/ttclz49.htm (accessed September 20, 2021).

Eisenberg, E.M 1984. "Ambiguity as Strategy in Organizational Communication." *Communication Monographs* 51, no. 3, pp. 227–242.

Eisenberg. E.M., A. Trethewey, M. LeGreco, and H.L. Goodall. Jr. 2017. *Organizational Communication: Balancing Creativity and Constraint*, Eighth ed. New York, NY: Macmillan.

Ellis, C. 2004. *The Ethnographic I: A Methodological Novel About Autoethnography*. Walnut Creek: AltaMira Press.

Encyclopedia Britannica. 2022. "Multilateralism." www.britannica.com/topic/multilateralism (accessed January 25, 2022).

Fatoki, O.O. 2011. "The Impact of Human, Social and Financial Capital on the Performance of Small and Medium-Sized Enterprises (SMEs) in South Africa." *Journal of Social Science*. 29, no. 3. pp. 193–204.

Fearnow, B. 2021. "One-Third of Unvaccinated Americans Don't Trust Scientists Who Made Vaccines, Survey Finds." *Newsweek*. www.newsweek.com/one-third-unvaccinated-americans-dont-trust-scientists-who-made-vaccines-survey-finds-1576031 (accessed May 20, 2021).

Folkman, J. 2014. "8 Ways to Ensure Your Vision Is Valued." *Forbes*. www.forbes.com/sites/joefolkman/2014/04/22/8-ways-to-ensure-your-vision-is-valued/?sh=7c4cc78c4524 (accessed November 19, 2021).

Foster W.L., P. Kim, and B. Christiansen. 2009. "Ten Nonprofit Funding Models." *Stanford Social Innovation Review*. https://ssir.org/articles/entry/ten_nonprofit_funding_models (accessed December 29, 2020).

Francis J.N., J.P. Lam, and J. Walls. 2002. "Executive Insights: The Impact of Linguistic Differences on International Brand Name Standardization: A Comparison of English and Chinese Brand Names of Fortune-500 Companies." *Journal of International Marketing* 10, no. 1, pp. 98–116. https://doi.org/10.1509/jimk.10.1.98.19528.

Galowich, D. 2018. "The Business Leader's Guide to Communication Across Generations." *Forbes*. www.forbes.com/sites/forbescoachescouncil/2018/07/16/the-business-leaders-guide-to-communication-across-generations/?sh=ce6ea3466565 (accessed August 22, 2021).

Gao, M.H. 2005. *The Invisible Handshake: Interpreting the Job-seeking Communication of Foreign-born Chinese in the United States*. Dissertation. Tampa, FL: University of South Florida.

Gao, M.H. 2013. "Culture Determines Business Models: How Home Depot Failed in China." *Thunderbird International Business Review*. Phoenix, AZ.

Gergen K. 1991. *The Saturated Self: Dilemmas of Identity in Contemporary Life*. Basic Books.

Gerontology Research Group. 2019. "Jeanne Calment 'Rehabilitated' as World's Oldest Person Ever." *GRG News*. https://grg.org/GRGNews2019.html (accessed March 14, 2023).

Gesenhues, A. 2013. "Survey: 90% of Customers Say Buying Decisions Are Influenced by Online Reviews." *Martech*. https://martech.org/survey-customers-more-frustrated-by-how-long-it-takes-to-resolve-a-customer-service-issue-than-the-resolution/ (accessed August 29, 2021).

Goffman, E. 1959. *The Presentation of Self in Everyday Life.* New York, NY: Anchor Books.

Granovetter, M. 1973. "The Strength of Weak Ties." *The American Journal of Sociology.* 78 (6)

Graziani L. 2019. "What Is Bilibili? A Look Into One of China's Largest Online Video Platforms." *Walkthechat Website.* https://walkthechat.com/what-is-bilibili-a-look-into-one-of-chinas-largest-online-video-platforms/ (accessed October 28, 2020).

Greenleaf, R.K. 2002. *Servant Leadership: A Journey Into the Nature of Legitimate Power and Greatness.* Mahwah, NJ: Paulist Press.

Hamblen, M. 2010. "Google CEO Preaches 'Mobile First:' Mobile Devices Have Displaced PCs for Computing, Communications, Schmidt tells MWC." www.computerworld.com/article/2520954/google-ceo-preaches--mobile-first-.html (accessed September 26, 2019).

Haq, S.N. and E. Jozuka. 2022. "Kane Tanaka, the World's Oldest Living Person, Turns 119." *CNN.* www.cnn.com/2022/01/03/asia/kane-tanaka-turns-119-intl-scli/index.html (accessed January 28, 2022).

Hayes, M.A. and M.D. Comer. 2010. *Start With Humility: Lessons From America's Quiet CEOs on How to Build Trust and Inspire.* Createspace Independent Publishing Platform.

Hofstede, G. 1991. *Culture and Organizations: Software of the Mind.* New York, NY: McGraw-Hill.

Hong Kong Economic and Trade Office in NYC. 2022. "Hong Kong Welcomes." www.hkwelcomesu.gov.hk/eng/ (accessed February 20, 2022).

Howell, J.T. 1972. *Hard Living on Clay Street: Portraits of Blue-Collar Families.* Prospect Heights, IL: Waveland Press, Inc.

Huangdi, N. 550 BCE. 《黄帝内经》. *The Yellow Emperor's Classic of Internal Medicine, or Yellow Emperor's Inner Canon,* Han Dynasty.

Hycner, R.H. 1999. "Some Guidelines for the Phenomenological Analysis of Interview Data." In *Qualitative research,* eds. A. Bryman and R.G. Burgess, Vol. 3, pp. 143–164. London: Sage.

Indeed Website. 2021. "The Importance of Networking in Business." www.indeed.com/career-advice/career-development/networking-in-business#:~:text=Networking%20in%20business%20is%20one,and%20opportunities%20for%20personal%20improvement (accessed February 19, 2021).

Interbrand Website. 2020. "Best Global Brands 2020." www.interbrand.com/best-brands/ (accessed September 28, 2021).

International Monetary Fund. 2021. "World Economic Outlook Database: EU Countries." IMG.org.

Jackson, S. 2022. "Airbnb CEO Brian Chesky, Who Recently Announced Employees Can Work From Home Forever, Calls the Office an 'Anachronistic Form' and 'From a Pre-Digital Age.'" *Insider.* www.businessinsider.com/ airbnb-ceo-brian-chesky-office-anachronistic-from-pre-digital-age-2022-5 (accessed May 9, 2022).

Jain, A. 2016. "The 5V's of Big Data." *IBM.* www.ibm.com/blogs/watson-health/ the-5-vs-of-big-data/ (accessed February 8, 2022).

Jassy, A. 2021. "Amazon Offering Teams More Flexibility as We Return to Office." *Amazon Website.* www.aboutamazon.com/news/workplace/amazon-offering- teams-more-flexibility-as-we-return-to-office (accessed January 28, 2022).

Johnston, L.M. and M.H. Gao. 2009. "Resolving Conflict in the Chinese and U.S. Realms for Global Business Entities." *China Media Report Overseas* 5, no. 4. pp. 22–36.

Jones, S. 2022a. "Reddit Anti-work Moderator Says Working was 'Degrading' and 'Pointless.'" *Business Insider.* www.businessinsider.com/reddit-antiwork- moderator-working-degrading-pointless-doreen-ford-2022-1 (accessed January 24, 2022).

Jones, S. 2022b. "American Express CEO Defends Hybrid Working, Saying It Makes No Sense for People to Trek Into the Office 'Just to Sit on Zoom.'" *Business Insider.* www.businessinsider.com/amex-ceo-steve-squeri-return- office-hybrid-working-zoom-calls-2022-2 (accessed February 6, 2022).

Jorgensen, D.L. 1989. *Participant Observation.* Thousand Oaks, CA: SAGE Publications.

Josephs, L. 2019. "Boeing Fires CEO Dennis Muilenburg, as the Company Struggles With 737 Max Crisis." *CNBC.* www.cnbc.com/2019/12/23/ boeing-stock-halted-pending-news-company-battles-fallout-737-max-crisis .html (accessed January 20, 2020).

Kaplan, R.S. and D.P. Norton. 2004. *Strategy Maps: Converting Intangible Assets Into Tangible Outcomes.* Boston: Harvard Business School Press.

Kasasa. 2021. "Boomers, Gen X, Gen Y, and Gen Z Explained. Kasasa Community Rising." www.kasasa.com/articles/generations/gen-x-gen-y-gen- z?hs_amp=true

Katriel, T. 2004. *Dialogic Moments: From Soul Talks to Talk Radio in Israeli Culture.* Detroit: Wayne State University Press.

Knapp, M.L. and A.L. Vangelisti. 2006. "Relationship Stages: A Communication Perspective." In *Making Connections: Readings in Relational Communication,* eds. K.M. Galvin. and P.J. Cooper, Fourth ed. Los Angeles, CA: Roxbury Publishing Company.

Knight, R. 2016. "How to Make a Great First Impression." *Harvard Business Review.* https://hbr.org/2016/09/how-to-make-a-great-first-impression (accessed December 28, 2020).

Koch, L. 2019. "The Three Ps of Gen X Tech Use: Plugged In, (Social) Platforms and Privacy." www.emarketer.com/content/the-three-p-s-of-gen-x-penetration-social-platforms-and-privacy (accessed August 22, 2021).

Kohll, A. 2018. "The Evolving Definition of Work-Life Balance." *Forbes.* www.forbes.com/sites/alankohll/2018/03/27/the-evolving-definition-of-work-life-balance/?sh=1a70be149ed3 (accessed January 25, 2022).

Laing, R.D. 1961. *Self and Other.* London, UK: Routledge.

Laozi. 老子. 471 BCE. *Tao Te Ching.* 道德经. Western Zhou Dynasty. Translated by Jane English at www.wussu.com.

Lee, Danny and Che, Claire. 2022. "China Eastern Lists Steps Needed to Return 737 Max to Skies." Bloomberg. www.bloomberg.com/news/articles/2022-05-20/boeing-max-faces-another-china-hurdle-as-airline-says-not-ready#:~:text=China%20was%20the%20first%20to,in%20the%20country%20to%20restart (accessed June 14, 2022).

Lewin, K, R. Lippitt, and K. White. 1939. "Patterns of Aggressive Behaviors in Experimentally Created 'Social Climates'." *Journal of Social Psychology* 10, no. 2, pp. 271–301.

Likert, R. 1932. "A Technique for the Measurement of Attitudes." *Archives of Psychology* 140, pp. 1–55.

Liu, C. and D. Wei. 2020. "Alibaba's Secret Three-Year Experiment to Remake the Factory." *Bloomberg News.* www.bloomberg.com/news/articles/2020-11-01/alibaba-s-secret-three-year-experiment-to-reinvent-the-factory (accessed November 2, 2020).

Local Government Chronicle. 2008. "Why 70% of Partnerships Fail." *Local Government Chronicle.* www.lgcplus.com/archive/why-70-of-partnerships-fail-05-10-2008/ (accessed June 2, 2021).

Maglio, T. 2022. "Who Is Winning the Streaming Wars? Subscribers by the Numbers." *IndieWire.* www.indiewire.com/2022/03/how-many-subscribers-netflix-disney-plus-peacock-amazon-prime-video-1234705515/ (accessed June 16, 2022).

Malinowski, B. 1923. "The Problem of Meaning in Primitive Languages." In *The Meaning of Meaning,* eds. C. Ogden and I. Richards. London, UK: Routledge.

Marketing Charts. 2022. *So How Many Millennials Are There in the US, Anyway?* (Updated). www.marketingcharts.com/featured-30401 (accessed June 16, 2022).

Marriott Website. 2022. "Marriott Executive Apartment Business." www.marriott.com/executive-apartments/travel.mi (accessed January 20, 2022).

Martin, J.N. and T.K. Nakayama. 2013. *Intercultural Communication in Contexts,* Sixth ed. New York, NY: McGraw Hill.

Martinuzzi, B. 2021. "Leadership Styles and How to Find Your Own." *American Express.* www.americanexpress.com/en-us/business/trends-and-insights/articles/

the-7-most-common-leadership-styles-and-how-to-find-your-own/ (accessed November 23, 2021).

Maxwell, J.C. 2008. *Leadership Gold: Lessons I've Learned From a Lifetime of Leading.* Nashville, TN: Thomas Nelson, Inc.

McCluskey, M. 2022. "Tim Cook, Mindy Kaling, and Bill Gates to Headline the 2022 TIME100 Summit." *TIME.* https://time.com/6183847/2022-time-100-summit/ (accessed June 16, 2022).

McMakin, T. and D. Fletcher. 2018. *How Clients Buy: A Practical Guide to Business Development for Consulting and Professional Services.* Hoboken, NJ: Wiley.

Morgan, G. 1998. *Images of Organization: The Executive Edition.* Oakland, CA: Barrett-Koehler Publishers, Inc.

Mullen, A. 2022. "What Is RCEP, the World's Largest Free Trade Deal That is Under Way?" *South China Morning Post.* www.scmp.com/economy/global-economy/article/3161707/what-rcep-worlds-largest-free-trade-deal-under-way (accessed January 28, 2022).

National Business Capital and Services. 2020. "2019 Small Business Failure Rate: Startup Statistics by Industry." www.national.biz/2019-small-business-failure-rate-startup-statistics-industry/ (accessed December 28, 2020).

Nix, E. 2018. "Did an Apple Really Fall on Isaac Newton's Head?" *History Channel Website.* www.history.com/news/did-an-apple-really-fall-on-isaac-newtons-head (accessed July 14, 2021).

Oldfield, N.D. 2017. *The Power of Trust: How Top Companies Build, Manage and Protect It.* Self-published Book.

Ortiz, A. 2020. "Chipotle to Pay $25 Million Fine for Tainted Food." https://www.nytimes.com/2020/04/21/business/chipotle-tainted-food-settlement.html#:~:text=Chipotle%20Mexican%20Grill%20on%20Tuesday,United%20States%2C%20federal%20prosecutors%20said. *The New Yok Times.* (accessed February 16, 2023)

Patel, N. 2021. "Why the Future of Work Is the Future of Travel, With Airbnb CEO Brian Chesky." *The Verge.* www.theverge.com/22783422/airbnb-pandemic-ceo-brian-chesky-interview-travel-decoder-podcast (accessed January 2, 2022).

Pearson, J. and P. Nelson. 2000. *An Introduction to Human Communication: Understanding and Sharing.* Boston, MA: McGraw-Hill.

Poynton, J.C. 1987. *Smuts's Holism and Evolution Sixty Years On: Transactions of the Royal Society of South Africa* 46, no. 3, pp. 181–189. https://doi.org/10.1080/00359198709520121.

Qiyuange Website. 2020. "Qian Motif in I Ching." www.qiyuange.com/zhouyi/22312.html (accessed May 1, 2020).

Redman, R. 2020. "Online Grocery Sales to Grow 40% in 2020." *Super Market News.* www.supermarketnews.com/online-retail/online-grocery-sales-grow-40-2020 (accessed June 5, 2020).

Regmi, K., J. Naidoo, and P. Pilkington. 2010. "Understanding the Processes of Translation and Transliteration in Qualitative Research." *International Journal of Qualitative Methods* 9, no. 1, pp. 16–26.

Reuters. 2022. "A Record 4.5 Million People Quit Their Jobs in November 2021." *NBC News.* www.nbcnews.com/business/economy/record-4-5-million-americans-quit-their-job-november-n1286930.

Richards, I.A. and C.K. Ogden. 1923. *The Meaning of Meaning.* Harvest/HBJ.

Robison, P. 2019. "Boeing's 737 Max Software Outsourced to $9-an-Hour Engineers." *Bloomberg.* www.bloomberg.com/news/articles/2019-06-28/boeing-s-737-max-software-outsourced-to-9-an-hour-engineers (accessed January 3, 2019).

Roush, C. 2021. "WSJ Launches New Ad Campaign Called 'Trust Your Decisions'." https://talkingbiznews.com/they-talk-biz-news/wsj-launches-new-ad-campaign-called-trust-your-decisions/ (accessed February 16, 2023).

Rushe, D. 2013. "Fake Online Reviews Crackdown in New York Sees 19 Companies Fined." *The Guardian.* www.theguardian.com/world/2013/sep/23/new-york-fake-online-reviews-yoghurt (accessed August 30, 2021).

Salinas, S. 2018. "Amazon's Jeff Bezos Launches a $2 billion 'Day One Fund' to Help Homeless Families and Create Preschools." *CNBC.* www.cnbc.com/2018/09/13/bezos-launches-day-one-fund-to-help-homeless-families-and-create-preschools.html (accessed September 13, 2020).

Seidman, I. 2006. *Interviewing as Qualitative Research: A Guide for Researchers in Education and the Social Sciences.* New York, NY: Teachers College Press.

Sendjaya, S. and J.C. Sarros. 2002. "Servant Leadership: Its Origin, Development, and Application in Organizations." *Journal of Leadership & Organizational Studies* 9, no. 2, pp. 57–64.

Shakespeare, W. 1597. *Romeo and Juliet.*

Shakespeare, W. 1605. *A Midsummer Night's Dream*, Act 1, Scene 1, pp. 132–140.

Shakespeare, W. 1623. *Tempest*, Act 2, Scene I.

Sheth, J.N. 2021. *The Self-destructive Habits of Good Companies: Great to Gone.* Tamil Nadu, India: Pearson.

Slingerland, E. 2007. *Effortless Action: Wu Wei as Conceptual Metaphor and Spiritual Ideal in Early China.* Oxford, NY: Oxford University Press.

Smith, J. 2011. "BRIC Becomes BRICS: Changes on the Geopolitical Chessboard." *Foreign Policy Journal.* www.foreignpolicyjournal.com/2011/01/21/bric-becomes-brics-changes-on-the-geopolitical-chessboard/2/ (accessed January 28, 2022).

Spears, L.C. 1998. *Insights on Leadership: Service, Stewardship, Spirit, and Servant Leadership.* New York, NY: Wiley.

Statista Website. 2022a. "Number of Smartphone Subscriptions Worldwide From 2016 to 2027." *Statista.* www.statista.com/statistics/330695/number-of-smartphone-users-worldwide/ (accessed June 16, 2022).

Statista Website. 2022b. "Office Vacancy Rates in the United States." *Statista.* www.statista.com/statistics/194054/us-office-vacancy-rate-forecasts-from-2010/ (accessed June 30, 2022).

Sunzi. 5th Century BCE. *The Art of War.* 孙子兵法.

Taylor, D.A. and I. Altman. 1987. "Communication in Interpersonal Relationships: Social Penetration Processes." In *Interpersonal Processes: New Directions in Communication Research*, eds. M.E. Roloff and G.R. Miller. Thousand Oaks, CA: Sage.

Teh, C. 2022. "Blackberry Phones Will Stop Working on January 4, Signaling the End of an Era for the Iconic Cellphone." *Business Insider.* www.businessinsider .com/rip-blackberry-phones-will-stop-working-on-january-4-2022-1 (accessed February 1, 2022).

The Coca-Cola Company Website. 2022. "A Deeper Look at Coca-Cola's Emerging Business in Alcohol." www.coca-colacompany.com/news/deeper-look-at-coca-colas-emerging-business-in-alcohol (accessed July 13, 2022).

Tighe, D. 2020. "Share of Purchases Bought on Impulse in the United States as of 2018, by Age Group." *Statista.* www.statista.com/statistics/826442/share-of-purchases-bought-on-impulse-by-age-us/ (accessed June 2, 2021).

Ting-Toomey, S. and A. Kurogi. 1998. "Facework Competence in Intercultural Conflict: An Updated Face-Negotiation Theory." *International Journal of Intercultural Relations* 22, no. 2, pp. 187–225.

Troitino, C. 2020. "Frito-Lay Launches Direct-To-Consumer Sites Amid Pandemic Snacking Surge." *Forbes.* www.forbes.com/sites/christinatroitino/2020/05/11/frito-lay-launches-direct-to-consumer-sites-amid-pandemic-snacking-surge/?sh=160b48466f18 (accessed January 1, 2022).

tvsdesign. 2021. *tvsdesign.* www.tvsdesign.com (accessed June 2, 2021).

Umoh, R. 2017. "The Tactics Self-made Billionaire Elon Musk Uses to Motivate His Teams." *CNBC.* https://www.cnbc.com/amp/2017/07/05/2-major-ways-executives-like-elon-musk-are-trying-to-stop-you-from-quitting.html (accessed March 14, 2023).

U.S. Census Bureau. 2021. *Plain Writing Act of 2010.* www.census.gov/about/policies/plain_writing.html (accessed November 26, 2021).

U.S. Congress. October 13, 2010. "H.R.946—111th Congress (2009–2010): Plain Writing Act of 2010." *U.S. Census Bureau website.* www.govinfo.gov/content/pkg/BILLS-111hr946rh/pdf/BILLS-111hr946rh.pdf (accessed November 26, 2021).

U.S. State Department. 2022. "1898: The Birth of a Superpower." *Office of the Historian.* https://history.state.gov/departmenthistory/short-history/superpower#: ~:text=NOTE%20TO%20READERS-,1898%3A%20The%20Birth%20 of%20a%20Superpower,a%20short%20but%20shattering%20war (accessed January 28, 2022).

Uhl-Bien, M., R.E. Riggio, K.B. Lowe, and M.K. Carsten. 2014. "Followership Theory: A Review and Research Agenda." *The Leadership Quarterly* 25, no. 1, pp. 83–104.

UNESCO. 2011. *"Yellow Emperor's Inner Canon" accepted by UNESCO as a "Documentary Heritage" for Inclusion in the Memory of the World Register.* www.unesco.org/new/en/communication-and-information/flagship-project-activities/memory-of-the-world/register/full-list-of-registered-heritage/ registered-heritage-page-4/huang-di-nei-jing-yellow-emperors-inner-canon/ (accessed October 1, 2021).

Venture City. 2020. "Elon Musk: The Scientist Behind the CEO Documentary." https://youtu.be/q-g7BPdSmP4 (accessed December 17, 2020).

Verizon. 2022. "A Timeline: Notable Milestones in the History of iPhone from Apple." www.verizon.com/articles/milestones-in-history-of-apple-iphone/ #:~:text=June%202007%3A%20The%20first%20generation,and%20a%20 breakthrough%20Internet%20communicator (accessed February 22, 2022).

Vinoski, J. 2021. "One of America's Best Manufacturers is this Japanese Zipper Maker." *Forbes.* www.forbes.com/sites/jimvinoski/2021/03/22/one-of-americas-best-manufacturers-is-this-japanese-zipper-maker/?sh=4af4 1df5fa2cs (accessed April 15, 2021).

Vivid IP. 2022. "Our Story." www.vividip.com/our-story (accessed January 3, 2022).

Vrbo Website. 2022. "The Story Behind the New Vrbo Brand." www.vrbo.com/ media-center/press-releases/2019/the-story-behind-the-new-vrbo-brand.

Ward, A. 2018. "BP: Rebuilding Trust After a Disaster; How the Company's Chairman Steered the Group to Recovery After the Oil Spill." *Financial Times.* Accessed 05/20/2021 from https://amp.ft.com/content/3e09d84a-489f-11e8-8ee8-cae73aab7ccb (accessed May 20, 2021).

Ward, S. 2020. "Why Business Partnerships Fail and How to Succeed." *The Balance Small Business.* www.thebalancesmb.com/why-business-partnerships-fail-4107045 (accessed June 2, 2021).

Watzlawick, P., J. Beavin, and D. Jackson. 1967. *Pragmatics of Human communication: A Study of Interactional Patterns, Pathologies, and Paradoxes.* New York, NY: Norton.

Weick, K.E. 1969. *The Social Psychology of Organizing.* Reading, MA: Addison-Wesley.

Weick, K.E. 1995. *Sensemaking in Organizations.* Thousand Oaks: Sage Publications.

Weiner, J. 2020. "LinkedIn CEO Shares Advice on Leadership, Hiring and Firing." *CNBC.* www.youtube.com/watch?v=W8RmWPqBiBo&t=749 (accessed January 5, 2022).

White, M.C. 2022. "CEOs Are Joining the 'Great Resignation,' Trading Fatigue for Family Time." *NBC News.* www.nbcnews.com/business/business-news/ceos-are-joining-great-resignation-trading-fatigue-family-time-rcna12223.

Willis, J. and A. Todorov. 2006. "First Impressions: Making up Your Mind After 100 Mini Second Exposure to a Face." *Psychological Science* 17, no. 7, pp. 592–598.

Wood, P. 2012. *Snap: Making the Most of First Impressions, Body Language, and Charisma.*

Xu, W. 2022. "YouTube Lecture Series on Modern Interpretations of Huang Di Nei Jing." *The Yellow Emperor's Classic of Internal Medicine.* 【徐文兵vs梁東】《黃帝內經》之上古天真論（上）音頻版 https://www.youtube.com/watch?v=lnrDk80B6kQ&t=5984s (accessed February 16, 2023).

Yuen, M. 2022. "Digital Grocery Will Be a $243 Billion Market in the US by 2025." *Insider Intelligence.* www.insiderintelligence.com/insights/digital-grocery-industry (accessed June 28, 2022).

Zalani, R. 2021. "Screen Time Statistics 2021: Your Smartphone Is Hurting You." *Elite Content Marketer.* https://elitecontentmarketer.com/screen-time-statistics/ (accessed August 3, 2021).

Zeng, S. 2013. "Zeng Shiqiang Lecturing on I Ching: Episode 15; Riding above Good or Bad Fortunes. 100 Masters Forum." *CCTV.* www.youtube.com/watch?v=FPGe4agklD4 (accessed June 14, 2022).

About the Author

Dr. May Hongmei Gao is a Professor of Communication and Asian Studies at Kennesaw State University in Atlanta, Georgia, United States. Dr. Gao has published extensively in communication, business, and Asian studies. Beyond many book chapters, Dr. Gao's research has been published in *Thunderbird International Business Review, Global Business Languages, China Media Review, International Journal of Chinese Culture and Management, China Currents, Asian Journal of Humanities and Social Studies,* and *East-West Connections.* Because of her expertise in business, culture, and communication, Dr. Gao has provided trainings for UPS, The Coca-Cola Company, tvsdesign, Euramax, Kimberly-Clark, Cobb Vantress, Equity Prime Mortgage, Enercon, and P&G.

Dr. Gao is the Founder and Chair of the *Symposium on ASIA-USA Partnership Opportunities (SAUPO)*, the largest Asia business conference in the United States. Both *The White House Initiative on AAPIs* and *Asian American Heritage Foundation* recognize Dr. Gao for her leadership in enhancing business with and education on Asia. *Georgia Asian Times* named Dr. Gao as one of the *25 Most Influential Asian Americans in Georgia* (GA25 in 2013 and 2016). U.S. Pan Asian American Chamber of Commerce SE acknowledges her as one of *Five Outstanding Asian Americans* (2019). Dr. Gao holds a PhD in Communication from the University of South Florida (USF), an MA in Mass Communication from Brigham Young University (BYU), and a BA in English from Shanghai International Studies University (SISU). Prior to coming to the United States, Dr. Gao was a TV Anchorwoman at China Anhui TV Station, and a PR Specialist at the University of Science and Technology of China. Dr. Gao lives in Atlanta with her husband Todd. She enjoys writing, gardening, traveling, and playing Guzheng music.

Index

OTHER TITLES IN THE CORPORATE COMMUNICATION COLLECTION

Debbie DuFrene, Stephen F. Austin State University, Editor

- *Technical Marketing Communication, Second Edition* by Emil B. Towner and Heidi L. Everett
- *The Thong Principle* by Donalee Moulton
- *How to Become a Master of Persuasion* by Tony Treacy
- *101 Tips for Improving Your Business Communication* by Edward Barr
- *Business Writing For Innovators and Change-Makers* by Dawn Henwood
- *Delivering Effective Virtual Presentations* by K. Virginia Hemby
- *New Insights into Prognostic Data Analytics in Corporate Communication* by Pragyan Rath and Kumari Shalini
- *Leadership Through A Screen* by Joseph Brady and Garry Prentice
- *Managerial Communication for Professional Development* by Reginald L. Bell and Jeanette S. Martin
- *Managerial Communication for Organizational Development* by Reginald L. Bell and Jeanette S. Martin
- *Business Report Guides* by Dorinda Clippinger
- *Strategic Thinking and Writing* by Michael Edmondson

Concise and Applied Business Books

The Collection listed above is one of 30 business subject collections that Business Expert Press has grown to make BEP a premiere publisher of print and digital books. Our concise and applied books are for...

- Professionals and Practitioners
- Faculty who adopt our books for courses
- Librarians who know that BEP's Digital Libraries are a unique way to offer students ebooks to download, not restricted with any digital rights management
- Executive Training Course Leaders
- Business Seminar Organizers

Business Expert Press books are for anyone who needs to dig deeper on business ideas, goals, and solutions to everyday problems. Whether one print book, one ebook, or buying a digital library of 110 ebooks, we remain the affordable and smart way to be business smart. For more information, please visit www.businessexpertpress.com, or contact sales@businessexpertpress.com.

CPSIA information can be obtained
at www.ICGtesting.com
Printed in the USA
BVHW050545180523
664350BV00005B/14